Music Therapy within Multi-Disciplinary Teams

Music Therapy within Multi-Disciplinary Teams

Proceedings of

The 3rd European Music Therapy Conference
Aalborg June 1995

Edited by Inge Nygaard Pedersen and Lars Ole Bonde

Aalborg Universitetsforlag

Inge Nygaard Pedersen & Lars Ole Bonde (eds.)
Music Therapy within Multi-Disciplinary Teams
Copyright: 1996 by the Authors (except H. Smeijster's artcle:
Barcelona Publishers, 4 Whitebrook Rd., Gilsum NH 03448)

ISBN 87-7307-532-9

Published by
  Department of Music and Music Therapy
  Aalborg University

Distribution
  Aalborg University Press
  Badehusvej 16, 9000 Aalborg
  Tlf. # 45 98130915
  Fax: # 45 98134915

Layout and word processing: Lars Ole Bonde
Print: Centertrykkeriet Aalborg University, 1996

Contents:

Introduction

Part 1. Research

Part 2. Mental Health

Part 3. Developmental Disabilities

Part 4. Training

Reflections on The 3rd European Music Therapy Conference, Aalborg 1995

by Inge Nygaard Pedersen and Lars Ole Bonde (DK)

Introduction

In June 1995 round 250 European music therapists participated in the 3rd European Music Therapy Conference in Aalborg, Denmark. Thereby the tradition of having a European conference every third year was continued - taking on the mantle of responsibility from Cambridge (GB 1993, 2nd conference) and putting it on the shoulders of the Belgians to organize the 4th European conference in Leuwen 1998.

The chain of European Music Therapy Conferences is promoted and supported by EMTC - EUROPEAN MUSIC THERAPY COMMITTEE.

The theme of the Aalborg Conference was:
"Music Therapy Within Multi-Disciplinary Teams"

Not all the papers presented here focus directly on this topic but it is addressed in all the papers. Some of them have made it their main focus.

In Denmark the history of music therapy has shown that the discipline developed witihin a multidisciplinary working area without an established professional identity. Today a professional identity is well established, and music therapists as professionals very much need and seek cooperation possibilities within treatment teams and other groups.

An overall principle of the conference in Aalborg was to invite all keynote and subkcynote speakers from within Europe and to give space to as many of the "newcomers" within our field as possible.

We received round 120 abstracts for the conference and it was difficult to reduce them to the 80 papers presented in the rich and very colourful conference programme.

The Proceedings

It has also been difficult to select the papers for this book as papers generally were of a very high standard. Our selection criterias have been:
(1) all keynote and subkeynote papers should be indcluded,
(2) concerning the rest of the papers we have taken geographical as well as topical considerations in an attempt to reach a certain balance of input in each area. Thus we have selected 21 articles by authors from 11 different countries.

Because of the great number of speakers not all of them had as big an audience as they deserved. But as the Scientific Coordinator said in her welcome address:

> *"The discipline of music therapy seems to have grown to the phase, where we all want to present - like in the fantastic developmental stage of children where they naturally seem to live in the attitude of: " SEE ME! HEAR ME!"*
>
> *And I think it is a very healthy stage to be in - gradually growing towards independency of fathers and mothers and at the same time naturally wanting to share experiences with significant others represented by our dear collegues throughout the field. I don`t think it shows that we don`t want to listen to one another - on the contrary - I think it shows that we all want to be balanced in giving and listening."*

The proceedings cannot transmit the very enthusiastic, warm and musical atmosphere of the conference, but we hope it can give you many hours of interesting reading and many memories of the conference days.

Acknowledgements

Before we introduce the content of the conference proceedings we want once again to bring our warmhearted thanks to all the members of the joint organising committee composed of representatives of the Danish Society for Music Therapy; the National Association for Professional Music Therapists (DK); Aalborg University, Institute of Music and Music Therapy; Aalborg Psychiatric Hospital, the Music Therapy Clinic; and the Aalborg School.

A special thanks to Aalborg University who gave us the necessary financial and encouraging support in the work, also stated in the closing speech of the Head of Aalborg University, rector Sven Caspersen. Also a big thanks to all the sponsors without whom the conference would not have been possible.

We want to emphasize the preparation work by the chairman Claus Bang who took over at the last moment. Together with Silvia Jensen he created the very nice conditions, exibitions, meals and parties. And as many of the readers will remember the chairman closed the last day accompanying farewell songs in 5 European languages!

We also want to mention the preparation work done by Dorthe Bergholt who arranged all the small concerts in the breaks, featuring a variety of Danish and ethnic musicstyles.

And we want in general to emphasize the very nice cooperation we have experienced in the joint organising group where we have used our different talents - we think - in the very best ways. Thanks to the head of the Society Nina Holten, and the head of the Association Per Muff Jensen for their support.

We have received a lot of lovely letters after the conference - all of them emphasizing two statements:
1) the high quality of the conference on all levels - especially the papers and

2) the nice and warm atmosphere.

We - the editors of the proceedings - want to thank all of the participants for their contribution to the inspiration of such statements.

Meeting and exchanging

In Denmark we think that all music therapists in some way are related in a spiritual sense, because our discipline demands - not only a high standard of musical and theoretical skills - but also a lot of personal engagement, empathy and courage to confront all aspects of being human. We believe that exactly these aspects of our profession create the very intense and intimate atmosphere whereever music therapists come together. It also create the need for ongoing personal growth together with collegues, in supervision groups and in multi disciplinary groups.

Some years ago music therapists were often very isolated in their workplaces. We know many still are, so we think the development of being more and more integrated in multy disciplinary teams are deeply important. We still need though also to meet with music therapy collegues within our profession to be filled up in depts during conferences, meetings, supervisiongroups etc.

We want to call attention to our two honoured guests, music therapist Synnøve Friis (DK) and Prof. Johannes Th. Eschen (D). They both have made important contributions to the development of music therapy in Denmark in the phase of building up an educational milieu. The two first ass. professors of the program in Aalborg were both educated by Eschen in the Herdecke Pilot Project in 1978-80. We both think (Inge Nygaard Pedersen and Benedikte Barth Scheiby) that Eschen's courage to endure the often chaotic proces in our (the student') search for meaning and knowledge based on our personal growth proces experiences gave space for a lot of creative and integrated ideas for the future work as trainers and tutors of music therapy students.

S. Friis is - together with Claus Bang - one of the outstanding pioneers of music therapy in Denmark. They are both in great demand all over Denmark and abroad.

Today Denmark has a broad variety of specialists in the field of music therapy. We are also very proud and grateful, because Aalborg University is the home base of the only current, formalised Ph.d.-program in Music Therapy in Europe - not least thanks to the work of the distinguished supervisors and guest teachers - the two keynote speakers in the area of research Prof. Even Ruud (N) and Prof. David Aldridge (D) and to our consultant and fascilitator outside Europe Prof. Ken Bruscia (USA) who unfortunately couldn't participate in the conference.

Contents

In the proceedings we have divided the text into sections parallel to the four main areas of the conference days: Research, Mental Health, Developmental

Disabilities and Training. In each section we include the keynote paper, the subkeynote paper and other selected papers.

RESEARCH

In the area of research we had two keynote papers presented by Prof. Even Ruud and Prof. Dr. David Aldridge.

As you will se the two papers give a very varied and well documented overview of the research arena in Europe today. Ruud emphasizes the overall development of qualitative research approaches which are - he states: holistic, empirical and naturalistic, descriptive, interpretive, empathic, based on "Grounded theory" and immidiate observation and spontanious interpretation. He also presents an interpretative paradigm and shows a way of outlining the roots of this new paradigm in music therapy research. Aldridge elaborates:

"Science is a process, an activity - not a set of commandments set in stone for all time as the basis for a dogma. In a post-modern world, where all the major themes are challenged and demonstrated, then it is our responsibility to construct themes that are appropriate to the knowledge that we need."

Seen from a philosophical perspective: *"This is a move away from the Cartesian position that separates mind and body as reflected in **cogito ergo sum** - I think therefore I am. What I am proposing here is **ago ergo sum** - I perform therefore I am"* and Aldridge sums up saying: *"- doing science - or the activity of sciencing - is a matter of deciding. It is therefore a moral activity."*

These perspectives of qualitative research as a "new" paradigm are supported by the two subkeynote papers from Dr. Henk Smejsters (NL) who emphasizes the possibilities and advantages of integrating qualitative and quantitative approaches and Prof. Edith Lecourt (F) who addresses also the problems and neccessity of research based on subjective experiences.Ideas from this new paradigm inspire several papers, as can be seen in the descriptive paper on Music Thinking and the Experiencing Body by Ruth Eckhoff (N) - one of the socalled "newcomers" in the official scenario. Chairman Claus Bang shares some of his experiences and reflections from 35 years of voice treatment and speech therapy with hearing impaired at the Aalborg School - focusing on the specific Tone Bar Therapy. This is an extraordinay testimony of a true pioneer, still going strong. Finally we have chosen an example of a pilot study by Gabriella Pirelli (I), in which she combines quantitative and qualitative methods.

Another topic addressed by Aldridge is the question of futher practice for editing and publishing our research. We now have a lot of new possibilities with the development of information technology like CD-Rom, databases etc.

To sum up the research area we want to quote Aldridge's important statement:

"What we need to avoid is that one group can make an exclusive claim to determine the doing of knowledge according to their own principles. To establish tolerance we need to understand each other and our varying purposes."

We think and hope that the conference mirrored the beginning of this phase within our profession.

MENTAL HEALTH:
In the area of Mental Health we are carried into the work with older people and the role of a multi-disciplinary team work by H. Odell Miller (GB) as keynote speaker. She addresses among other things the problems of working with a client population often not very highly estimated as a working area. She has succeeded in integrating several methods of music therapy in her own work and is still very conscious of her psychoanalytical concepts concerning how this can be *"useful in helping the music therapist think, and understand, more about the work and its team context. This enables music therapists to remain hopeful in a field where otherwise the overwhelming emotion could be one of despair."*

In the area of mental health the proceedings offers the reader papers on a wide range of topics: countertransference problems in the multi-disciplinary teamwork with emotionally disturbed children (Alison Levinge, GB); the importance of integrating music therapy with other treatment offers for in hospital psychiatric clients, in order to make group music therapy visible and a common treatment offer at the hospitals (Almut Pioch & Albert Berman, NL); and the specific possibilities of using music therapy in Cancer Care (Anne Olofsson, S).

We also meet another "newcomer", Helle Nystrup Lund (DK) presenting a well documented case study and reflections on using music therapy with High Functioning Autistic Clients.

Two other case studies address as different client populations as a musician suffering from identity problems and alcohol abuse, written very sensitively and personal by Kimmo Lehtonen (SF); and the harsh reality of music therapy with women in forensic psychiatry - the forgotten women, by Katie Santos (GB).

As a whole music therapy in mental health areas seems to develop very much within improvisational approaches, often based upon psychoanalytical or psychodynamic concepts emphasizing the understanding of the form and intensity of the musical and verbal relationship. Most music therapists in this area seem to reflect on their own roles as therapists and seem to address ongoing countertransferential questions as a basis for understanding the clinical proces.

DEVELOPMENTAL DISABILITY
In the area of developmental disability - introduced by the keynote speech of Anne Steen Møller (DK, another "newcomer") - we are gently and sensitively guided into the world of multiply handicapped children. Her focus is defining levels of contact with this client population, where one tiny movement with one hand can show a magnificant progression in communication ability. Also

Eyulfur Melsted (AU) works with this client population. He ends up stating:
"-provided you offer these children that accurately balanced mixture of aimed music and humane approach, which we in common language call music therapy at their optimal level of perception ,they seem to do better!"

Music Therapy with infantile deafness is represented here by the subkeynote speaker Giulia Cremaschi Trovesi (I) addressing the importance of knowing and using the basic sounds and rhytms within the maternal womb when building up contact with and developing expression possibilities for these children. Wolfgang Mahns (D) presents a case study from his work in an integrated primary school where the job of the music therapist is a mixture of both individual clinical work and integrative music therapy work in class situations.

TRAINING
Papers within the area of training were spread over the three days of the conference. This doesn´t mean that we consider this area less important - on the contrary - and the weight of the two papers included here will impress the reader, introducing and developing some of the creative and systematic ideas which take form within training programs these years.

The area was introduced by the subkeynote of Gianluigi di Franco (I) who gave a systematic overwiev of the elements in music therapy supervision. Tony Wigram (GB/DK) presents one of the experiential concepts of learning by "being clients" at Aalborg University. He has adapted the long tradition of learning by being clients at the M.A. program. Wigram has developed especially this discipline in a very personal and professional way, emphasizing the importance of this specific training of the students before they go to practicum. We think Wigram's description is very clear and inspiring for all trainers of music therapy students.

Final statements
We want to give a perspective to this introduction with statements from some of the closing speeches.

First we want to mention the third honoured guest, neurobiologist Keld Fredens (DK) who emphasized how therapy allways has been and allways will be a branch of education - learning about one self and developing skills presented by others. We think that in our profession especially the self experience learning process is important also in the development of personal and professional identity.

We want to quote the scientific Coordinator and editor Inge Nygaard Pedersen (DK): *"Many music therapists have obviously chosen their profession from an experience of being in one way or another in an outsider position. Maybe we can say with the Danish author Harald Engberg:"I grew up and became a boy/girl of the sort my mother wouldn`t like me to play with.""*

But the conference and the proceedings show that we certainly want to play with and share with each other, on a level as expressed by Prof. Eschen in his final statement:

"Thanks also to all of us who gave us through their lectures, workshops etc
- such broad overview on fields of music therapy
- such clarity of thought   and
- such deep and touching highlights of the very Music Therapy practice."

We think we should be very proud of this statement as all music therapists seem to live with the fact - as stated in the wellcome address of the head of the Society, Nina Holten (DK):
"Music therapists are brainy on several levels, communicators on all levels with body and soul, flexible, half artists, half scientists , whole humanists, and very containing. Very qualitative."
The scientific subcoordinator and editor of this book Lars Ole Bonde (DK) made a poetical statement on the same topic - in a short limerick at the closing down ceremony:

> *"Our profession is science and art;*
> *therapists may talk clever and smart.*
> *But we all know for sure:*
> *There is nothing so pure*
> *as the non-verbal, musical part"*

The Danish musician, philosopher and composer Peter Bastian gave a true *live* concert at the beach party with his band *Bazaar*. In his book: "Into the music" he defines the musical experience this way:
"The total experience of a composition is what we call music, but the total experience of anything is what I call music."
We think this conference was very musical from this point of view. We hope the conference proceedings will transmit some of those experiences to the readers.

AALBORG in JUNE 1996

INGE NYGAARD PEDERSEN & LARS OLE BONDE, editors

Music Therapy — the science of interpretation

by Even Ruud (N)

Lately, European music therapists have fully come to discuss the scientific status of their profession. I am consciously using the term "profession" and not "music therapy" or the music therapist. That is because "science" to many people means to measure the effect of something, to establish correct or predictable procedures, to establish some kind of truth. When I talk about the importance of science for ourselves as a profession, I want to underline the importance of establishing some way of talking about and discussing music therapy as a profession, as a field of theory and practice, or as a kind of metadiscourse. This meta-discourse, or rather meta-critique should hopefully enable us to maintain a rational dialogue concerning our way of thinking about ourselves.

Pathways to music therapy
This understanding of science as a kind of metacritique rather than a way of establishing the truth value of music therapy practice needs some historical context. When I first entered my training as a music therapist at Florida State University in 1971 I was immediately immersed in a scientific climate, that is, the ideal of natural science transferred to the field of music therapy. This showed itself in two ways — the established E. Thayer Gaston tradition of music therapy as a university discipline (represented by my supervisor Dr. Donald Michel), and the newly established music therapy as behavioral modification (Dr. Cliff Madsen), which had a firm grip on the training program in Tallahassee. The Gaston tradition meant for instance a basic natural science outlook on research in music psychology. Physiological measurement to register the experience of music, acoustical data on music to reveal the nature of music and so on. This could easily be documented by referring to the first American standard textbook in music therapy - Gastons (ed.) *Music in Therapy* from 1968 — where the articles on research clearly reflect the natural science attitude of the time. Which of course is clearly understandable, taking into consideration the marginal position of music therapy as a new paramedical profession striving to be recognized by the scientific community.

Music therapy was of course not totally new for me. Coming from the more humanistic and indeed charismatic influence of Nordoff and Robbins, I was familiar with the humanistic, improvisational, idealistic, or some would at that time perhaps say speculative tradition in music therapy. I hesitantly accepted my new curriculum, carefully navigating between my new teachers and a useful library. I listened to lectures on acoustics and Skinner in the morning, and wrote papers on phenomenology, Buber, Freud and Zuckerkandl in the evening. If the files in the Music therapy department at FSU still are kept, you will perhaps find some incomplete papers on Buber and the I-thou relation among all the "contingent use of music"-papers.

One thing I learned to accept, and which probably has made a lasting impression on me, was Dr. Michel´s midwest scepticism and the over-all pragmatism which infused the North-American outlook on life. "I am from Missouri, I am a sceptic — show me", dr. Michel used to say, holding his closed fist up in front of us". I often remembered this later when I met with music therapy students and therapists who claimed some hidden truth or nature within music which would have an universal effect upon man. When I later undertook an extensive study on the history of music therapy as a part of my doctorial work, I would constantly run into these narratives which claimed that music had some kind of metaphysical status (Ruud 1980, 1990). Scepticism, or rather in the Popperian edition, which claims that statements about reality ought to be given a form to be refuted, gives some sense to the field of music therapy, who still have believers in the supernatural powers of music. One should constantly remind oneself that the discipline of music therapy is surrounded by lots of mystical and speculative thinking. Persons and ideas keep coming into music therapy, which are not always concerned about standards of rationality.

Pragmatism also keeps turning up in my thinking. When it has been so hard to establish "the truth", the pragmatic values of theories and explanations seem to be a way to deal with competing claims of knowledge as I will discuss later.

Coming back to Europe, and after having written the book "Music Therapy and its relationship to current treatment theories" - based on my master thesis in 1973 (Ruud 1973, 1980b, 1990b,1990c, Ruud and Mahns 1991) — which was really an effort to solve the dilemma I felt myself torn between different therapeutic or scientific schools of thought — two rather heavy issues seemed to bother me in the following years.

Going to the United States to study music therapy did not become the pilgrimage-journey which I had sought. FSU was the Mecca of the behavioral or positivist school of music therapy. On the other hand, it was in fact one of the only places in the US which had a graduate program and was concerned about research in music therapy.

In the years to come I made several trips around Europe. I learned through my friends Unni Johns and Trygve Aasgaard the more eclectic attitude of Juliette Alvin in London. Together with my friend and collegue, the Nordoff-Robbins therapist Tom Næss, I visited Alfred Schmölz in Vienna and touched the ground of Freudian and Adlerian therapy. I went to Paris and learned other psychoanalytic narratives from Edith Lecourt. We met with Johannes Eschen in Hamburg and tried to catch up with Mary Priestley´s analytical music therapy — this time it was Jungian version. One afternoon in Hamburg with Lilli Friedemann´s group improvisation — she talked Swedish to us and served homebaked applecake — made an lasting impression. There was more in Hamburg; Isabelle Frohne showed us how to use receptive techniques combined with deep analytic work, and Hans Helmuth Decker Vogt invited twenty of us to his center in Lünenburger Heide to demonstrate videos of music therapy in an adult clinical setting. Later I was impressed with the new "Herdecke generation" of music therapists and learned more from Wolfgang Mahns, Inge Nygaard Pedersen and Benedicte Scheiby the value of the psychoanalytic approach in music therapy.

All these trips, often with the students, sometimes going for myself to congresses and symposiums all around Europe made me drift further away from the positivist school of music therapy.

This, although the behavioral approach seems to solve some basic problems concerning measuring the effects of a certain music therapy approach, I was intrigued by the challenge of answering not only how music was effective, but *why*. I thought there would have to be an answer to the problem of the nature of music, some way to explain how music was constituted in order to function as a therapeutic means. I felt that the positivist approach, all the measurement of blood pressure and galvanic skin responses never said anything about the experience of the person, or the structure of the music. I remember one passage from the music philosopher Zuckerkandl, who wrote critically about how the essence of the experience of music really could not be captured by the measurement equipment of the positivist researcher, how the richness and complexity of the mind really outplayed the machines. Instead there seemed to be a route to knowledge through the phenomeno-logical description or hermeneutical interpretation. Although these approaches were both hard to grasp and apply, and I struggled with their meaning for many years.

But there was another challenge, not really dealt with in the North-American scientific climate. That was critical theory, or the Frankfurth school of thought. Music therapy had a long tradition of claiming general cultural value in the sense of serving prophylactic purposes (cf. Ruud 1988). Much contemporary music therapy seemed to have become too centered around the individual in an institutional setting, thus forgetting the surrounding society. Also, much music therapy seemed to be in compliance with a repressive psychiatric practice, much criticized from the sixties and onwards by the anti-psychiatry movement. It seems to be a challenge for music therapy, both to be able to serve the community at a broader level, and further to serve some emancipatory needs of the individual instead of becoming part of a medically dominated psychiatry. Psychoanalysis and a radical social attitude had for some of us to be integrated into the expanding field of music therapy.

This was the seventies, and it was obvious that the whole concept of science had become problematic for an interdisciplinary profession which tried to combine art and therapy, biological medicine and sociological critique, concern for the individual as well as for the relation between the individual and the surrounding community. Not least, if you had adopted the method of improvisation, so strongly implemented by Paul Nordoff and Clive Robbins, Alfred Schmölz or Mary Priestly to name some of the pioneers, you really had problems with the positivist or natural science attitude, which meant methods based on prediction and replication as a way of establishing a scientific truth. There was really no way you could repeat a study based on musical improvisation. And it was just as hard to make methodological predictions based on the rules of improvisation.

There was a problem, though, with the somewhat idealistic and sometimes loose and speculative grounding of much music therapy theory and practice. I remember writing letters to Paul Nordoff and Clive Robbins advising them to move more explicitly towards humanistic psychology. And Clive came to Oslo and lectured brilliantly on Maslow and music therapy as well as reading from the Sufi stories after we had discussed the future of music therapy... Thus reminding us of the wisdom in the art of music and improvisation not so easily adapted to the scientific discourse.

And in Oslo, while establishing the first nordic training program in music therapy in 78, I felt increasingly the need to find a new theoretical base for music therapy — without leaving the idea of the art of improvisation. One should remember that the nordic countries had a strong tradition for music therapy in special education. Pioneers such as Claus Bang and Olav Skille had made significant contributions to this particular field, and politically it was a right move to establish music therapy along the lines of special education. Piaget and cognitive psychology seemed to make a good starting point in the effort to combine developmental psychology with aesthetic theories of music. From musicology, Leonard B. Meyers theories of music and expectations proved to be a valuable input in the therapy-theory-dominated field. This constructivist approach to learning and interaction in music made sense when we tried to understand how the child learned from his improvisations, how he used his skills to construct a musical and personal identity as a tool for communication. The field of communication theory was a natural path to follow.

In the eighties we gradually saw a shift away from the positivist dominance within music therapy. In 1982, Barbara Hesser invited music therapists from all around the world to partake in the New York symposium "Music in the life of man." Things had changed in the US since I went there ten years earlier. A new organization, AAMT, had been initiated by Kenneth Bruscia and Barbara Hesser in order to take care of the neglected humanistic tradition. In the context of the NAMT/AAMT struggle the New York symposium was a politically important move in reconciling the small group of humanistic music therapists mainly on the east coast with a larger international community. Meeting with south-american music therapist, for instance Lia

Rejane Barcellos from Rio I learned that Heidegger and the phenomenological school of thought was not only an European tradition. In this symposium I also met Carolyn Kenny who had made an explicit critique of the positivist dominance of music therapy in her thesis *The Mythic Artery* (Kenny 1982). Later she emphasized the theory building aspect of music therapy in her *The Field of Play: A Guide for the Theory and Practice of Music Therapy* (1989). Leading AAMT-universities, like New York University (Barbara Hesser) and Temple University (Kenneth Bruscia, Cheryl Maranto) now started Ph.D-programs with an emphasis on qualitative methods. Increasingly phenomeno-logical and hermeneutical approaches were explicitly put into work within music therapy research (Ruud 1988, Amir 1992, Bruscia in Kenny 1995, Wheeler (ed.) 1995, Forinash & Gonzales 1989) In Europe RoseMarie Tüpker (1988) wrote books and articles on qualitative methods. The First Symposium in Qualitative Research in music Therapy in Düsseldorf in August 1994 made the effort to gather some of these researchers and thus made a significant contribution to the development of this new formation in music therapy research.

This small historical narrative should help to align the field of music therapy with the current multi-paradigmatic situation within the field of science. In this situation, which I will elaborate a bit further later on, science is no longer occupied with finding a single truth, or even defining a single reality. Together with the new paradigm of naturalistic or qualitative research there is a growing acceptance that people interpret reality differently, that our lifeworlds inform our interpretation of music in a way that makes all concerns for universality in music problematic. This situation could, however, invite long forgotten speculative tradition within our field. The problem of competing claims of knowledge and interpretation seems to demand serious attention.

Reflexivity — or science as metacritique
In the following I will argue that when science no longer is concerned with explanations, predictions or truth, the focus shifts towards dealing with the presupposition behind a certain scientific school of thought. In order to maintain a rational dialogue within the field of music therapy we have to make explicit our concepts of music and man which lie at the bottom of our theories about the therapeutic application of music.

There is a definite connection between our values, interests and norms and how we come to experience reality. If we accept as fact that people define or even experience reality differently, it will be an important task for a scientific attitude to understand the inner relationships between our values and the way we perceive the world. Let us take an example from music therapy to illustrate this.

One of the more celebrated examples from recent music therapy is to be found in the book "Creative music Therapy" (1977) by Paul Nordoff and

Clive Robbins. The case of Edward is discussed in the text as well as demonstrated in the cassette published with the book.

In the first session we may while listening to the tape experience how violently Edward protests even before he enters the music therapy room. That is, it makes sense to categorize his vocalising as screaming as "rejecting". However, and this is important, this "sonoric reality" may be interpreted and categorized differently by different therapists coming from different therapeutic or theoretical traditions. And of course, the therapeutic actions originating from these interpretations will be different. To be stated differently: The theoretical narratives used to interpret Edward´s vocal behaviour will lead to different sonoric realities, and different therapeutic strategies. Talking to different therapists, Edward´s vocalizing may be perceived as "crying", "defiance", "attention-seeking behavior", "high frequency sounds", "communication signals". Reflexivity concerning music therapy practice, will take into consideration how our categories of observation are not only theoretically biased, but in turn will determine what we will hear, how we will perceive the sounds or interpret the boy´s sounds. This again creates the basis for the choice of methods.

It is one of the basic tenets of the critical school in the philosophy of science that there is a correspondence between values, interests and how we perceive the world. The ideals of a value-free science were met with a critique from the hermeneutically inspired tradition. As we saw in the early conception of science held in music therapy, objectivity was held as one of the basic conditions of a scientific approach, i.e. to claim that the status of scientific results has to do with reducing possible sources of error, or to be systematically open to critique in advance by trying to reduce some of the most characteristic sources of errors.

There are however different types of errors. Our observations and theories may be influenced by our personality, our cultural, social or political background. Or they may be influenced by the particular scientific tradition we belong to. Objectivity addresses the possibility of dealing with such sources of errors and scientific activity has developed procedures and methods to secure objective access to the phenomena we are studying. This is a type of objectivity we name intersubjectivity and should secure that researchers will reach the same results when they apply the same methods of study.

There is however a type of presupposition we cannot handle in this manner. Researchers will always be informed by different interests or values which will influence their research activity. This pre-understanding does not only concern what we actually see and describe as researchers, but also what we look for. As we saw in the example of Edward, how we perceived his sounds was dependent upon the categories available to us, or chose to use. His sounds could have been perceived as a "scream", as "inappropriate behavior", as a "signal", or as a "possibility for communication". This example demonstrates how different people bring to the situation different values and interests attached to the use of different categories. For music therapists, in general we are faced with a professional identity which is trained to perceive sounds as possible signals of communication. Or, we could say that within a certain music therapy paradigm, the music therapist is concerned with an interest to maintain such signals in order to develop a pattern of interaction and expression.

In this sense we may trace systems of values originating within particular concepts of man and music. A music therapist within the humanistic tradition who for instance tends to think in these terms, regards man as active and in a search for meaning. At the same time music may be conceptualized as a "language", "system of symbols", "non-verbal system of expression", or a "system of communication" and so on.

A positivist ideal of science would insist upon the necessity to separate values and interests from the description of the phenomena. Their ideal is to insist on value neutrality. A positivist researcher within the field of music therapy would however be forced to make some kind of categorization. Often terms from physics would be used to describe Edward´s sound — frequency, timbre, duration and so on. As a general term Edward´s sounds may have been characterized as "discriminative stimuli".

The question is if such terms are more neutral than other systems of categories. Or if we really come closer to reality by using metaphors from physics rather than other areas of life. It is also possible to characterize the term "discriminative stimuli" as a particular concept of music.

My point here is to demonstrate that there is a certain connection between perception and knowledge, and norms, values, interests and actions. In other words, there is an inner connection between interests and perception in the sense that our values and interests inform and govern our way of perceiving the world.

If we translate "action" into "music therapeutical methods" we may draw the following triangle which illustrates the connection between these concepts:

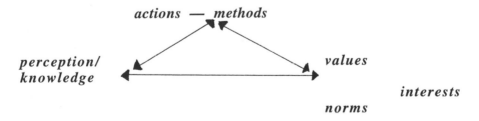

(after Jacobsen, Schnack and Wahlgren, 1979)

The term "norm" means the rules that regulate perception and action. In the case of Edward the music therapist may apply rules like: "you should use all the sounds the child makes as a point of departure for communication and interaction", "you should try to develop the child´s sounds in such a way that they can be developed within a communicative context." As I said earlier, values are for instance attached to a certain concept of music. But values also inform us about why this concept of music or definite actions based on this concept may benefit the child. It will be a part of the competence and training of the music therapist to master different ways of arguing for the possible beneficial influence of music. The music therapist, in other words, acts from a belief in the value of the type of activities she may want to initiate. When the term "interest" is used here, it is because we may always ask who may benefit from the action. The music therapist may argue that it is in the interest of the child to develop her repertoire of sounds and place this in a communicative context.

We may however imagine that behind other ways of categorizing the child´s sounds, for instance as "scream and noise", we may find more short term interests concerning creating an endurable work situation for the staff. Not to be moralistic about interests or ways of categorizing the world, factors such as wage and work condition, number of staff and so on will influence what systems of categorization are used. This again has to do with how society makes its priorities.

What I want to make explicit is that there is a definite connection between interests and perception/knowledge and that this connection may be coloured by prevailing ideas and attitudes in the society. In this connection one may also raise the discussion about whose interests govern the work of the music therapist. For instance, it is the values of the music therapists as a professional group who inform the work of the music therapist. Or we may ask if this work really is in the interest of the child, or if it is informed by the interest of society, whose interest it is to develop everyone within a limited concept of normality. In other words we may always ask critical questions of our own practice if it really is in the interest of the child to develop certain forms of competencies.

Qualitative methods

As I mentioned earlier, any scientific investigation of the improvisational music therapy, as for instance with the case of Edward, would meet with a lot of difficulties if we were to follow the procedures of positivist science. Lately we have seen the emergence of a qualitative research approach which, we might argue, will be better suited to capture the uniqueness of the improvisational method. Some of the main characteristics of the qualitative approach may be listed as follows:

1. Qualitative research is holistic. This may mean that research is organized around a case, a group, a classroom and so on. The purpose of the research may be to understand particular incidents. Its focus may be on the person, the experiences of persons involved, events or materials (Aldridge

1994, Bruscia in Wheeler (ed.) 1995). Thus, it seems reasonable that a particular improvisation (or several) could serve as a possible focus for study.

2. Qualitative research is empirical and naturalistic. This means that research takes place in the natural setting, that is, where music therapy is actually taking place. This natural setting is the direct source for the gathering of data.

3. Qualitative research is descriptive. Sounds/music, words and pictures rather than numbers. Interpretation starts from information contained in the situation and includes experiences or transcripts of music, outprint of interviews, fieldnotes, videotapes, audiotapes, personal documents and more. Since music therapists who are doing research on methods involving improvisation (or doing clinical research in general) cannot replicate their studies, *documentation* seems to be crucially important. What the Germans calls "Nachvollziehbarkeit" — the ability to trace and follow any statement about the world, description or representation of the situation/event back to the sound, verbal statement, picture (tapes, video, paintings), and so on seem important to music therapy. Since there is no way to repeat an improvisation, which in itself excludes a scientific paradigm based on replicability, research has to document the sounding behind the interpretation. This is especially important when dealing with music. This is because of the polysemic quality of music, the innumerable ways music may be represented through verbal metaphors.

4. Qualitative research is interpretive. It is a basic condition for our interaction with the world that we build our concepts and understanding upon our interpretation of what the senses give us. Thus, the basic scientific tool must be hermeneutics or the science of interpretation.

5. Qualitative research is emphatic. It is directed toward the intentions behind what is observed. It is concerned with the perspective of the participants or observed. If the purpose of research is to grasp the concrete and immediate meaning in an improvisation, or has the intention of understanding the intention behind a certain way of expression, qualitative research may be the answer. Qualitative researchers will differ, however, in their view of the nature of the meaning of music. Some may look into the structure of the material/event to study a sort of "embodied" meaning. Others may adopt the relativist attitude of the anthropologist to study how people construct meaning within a particular context.

6. Qualitative research is based upon "grounded theory". This means inductive analysis of data, or what is called a "bottom-up"-perspective.

7. In qualitative research emphasis is placed on immediate observations and spontaneous interpretations. As Tüpker (1990) has argued, this would satisfy the need for closeness in understanding with resepct to the improvisation in question. This would also provide for the necessary flexibility, the ability to let oneself be moved by the situation, the music. Instead of trying to live up to the positivist ideal of the neutral, objective

researcher, qualitative methods take advantage of the participating researcher who stands in a particular relation to the phenomena under study. This way of acknowleding subjectivity of course raises serious questions of validity. Tüpker asks for what she calls "controlled subjectivity", which involves the ability to avoid distracting or harmful influences. Other qualitative researchers emphasize various methods of triangulation (See Aldridge 1994).

This also means that we do not lose our primarily pre-scientific and immediate understanding, but that we try to contain such experiences within the scientific statement. This is also especially important if we want to contain the bodily expression often behind the musical gesture. In Husserls term, the spontaneity of the interpretation would try to secure that we capture the bodily "Fundierung" in the verbal representation (Merleau-Ponty).

Such an interpretative perspective where the "nature" of the phenomena are made explicit and relate to the pre-understanding of the interpreter may well suit the demands of reflexivity or metacritical activity which were discussed earlier. Generally it could be stated that music therapy, as a human or interpretive science, is mainly interested in investigating the relationships between the musical signs that originate in the transactions between the client and the therapist and those changes in the experience or behavior of the client which stem from those processes of signification which happen within or between the client and therapist as a result of the musical interaction.

This would imply developing some tools of interpretation which make it possible to read the interplay between musical structures, the experiences of the client and the interventions of the therapist. One possible strategy in the deconstruction of this triadic process would be to postulate the whole music therapy situation as a text. Then we could benefit from the theoretical and methodological diversity developed within the field of human sciences, that is for instance literary and cultural studies, narrative analysis, rhetorics, semiotics, discourse theory, structural analysis and so on.

Competing claims of knowledge

It is an underlying assumption within the field of qualitative research that the aim of qualitative research in music therapy is not to reach some kind of truth, in the sense of describing a single reality. There is also an assumption that a particular method does not guarantee that the results can be compared with some pre-set standard of truth. Or, as Ken Aigen said in his opening address to the First Symposium on Qualitative Research in Düsseldorf in August 1994: "Method is neither a guarantor nor an arbiter of truth. Because so much of qualitative research is dependent upon the skills, personal qualities, and insight of the researcher, it is possible that a given method could be meticulously followed and still not produce valuable or trustworthy findings." (1994:11) Instead, qualitative research acknowledges the existence of multiple realities, or as Ken Bruscia states, "that truth and reality exist in the form of multiple, intangible mental constructions" (Bruscia 1994: 6). Thus the best we can accomplish is to reach a better understanding of the particular reality we are involved in or share in some areas with a particular client. Does this mean, then, that qualitative research is not concerned with possible competing claims of knowledge? Or, how are various aspects of "validity" dealt with in the field of qualitative research?

We will find that there are approaches which live up to this ideal of relative truth and reports which try to obtain some kind of validity in the traditional sense. Henk Smeijsters, for instance, although he recognizes the importance of qualitative designs in music therapy research, claims that it is important not to give up "the accepted criteria for sound scientific research" (1994:1) Smeijsters, then, argues that we need criteria for validity, and he thus sees the problem of validity as a methodological one. It is a problem to be solved within his empirical or positivist epistemology. It could be questioned, however, if the problem of conflicting claims of knowledge is a methodological one, or if it belongs to the epistemological domain. If the latter is the case, we have to deal with different epistemologies pertaining to various methodological approaches. It is not, then, a question of taking traditional methodological precautions to install validity.

In the positivist paradigm we find a concept of truth where the data are looked upon as being in correspondence with the reality, what is called the "correspondence theory of truth". Opposed to this, data in qualitative research are considered in some way "constructed". Since there is no way of knowing the reality directly, only through language and perception, the qualitative (or hermeneutic) effort aims at revealing some kind of meaning or significance in the data. This is in accordance with the broader interpretive background, the hermeneutic concept of truth, or what is sometimes called the "coherence theory of truth". The coherence criterion refers to the unity, consistency and internal logic of a statement (see Kvale 1989). Thus qualitative researchers, when they talk about accuracy, do not mean 'correspondence', but 'appropriate (metaphoric) representation'.

But we also have a third concept of truth prevailing in the contemporary theory of science, i.e. the pragmatic point of view, which is concerned with "truth" being measured against its practical consequences, its usefulness (see Alvesson and Sköldberg 1994).

We could draw the following triangle to represent the various positions.

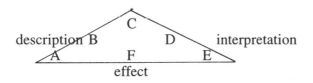

This model could help in understanding some of the paradigms dominating different schools of research in today´s music therapy. Let us first take a look at the traditional conception of science. If research in music therapy is wholly identified as "outcome research" we could apply a pragmatic criterion to evaluate whether the knowledge we have produced is "true". This is recognized in the model as a position F. Behavioural studies, for instance, are concerned with the "contingent use of music", that is with its effect upon behaviour, not its meaning for the patient.

The problem with such a position is that it would tell us nothing about the processes leading towards change in behaviour, or describe the music being an important facilitator in the process. Moving left in our model, we will find researcher A who not only will try to account for the changes in the behaviour of the client, but will have made a description, or an operational definition of the music being used, or the behaviour involved. This is often done within the paradigm of empirical epistemology by applying concepts from physics or acoustics in order to obtain "correct" data or intersubjectively shared statements. Therapist A, then, finds herself in a descriptive-pragmatic mode where the question of the significance of music is downplayed and where descriptions (of music or behaviour) are close to data. This is also a practice where the theory building has lesser importance than theory corroboration and verification. (In this sense *Journal of Music Therapy is the most recognized chronicle of the music therapy verification-proletariat.*)

Position B is assumed by the positivist researcher most concerned with describing the data. In research where the analysis of music is put into focus, this will lead to a detailed description of the musical parameters according to some system of analysis. In some of these systems, analysis often starts from this level, either close to the score, transcription or (phenomenological) experience. Some close readings of the music done by phenomenologists would belong in the area between B and C, depending upon the recognition of their own preunderstanding (Husserl-Heidegger). It is interesting then, to see how phenomenology is coming close to positivist standard of truth when insisting upon describing 'the essence' of a phenomenon — a so-called naive realism.

The analyst taking position C would try to take a stand where the investigation of the phenomenon reveal the nature of the phenomenon, in the sense of saying something about its significance. Although not fully recognizing that this meaning is a construct, or taking the full account of a deeper cultural or biographic meaning into focus, analysis would tend to stay close to the structure of music or the supposed "natural categories" evolving from the close investigation of the experiences of the patient.

D position, however removes itself from the idea of the possibility of describing music or the experience of the patient "as it is", or the "true experience" of the client. For the hermeneutic interpretation there is always a deeper underlying theme, a significance which may be *interpreted*. We can clearly see this in Dorit Amir´s research paper which states: (1994:2) "I

26

wanted to find out more about the meaning of the experience of music therapy for those who are involved as therapists and clients." Although Amir explicitly describes the process which leads to her categories, it could be discussed to what extent her categories are constructed. Amir seems to be faithful to the orthodox tenets of grounded theory, thus focussing the empirical nature of their categories. This empiricist turn is supported by her list of credibility measures: intensive contact with subjects, triangulation, peer debriefing, negative case analysis and member checks. Thus Amir's hermeneutic approach to the "meaning behind" is somewhat influenced by the empiricist epistemology.

There seems to be less of the postmodern turn in qualitative research in the recent qualitative approach. One exception may be Carolyn Kenny, who brought narrative and critical theory, as well as a deconstructive attitute to the question of methology in her contribution to the Düsseldorf Symposium (Kenny 1994). Future will tell if even music therapy researchers may find the text (music, experience) irrelevant as an "authentic expression" informing us about the "inner life" of the patient, taking into consideration only the text as being produced within the context of other texts. That is, music improvised, for instance, is not understood with reference to some underlying structure of the music or to the biography of the patient, but to the musical code developed throughout the previous sessions.

Moving towards E would also allow the narrative and rhetorical character of our knowledge to partake in the important task of theory building in our field. At the same time we would have had some necessary feedback from the larger intersubjective community of therapists about the reality of our thoughts and actions.

Conclusion
Summing up it may seem that this route through the field of music therapy has led me into the inpreprelative paradigm I have learned from a community of music therapist how they have come to perceive reality and the nature of their work differently. I have learned how their outlook on life, how their values and interests coloured their way of looking at the process of research, their way of pursuing a truth. As I have argued, however, there is no single truth, no single reality.

The field of music therapy is forever populated with persons and paradigms with competing claims of knowledge. The only answer is to learn and to communicate.*

* Thanks to Carolyn Bereznak Kenny for critical remarks and help with editing.

References:

Aigen, Kenneth. "The Role of Values in Qualitative Music Therapy Research." Paper presented at the First International Symposium for Qualitative Research in Music Therapy, Düsseldorf, July, 29. - 30, 1994.

Aldridge, David 1994. "Single Case Research Designs for the Creative Arts Therapist", in *The Arts in Psychotherapy*, 21(5)

Alvesson, Mats and Kaj Sköldberg 1994. *Tolkning och reflektion.Vetenskapsfilosofi och kvalitativ metod*. Lund: Studentlitteratur.

Amir, Dorit 1992. *Awakeing and expanding the Self: Meaningful Moments in the Music Therapy Process as Experienced and Described by Music Therapists and Music Therapy Clients*, Ann Arbor: UMI Dissertation Service.

Amir, Dorit. "Experiencing Music Therapy: Meaningful Moments in the Music Therapy Process." Paper presented at the First International Symposium for Qualitative Research in Music, Therapy, Düsseldorf, July 29. - 30, 1994.

Bruscia, Kenneth E. "Authenticity Issues in Qualitative Research", Paper presented at the First International Symposium for Qualitative Research in Music Therapy, Düsseldorf, 29. - 30. July, 1994.

Bruscia, Kenneth E. 1995. "Modes of Consciousness in Guided Imagery and Music (GIM): A Therapist´s Experience of the Guiding Process", in Carolyn Bereznak Kenny (ed.) *Listening, Playing, Creating. Essays on the Power of Sound*, New York: State University of New York Press.

Gaston, E. Th. 1968. *Music in Therapy*, New York: The Macmillan Company.

Jacobsen, B., Schnack, K. og Wahlgren, B. 1979.*Videnskabsteori*. Gyldendal, København.

Kenny, Carolyn Bereznak 1982. *The Mythic Artery. The Magic of Music Therapy, Atascadero, Ca.:Ridgeview Publishing Company*

Kenny, Carolyn Bereznak. 1989:. *The Field of Play: A Guide for the Theory and Practice of Music Therapy*. Ridgeview Publishing Company.

Kenny, Carolyn Bereznak "The Story of the Field of Play." Paper presented at the First International Symposium for Qualitative Research in Music Therapy, Düsseldorf, July, 29. - 3 0, 1994.

Kvale, Steinar 1989. "To Validate is to Question." In Kvale (ed.) *Issues of Validity in Qualitative Research*. Lund: Studentlitteratur.

Langenberg, Mechthild, Jörg Frommer and Michael Langenbach. "Fusion and Separation. Experiencing Opposites in music, Music Therapy, and Music Therapy Research." Paper presented at the First International Symposium for Qualitative Research in Music Therapy, Düsseldorf, July, 29. - 30, 1994.

Nordoff, Paul and Clive Robbins 1977.*Creative Music Therapy*. The John Day Company, New York.

Ruud, Even 1973. *Music Therapy and its Relationship to Current Treatment Theories*. Masters Thesis, Florida State University.

Ruud, Even 1980. *Hva er musikkterapi*? Oslo: Gyldendal

Ruud, Even 1980b. *Music Therapy and its Relationship to Current Treatment Theories*. St. Louis: Magnamusic-Baton.

Ruud, Even 1988. "Music Therapy: Health Profession or Cultural Movement. *Music Therapy*, Vol. 7, No. 1, 34 - 37.

Ruud, Even 1990: *Musikk som kommunikasjon og samhandling*. Solum, Oslo. (Music as Communication and Interaction, Ph.D-thesis, University of Oslo 1987)

Ruud, Even 1990b. *Caminos da musicoterapia*. Sao Paolo: Summus editioral

Ruud, Even 1990c. *Los Caminos de la Musicoterapia*, Bueanos Aires: Editorial Bonum.

Ruud, Even and Wolfang Mahns 1991. *Meta-Musiktherapie*, Stuttgart: Gusrav Fischer Verlag.

Smeijsters, Henk. "Qualitative Single-Case Research in Practice: A Necessary, Reliable and Valid Alternative for Music Therapy Research." Paper presented at the First International Symposium for Qualitative Research in Music Therapy, Düsseldorf, July, 29. - 30, 1994.

Tüpker, Rosemarie 1988. *Ich singe, was ich nicht sagen kann*. Gustav Bosse Verlag, Regensburg.

Towards the Development of a European Research Culture in Music Therapy

David Aldridge (D)

Over the past ten years we have seen an emerging demand for music therapy research in Europe. A number of individual researchers based in different countries have attempted to promote music therapy research. Music therapy itself, like nursing, psychotherapy and various other forms of helping professions, is also being challenged to produce research results.

The source of that challenge is coming both from within the profession itself, and from without. From within the profession, a new generation of music therapists is demanding academic credibility, and this need is linked to the establishment of postgraduate music therapy courses leading to masters qualifications. Music therapists, too, are demanding within their own career trajectories that they can deepen their understanding of what they are doing and gain academic credentials by further study. Combined with this internal demand, we are seeing throughout the European Union a demand for outcomes research related to varying therapeutic initiatives both from third-party funders and from employing health institutions. With Government cut-backs in health and education, enhanced scrutiny in University spending, and fiscal demands for efficiency and productivity, then music therapy departments are having to either justify their existence by producing material evidence of their efficacy or produce research papers to improve their academic points rating.

This means that a relatively new profession is being forced to develop research results without having had the chance to establish research training, without a satisfactory background of research material and without the opportunity to negotiate an acceptable way of doing research that is related to therapeutic outcome. Indeed, we are not alone in this, rehabilitation medicine and general medical practice in the Western world stands under the same spotlight of scrutiny.

In addition, we are faced with a relative lack of research expertise. Some of us have a research career that has experience of various forms of research projects. However, few of our colleagues have had the opportunity to do post-graduate research and are being expected to teach research methods and supervise research projects. While this may be a necessity, driven by need, I suggest that in some cases we will find that colleagues are being prepared for an over-idealised world of academic research that reflects maybe the lack of experience within the profession, rather than research that is focused upon clinical practice. It is vital that we develop a sound basis of research-orientated clinical practitioners.

However, take heart, for within Europe there are several moves that have been underway during the last ten years to provide a research infrastructure within individual countries, and which I hope will meet the challenge to cooperate on an international basis. Many of us are trying to provide research support that suits the music therapists themselves, while serving their needs to reach out to an external community.

At the heart of much of this debate is the difference between process research and outcomes research. Many music therapists will be interested in what happens when they do music therapy. They ask the question, how does the music unfold and what has this to do with the changing status of the person with whom I am working? This changing status may be musical, aesthetic, psychological, clinical or indeed social. External parties, however, may be more concerned with the differences before a person has music therapy when compared with what happens after a person has had music therapy. The question will be related to the material benefit associated with doing music therapy. This question is not so much concerned with how that process is carried out rather it is concerned with the actual clinical outcome itself (and sometimes the costs incurred related to that outcoem). Within the whole field of health-care delivery in the Western world such questions are being placed in the foreground of research initiatives.

Furthermore, there is also a difference between the purposes of research. At the moment, in a junior profession we have researchers preparing masters material and doctoral studies. These studies are often of a different nature to post-graduate research studies and research contracted to outside agencies. Doctoral studies are focused on the development of the doctoral candidate. They are there for the sole process of developing someone who will later be able to carry out research. Therefore the work itself will often be of an intensely deep and inward-looking nature. The research that is carried out by experienced researchers will be more outward looking and often be at the request of some external agency wanting to see some material benefit from their investment. Therefore, the purposes and the methods used will differ. I am arguing that we need both these forms of research, and only to foster an inward-looking research will restrict the nature of music therapy research, and thereby practice, in the future. As a rational step forward several of us have proposed that single case research designs are a positive way forward fostering both process oriented work combined with the possibility for assessing outcomes

What kind of research we do, and the methods we use to go about researching, will be influenced by the philosophy of science that we have. My main proposal is that science is a process, an activity not a set of commandments set in stone for all time as the basis for a dogma. In a post-modern world, where all the major themes are challenged and deconstructed, then it is our responsibility to construct themes that are appropriate to the knowledge that we need. While this debate is often set out as differences in truth claims; that is "Is truth relative?" or "Is there one truth ?", my argument is that such a position belongs to a previous era of debate. Claims about truth have already been discussed in various other scientific disciplines. What we are really making claims about are objectivity and subjectivity. And this debate can be currently found in the nursing literature, in the world of psychology, in journals dedicated to social science and particularly over the last ten years in the field of complementary medicine.

First, let me make an observation about science in a broad sense. The word science itself in its English usage springs from the Latin *scire*, to know, originally meaning to cut, and thereby to decide, and has a relationship with the Latin adjective *scius* , that means "knowing". So, on the one hand we have a derivation of science that appears to be about making decisions, to cut and to separate. Or, we can follow another route and look at the adjective *scius* as it refers to knowing, and as it occurs in the Latin word *conscius*, literally con=together scius= knowing). Perhaps this is what we are searching for in our scientific activity, how we can share knowledge, or how can we bring knowledge into consciousness.

Yet another perspective would take us to the German word for science, "Wissenschaft". *Wissen* is to know or to know about, and is related to knowledge and judgement, and *schaffen* is to make or create, or to manage or accomplish. So, from another European perspective we can see science as an activity of creating knowledge, and perhaps it is this creative activity that may appeal to many of us today, and perhaps some of us feel this has become lost to the scientific activity. Knowledge is something that can be done, it is a creative activity, a process not a fixed product. Indeed the word knowledge in English is distantly derived from a root that means "I can" (Middle English Ic can, German können and kennen) and is perhaps best described as the statement "I can know". Once we take such a position of knowledge being actively acquired, then we can speculate upon the various arts of doing science.

This is a move away from the Cartesian position that seperates mind and body as reflected in cogito ergo sum - I think therefore i am. What I am proposing here is ago ergo sum - I perform therefore I am.

What remains to be added to these descriptions from the Latin and the Gerrman roots is the notion of decision or judgement, therefore doing science - or the activity of sciencing - is a matter of deciding. It is therefore a moral activity.

How do we create knowledge, then? This question lies at the centre of many modern scientific debates, and is a question of methodology. One of our critiques of modern science doing is that the argument rarely concentrates on the subject matter of our inquiry that leads to a new creative discovery for the person who wants to know. The activity of science seems more like the pressure for us to conform in our knowing to a set of prescriptions that are applied to a given body of knowledge, that is, *methodolatry not methodology.* It is this struggle with an appropriate methodology that we find in the current creative arts therapy literature, and one that has been hotly debated during the last decade within other fields of applied therapeutic practice.

Some of the basic assumptions of science in the seventeenth century were that a reality really existed outside of the mind of the observer and that objectivity, detached from the mind of the observer, is a desirable goal. From such a perspective it is possible to propose that all phenomena obey scientific laws, and that science is the activity of measuring and quantifying that reality. However, philosophies of modern science have had to abandon such a perspective and undertake the assumption that *consciousness is fundamentally present within the universe.* The observer and the observed are intimately linked. For many of us in the field of research, the nature of which observations are made about people, and the methods used to make such observations, is a matter of ethical importance that lies at the heart of our culture. While measurements are sometimes necessary, and speak to a given audience, there are times when our human capacity cannot be adequately perceived filtered through a machine or calculated form a series of questionnaire response, as if feelings could be weighed like ballast. To know another person is to engage him or her directly in performance - ago ergo sum. Knowledge is something that can be sung or played.

One of the many reasons we may feel that our research is pressed into a particular methodological strait-jacket is the demand for external validation. Such validation often means quantification and a statistically relevant result. All too often the statistics of frequency that are used, and the underlying philosophy of science, stem from another era of therapeutic research. The science of statistics developed in eighteenth century France was part of the centralized apparatus of the State. ``Statistics´´, *as the science of state* , was the empirical numerical representation of the resources available to the State and formed the components of a new power rationality. The *purpose* of such knowledge was to achieve a political objective. *Individual* needs were subsumed within the goals of the collective, the private ethic was informed by the public ethic and objective empirical data were the means by which goals were assessed Such data were related, as now, to the economic regulation of health care delivery (health as commodity); public order (the regulation of deviance), and hygiene (the quality of food, water and the environment).

From this viewpoint we have the notion of health care, and knowledge about that health care, which is regulated by the State. The objects of that health care (patients) , the practitioners of that health care (therapists), and the providers of that health care (health and State insurance) are informed by the same world view. Such was the strength of modern science, it offered a *replicable body of knowledge* in the face of the ever increasing solipsism of metaphysics in the eighteenth century.

In such a science, people are observed, *classified and analysed as `cases`* according to their deviance from a given norm. How often do we hear the statement "I work with anorectics" or "That is how it is working with depressives" ? When, in reality, we are working with individuals that are suffering, and that suffering may sometimes need to be coded as a medical category, for whatever purposes. But none of us really is such a category. If the experience of disease becomes a category like any other, then it loses the unique experience that it is. If our experience is coded to the categories of others , then we must be aware of the purposes that categorisation serves. While categorisation is the bed-rock of most forms of inquiry, the purposes of that inquiry should be made clear.

The epistemology of this normative process is that of natural science emphasizing reason, constancy and predictability. In the face of death and disruption the imperative of health is to maintain continuity and control. It is a philosophical assumption that what once was will be so again in the future. The basis of normative science has been that the future can be accurately predicted from the past, and is dependent upon the past. Thus, there is no room for spontaneity. I regard this as an existential anxiety in the face of death. Scientists, working from this perspective, have failed to face up to the uncertainty of life and the possibility for spontaneity. Such a basis for living, that there are fixed ultimately knowable scientific laws in a predictable universe, is no less a metaphysical statement as my saying that we are composed in the moment, that meanings are constructed and negotiated and thereby we achieve but momentary shared experiences of reality.

What I am arguing for then is that, if science is a *creative doing of knowledge,* then the way that we can do knowledge about being human is not restricted to instrumentation through machines, rather, that *knowledge is something that can be sung, or played, or danced or acted.* Underlying this approach is a philosophy of the world that moves away from a solely materialistic perspective, and its associated technologies, to a perspective on the world that sees it as **a** *living organism improvised in the moment in which we are all taking part.*

Subjectivity	We will need to include an experientialist perspective to our scientific activities that includes subjective data as primary, rather than limiting inquiries to so-called objective, physical sense - machine sense data.
	Objective data are really agreed codes for sharing private experiences and establishing the legitimacy of some experiences and not others.
	There will be a place for first-person descriptions, and therefore subjective feelings.
Participatory	Understanding does not stem from detachment alone, there are times when co-operation is called for, when identification with the subject is needed.
	We have a shared culture and there are activities that we can explore together.
Experiential	Consciousness is the observer and the observed, the experience of observing
	The researcher will be changed by the experience.

As in the age of Romanticism, the primacy of the self as perceiver is once more being emphasised. Subjectivity becomes paramount, on the one hand reifying the individual, but on the other hand running the risk that the individual will become *isolated*. Indeed, while post-modernism is perhaps itself characterised by a revolt against authority and tends towards self-referentiality, its very *eclectic*ism leaves the individual valued but exhausted of significance - *"the saturated self"*. The inflated potential for self-hood, dislocated from traditional value sources, increases the potential for *despair* and, while individuals may rise to the challenge of pluralism, there are some individuals who will seek to join groups who offer some form of reassurance by offering a given orthodoxy of beliefs and actions. The danger in modern Europe is that the romantic notion of individualism, becomes perverted into *tribalism,* and the dislocated individual seeking to construct his or her own identity, joins a group intent on the limitation of others freedom of self-definition. Concensus is fragile in a context where individual demands are reified. *Conscius* - knowing together- is also difficult to manage without tolerance.

We see this breaking out in the debate about quantitative or qualitative research, where one is proposed as the only form of research inquiry. While music therapists in the United States, partly because of their education structure have a tradition of music therapy research, that tradition has often been polarised into two opposing camps; qualitative research versus quantitative research. The grounds for this polarisation appear to be historically-based in the establishment of a political professional identity within the field of practice. What some of us have been trying to do is to avoid such polarisation and foster a climate of tolerance that allows us to develop music therapy research that suits music therapists and their various purposes. All too often this debate has been at the foreground of research initiatives and has masked the underlying political debate about which group should hold political sway within the profession. We could just as easily translate this debate into the intolerance of varying music therapy schools for one another. Such arguments really are superfluous at a time when the profession itself is ripe to develop, and in its maturity should be ready to extend the tolerance necessary for knowing together.

What I am arguing for is that if science is a *creative doing of knowledge,* then the way that we can do knowledge about being human is not restricted to instrumentation through machines, rather, *knowledge is something that can be sung, or played, or danced or acted*. Underlying this apporach is a philosophy of the world that moves away from a solely materialistic perspective to a perspective that sees the world as a living *organism improvised in the moment in which we are all taking part*.

If truth in post-modern society is relative, and the self is constructed to meet the variety of life's' contingencies, then we move

35

away from the model of one generation initiating the next generation into the truths of its own beliefs. Instead, we have a *pool of experts and advisers* to whom we can turn for advice. In some modern alternative healing approaches, traditional forms of teaching by initiation and learning by apprenticeship, are rejected in favour of an eclecticism that take techniques assembled according to the situation. A new generation of music therapists is being trained that demands *a choice of learning approaches* which suits their approach to music and to therapy. The pioneer approach of the teacher/ pupil relationship no longer holds sway, and while the restriction of the relationship may be lost, so too is the security. Furthermore, as there is no established tradition of music therapy research, we have the luxury of deciding what methods are appropriate to use in our scientific endeavour. While some of us will research alone, others will decide to work together in groups. What we need to avoid is that one group can make a an exclusive claim to determine the doing of knowledge according to their own principles. To establish tolerance we need to understand each other and our varying purposes.

The activity of doing research, or sciencing as knowing, is concerned not with restricting us to a one-dimensional sense of being according to an accepted orthodox world-view, but the possibility for the interpretation of the self as new. What we choose to know, and how we know is a matter of judgement, and therefore one of moral agency. How each one of us decides to know in the future, with whom we share that knowledge, and how we tolerate and incorporate what others know, will determine the scientific culture of music therapy.

	Physiological work	Clinical applications	Theoretical work	Publica-tion
Phase One	establish physiological criteria of change in therapist/ patient interaction	single case studies, develop working methods appropriate to a hospital setting	literature reviews, theory development	case studies and position papers
Phase Two	refine hypotheses and test out methods, establish experimental method	develop working relationships with the hospital staff, attempt feasibility study of co-operative work	collect case examples from recorded work	case studies and clinical outcome material
Phase Three	continue work, identify clinical problems and refine hypotheses	look for larger scale clinical trials, establish contacts with other clinical groups	develop theory and refine techniques	develop database produce collected works CD ROM

We see from the differing phases that there are continuing themes related to our work. These themes are related to the needs of our colleagues in practice. The theme of physiological change was the basis for the doctoral work of my colleagues Lutz Neugebauer and Dagmar Gustorff, and is continued in our current work. The clinical research continues and will form the backbone of our published material as the main area of interest for clinicians is clinical practice. What I hope to do with this clinical work however is to graft that work onto the underlying theoretical structures that exist within our music therapy approach and within clinical practice in general. This is surely the purpose of an academic department. Such clinical and theoretical work then leads outwards into the world with various publications and inwards by feeding the teaching of the music therapy students in training.

Coupled to this research material we have tried to introduce an element of research teaching in the second year of the masters training program through individually-based case-oriented research. While it is possible to gain a doctoral qualification within the faculty of medicine at the University of Witten, we have also seen the necessity that the Aalborg PhD program identified, and that is for a qualification of Doctor Music Therapy. When we have so much limited, albeit valuable, experience and expertise it makes sense then to pool that expertise and knowledge between University centres. It is only by our differing countries coming together that we can begin to meet the research challenges that are being made of us.

Within our program we have initiated a literature support service that is being shared currently with Denmark, Holland and other Nordic and Scandinavian countries. This has been based on our recognition of a simple research support service within Germany to meet the needs of students who have trained with us and are now colleagues in practice. In addition there are other colleagues who do not have the benefit of institutional support and it is our responsibility to at least support them in whatever way they can should they wish to begin clinical research.

In addition, we also see the need to offer research methodological advice, and in some cases specific teaching. I see no reason why this should be restricted to our own national interests and call upon my colleagues to find a way in which we can collaborate to offer a European "college", in the sense of a group, that will offer such support. Such an aim is surely the basis of European funding.

Next steps:
It is important that we continue to further establish European connections. One way to accomplish this will be by exchanging teaching staff interested in research, or providing the opportunity for extended visits. Promoting research placements for higher-level students, or junior members of staff, would also be a possibility that would benefit the institutions. For example, we have had visiting music therapists who have sat in on the teaching sessions, experienced a series of therapy sessions and made a review of literature on a theme that has interested them. There are a number of institutions throughout Europe that have special areas of interest for music therapists, and an extended working visit is a good way of getting to know other institutions.

It may be time to consider a European journal for music therapy. There are, I know, national journals and I am aware that this is a sensitive matter. However, we do need to encourage a standard of music therapy writing that will bring the exciting clinical work that is being done throughout Europe to the attention of other clinicians. Furthermore, we also need to encourage the possibility for academic writing and theoretical discussion. This can only be achieved by an journal that will act as a forum for such debate. As our chosen medium is music, and non-verbal, then the challenge arises in these times of modern technology of developing new media possibilities. We do not need a new *printed* publication. I suggest that we investigate the publication of music therapy material on CD Rom. Material published in this way could be both text, musical scores, musical extracts as recorded sounds, video clips, photographs and database items.

We certainly need to collaborate on providing a research infrastructure. By this I mean that we have to share our various resources for offering methodological advice and teaching research methods. There is enough expertise, the problem remains of how to utilise it and coordinate it. We have access to databases and literature archives. What we do not have, as yet, is a means of giving a broad access to such material. I have previously suggested that we set up cooperating centres within the differing countries, but that would mean that institues would have to communicate with each other!

One important way forward would be to promote a "single-case" agency where we could co-ordinate single case methods teaching, offer a suitable research format and collect research examples. By doing this we could develop a set of clinical studies as a clinical studies database. This would necessitate translating the clinical studies into a common set of European languages, but would offer clinical researchers a pool of comparative data.

Finally, the benefit of music therapy is that it promotes indiviualism and allows for the unique expression of clinical expertise. The danger is that groups then form that are so convinced of their own unique value that they believe that all others should work in their superior way and that they have the right to dictate the standards of individuals. This is tribalism and is the ultimate danger in a post-modern society.

Research in Music Therapy on a Multi-Disciplinary Background

Edith Lecourt (F)

Introduction
This paper is in two parts:
1) the historical background of music therapy research in France,
2) my current research work with a multi-disciplinary participation.

1. Historical development of previous French research in music therapy
This presentation will illustrate the variety of disciplines that have successively developed within the mentioned research areas.

A - Cosmogony and Religion
From Antiquity to the end of the Middle Ages music therapy has been considered a part of cosmogony (mainly in Boece's model of the Four Elements which govern the world) and has been used in religion (see the Bible) as well as in medicine.

This orientation is still present in India, where there is no place for a specialization in music therapy, because music by itself has, in certain conditions, God's power: Music is God's language. This point of view - shared in many religions - gives no access to true research, as God's evidence cannot be founded on experimentation.

B - A tentative of rationalism
As I represent here Descartes' University I should like to give an homage to Descartes' interest and personal contribution to our field.
In the XVIIth century Descartes tried to rationalize the way music touches the human being in his *COMPENDIUM MUSICAE*(1618).

Mathematics and physiology were for him the rational basis for an explanation of the influence of music on the human being, and especially on humans' passions. The effect of consonance is explained within two parameters, one physio-mathematical (resonance) and the other psycho-physiological (wish, desire, expectation). Rhythm has an important place in this theory, with its powerful influence on emotion (more than harmony) and its direct relation to passions (e.g.: fast/slow).

Descartes was interested in the relation between the sensorial pleasure and the structure of its object (the opposite of Aristoteles' point of view). For him the properties of audition together with the properties os sound determine passion. Descartes' dream was to live long enough to be able to write a theory of music, explaining how every movement of the soul is excited by music, and how the movement is determined by a specific part of the music.

C. - A romantic, sentimental approach

During the Romantic period (from the end of XVIIIth century); the power of music was considered more a sentimental evidence than a religious or a scientific topic. And this way of thinking is still active today in many practice fields of music therapy. It was the case, for instance, in France with Jost's approach of receptive music therapy in the Seventies. Romantic pieces of music are used and considered in a Manichean way as "good" or "bad" for the client,"beneficial" or "dangerous" in consideration of his psychopathology.

This judgement is dependent on the sentimental state of research.
This concept can easily be operant from a behavioural point of view as it was the case with the first psychiatric approaches of music therapy a century ago.

D. - Research of the first psychiatrists

In France a new approach of music therapy appeared first in the beginning of the XIX. century. At the birth of psychiatry - at the origin of a medical (and not only social or religious) approach of alienation, Philippe Pinel, the pioneer, took the initiative to bring expressive activities such as music in Bicêtre Asilium in Paris. His disciples have developed experiences in music audition (listening to music) and music practice with the patients. This was the first clinical research which was composed of a set of clinical observations of patients' behaviour during the listening to concerts. These concerts were given by the first students of the National Conservatorium, created in Paris at the same time (Hospitals of Bicêtre, Salpétrière, Charenton, were the most famous at this time about 1820). J. Arveiller's book (1980) shows the development of these trials of the "moral" efficiacy of different pieces of music observed by the first french psychiatrists, some of them as famous as Esquirol, Leuret or Nathan. But progressively these explorations of the power of music on hundreds of patients gathered for concerts gave birth to criticism, and the results seemed to be too contingent for other psychiatrists like e.g. Moreau de Tours.

This first research in music therapy was the initiative of the psychiatrists, who used musicians to make it concrete. At the end of the nineteenth century and the beginning of our century music therapy was limited to a tool of socialization. This opened the place for musicians in the occupational therapies, but this movement has been more developed at this time in USA than in France where it didn't open to research.

E - The psychophysiology of music: Dental research

In the 1970es mainly a new hope was born for research - with a psychophysiological approach to music's efficiacy on behaviour. This was the origin of fifteen years of French research in sophrology - a sort of medical hypnosis - mainly developed at that time by dentists for surgery. The effects of listening to music have been explored in this context, as part of the psychophysiological preparation of patients, and also during the surgical act itself. Psychophysiological measures have adressed this influence of music listening on physiological parameters such as breath and cardiac rhythms, muscular tension etc. Dr. Maurice Gabai was the initiator of this research and many dentists have - during that period - presented results to validate the place and functions of music to create in the patient a diminuation of anxiety, a state of relaxation and analgesia which facilitates the surgical act. It also shows efficiacy on the immediate physiological consequences of it.

During the same years they observed improvement in quality of the dentist-patient relationship.

But these experiences also made it clear for music therapists that the psychophysiological research could not teach them a lot about psychological states such as affects or representations of moods.

These research approaches were extended to obstetrics - either in childbirth preparation (fighting against anxiety, and creating analgesia) as in fundamental research on the foetal audition with Dr. Jean Feijoo's findings (the precocity of the foetus' audition and its improvement in grave tones).

This rapid history of French research areas within music therapy shows already a multidimensional approach; from a sentimental point of view (dependant on specific types of music) with its applications in psychiatry for its behavioural effects on patients, to a more limited approach (relaxation, excitement); and finally to the psychophysiological and more experimental research centered on one parameter which is essential to analgesis: tension versus relaxation.

But in this reduction the mood approach of music therapy (which was already Descartes' question) was left behind.

F - A tentative to objectivate the mood influence of the music listening
In 1969 I participated in a research project with six extracts of pieces of music and 50 students. it was my first personal research (Guilhot, Jost, Lecourt, 1973, p.118-130): I have used the lists of moods already developed in American research and have compared the subjective responses with the subjects' results on the Cattell's Questionnaire of personality (16PF). I found that this second variable gave a very different lecture of the first responses (on the list of moods). For instance the consideration of personality factors such as distrust, anxiety and emotional stability led to opposite results, and for one of these factors, the responses diffcred also on moods and on pieces of music. (For instance: many differences were observed with these two pieces of music: Saint-Saëns' *Symphony No 3* Opus 78, and Fauré's *Requiem* Opus 48: In

Paradisum): This result was not a total surprise for me but a corroboration of the daily experience of the variety of our reactions to different pieces of music. And it encouraged me not to continue in this way (trying to develop a sort of "repertoire" for music therapy, considered as an "objective" result of scientific research).

At the same time and after Robert Frances' book "Musical Perception" (1958), in a much more elaborate experiment than mine, Michel Imberty (1979, 1981), gave an objectivation of the affective apprehension of extracts of Ravel's and Debussy's pieces of music with a statistical approach (based on the Osgood`s semantic differentiator): In this last case the objective was not music therapy but psychology of music from an experimental point of view.

This example is significant of the big gap which exists between some form of psychology of music and music therpy. This last domain being either too pragmatic for research or too subjective or both.

2. My actual research

From 1980 onwards I have tried to show in my own research that the subjective part of the musical experience cannot be considered as a handicap (or a bad artefact for research), because it is the heart of music itself! This subjective experience, which is essential in music therapy and in psychopathology can be approached in a clinical scientifical way. That collaboration has to take place in different areas in order to adapt methodologies and concepts.

I shall present some of these boundaries:

- an acoustical, environmental research project: my exploration of the sonorous experiences of patients (their "Sound landscapes" to speak in the language of Murray-Schafer) have had echoes from architects' research (in the School of Architecture of Grenoble) on three points: the object, the method and some concepts. These echoes were the beginning of new exchanges between our laboratories (1991), and gave birth to some original ideas.

- the interest manifested by students of musicology opened, with the agreement of some musicology colleagues (Universities of Paris and Strassbourg), gave birth to a confrontation of methods and topics, e.g.:

-       research on the role of music education as prevention against manifestations of psychopathology in children,

-       or a methodological comparison between a psychoanalytical interpretation of sound/musical productions of groups and the musicological interpretation of the same productions.

-       In the same way an actual research is going on concerning musical analysis of autistic patients' spontaneous sound/musical productions, with interactional observation, ethiological and psychopathological approaches and with the psychoanalytical lecture itself.

More generally my approach of the musical structure as a group structure has opened the possibility to combine aspects of musicology, psychopathology, music therapy and psychoanalysis in a synthetical, reflexive way.

I reflect on this group dimension not only from a social point of view (the musician's group) but also as a structure that expresses typically the group dimension of the psyche itself - as studied by Freud and other group analysts. This point of view has made bridges between a musical approach and a clinical psychoægical approach (1974); mainly a bridge between the objective structure of a musical production and the psychoanalytical group analysis theory (with the two principal schools: the English of Foulkes and Bion, and the French of Anzieu and Kaïs, cf.1993).

One of the practical consequences is the opening of music therapy to cultural difficulties (with the musical model of polyphony), - difficulties my new research project is addressing mainly with the European Association of Transcultural Group Analysis (1994).

This works opens the understanding of many colleagues, psychologists, psychiatrists and psychoanalysts to some form of music therapy and supply their interest in some specific forms of psychopathology. In this way it enlarges possibilities of research.

To conclude: From a training point of view this domain of research needs a extensive theoretical and methodological background to give the new coming music therapists the interest for research and the opportunity to discover and manage such necessary bridges.

Discussion: Psychology of music versus music therapy

The psychology of music is ususally defined as a part of the experimental and cognitive psychology (as for instance in the "Bible" of musicology: the Grove's Dictionary).

Though intellectually interesting the experiments within this area have rarely provided theoretical framework or methodological basis for applications in music therapy. Even in research it was realized that the perception of music have had few consequences in receptive music therapy (R.Frances, M.Imberty e.g.). And I think mainly for two reasons:
1) the experimental approach needs to atomize the object, in opposition to a clinical approach that must to consider the patient's allround situation
2) many music therapists don't have the curiosity or the scientific basis to understand and discuss this kind of research.

I think that the psychology of music as a scientifical domain has to recognize not only the experimental point of view, but also the clinical approach and its decisive contribution to the understanding of the musical fact. The clinical psychology of music has as its object the subjective experience of music by children, adults, older perople, individuals, situations as in groups and its cultural particularities.

The music therapists of today have to collect observations, to gather precious data for this research. I hope that they will benefit of a high level of general culture and specialized training to grasp the capacity and to develop this clinical part of the psychology of music, which I have named the "psychology of the sonorous and musical experiences" in an article for *The Psychologists`s Journal,* some years ago (1988).

References:

Arveiller, J. (1980). *"Des Musicothêrapies".* Issy-les-Moulineaux Ed. E.A.P. (On Music Therapies)

Descartes R. (1618). *Compendium musicae.* "Abrégé de musique",. Paris. P.U.F. (1987).

Feihjdo, J.; Renner, J.P.; Marcel, J.L. (1985). *"Traité de sophrologid", III et V.* Paris. le Courrier du Lievre. (Treatise of Sophrology)

Frances, R. (1958). *"La perception de la musique",* Paris . Vrin. (the perception of music)

Gabat, M.; Jost J., (1972). *"La déntente psychomusicale en odontostomatologie".* Paris. Meloine.(the psychomusical relaxation in dentistery).

Guilhot, J. & M.A.; Jost J.; Lecourt, E. (1973).*La Musicotherapie et les méthodes nouvelles d`association des techniques.* Paris. E.S.F.

Imberty, M.(1979). *"Entendre la musique - Semantique psychologique de la musique"* (to listen to music - a semantic psychology of music) and (1981) *"Les écritures du temps"* (the writings of time). Paris. Dunod.

Lapoujade, C., Lecourt, E. (1994). "Les recherches en musicothérapie en France de 1970 à 1993". La Revue de Musicothérapie, XIV, 4, 1 - 110. (the research in music therapy in France from 1970 to 1993)

Lecourt, E. (1987). "The musical envelope", in D`Anzieu and al. *"Psychic envelopes",* Karnac Books, London 1990
(translation of the book published in france)

Lecourt, E.(1988). "Une psychologie des experiences sonores et musicales", le Journal des Psychologues. No 63, 22-24 (a psychology of sonourous and musical experiences)

Lecourt, E. (1989). "Polyphony instead of harmony". Journal of The American Association of Music Therapy. 8,1, 112 -115

Lecourt, E. (1991). "Off-Beat Music Therapy: A Psychoanalytic Approach to autism",in K. E. Bruscia, *"Case Studies in Music Therapy,* Barcelona Publishers, Phoenixville, p.75-98

Lecourt, E.(1991). *"L`investissement de l`espace sonore par un groupe, approche thérique et multiculturelle",* Grenoble.

Colloque International "La qualité sonore des espaches habités". Actes. p.17-23 (the group`s investigation of the sonorous space, a theoretical and multicultural approach).

Lecourt, E. (1992). "The History of Music Therapy and Training in France". Music Therapy International report. Vol.8, 46-48

Lecourt, E. (1992). "The Functions of Music Therapy in France", The Arts in Psychotherapy, Vol.19, pp. 123-126

Lecourt, E. (1993). "Music Therapy in France",in CH.D.Maranto (Ed.) *"Music Therapy: International Perspectives.* Pipersville (USA). Jeffrey Books pp. 221-237

Lecourt, E. (1993). *"Analyse de groupe et musicothérapie".* Paris. les Editions Sociales Francaises. (Group Analysis and Music Therapy)

Lecourt, E. (1994). *"L`expérience musicale, résonances psychoanalytiques".* Paris. L`Harmattan. (the musical experience, psychoanalytical resonances)

Lecourt, E. (1994). "Modéles de groupes et cultures; la musique comme révélateur". Connexions, 63,1,159-168. (Models of groups and cultures; the music as revelator: this article is actually in print in a collective publication, (in english). "Group Analysis. No 63 and 64. 1995.

Qualitative Research in Music Therapy:
New Contents, New Concepts, or Both?
A Dialogue

by Henk Smeijsters (NL)

This dialogue is a result of the discussions which took place during the 1st International Symposium for Qualitative Research in Düsseldorf (1994). Reprinted from: Langenberg, M., Aigen, K., and Frommer, J. (eds), (1996). Qualitative Music Therapy Research: Beginning Dialogues. Gilsum NH: Barcelona Publishers.

Introduction

For me one of the most important experiences during the 1st International Symposium for Qualitative Research in Düsseldorf 1994) was the discussion about 'criteria', 'rules' and 'guide lines' in qualitative research. Most researchers argued that qualitative research - because it starts from a very different paradigm with its own conceptions about reality, about how to achieve knowledge, about generalization, causality and objectivity - needs its own criteria. Because I felt their way of doing research in essence did not differ from the way I do, I asked myself why without any cognitive dissonance I still used the traditional criteria. When preparing this dialogue to me it became clear that I used the traditional concepts to describe the new qualitative procedures. Other qualitative researchers in The Netherlands also do it that way. But I could not feel satisfied by telling myself that I was doing the right thing because other people in The Netherlands do the same.

So I wanted to ask myself whether as a qualitative researcher I perhaps kept on holding to preconscious quantitative thoughts. This dialogue is an expression of my search into this matter, why I want to use the old concepts when talking about new contents.

Criteria for Qualitative Research

Since Lincoln and Guba (1985) introduced 'trustworthiness' qualitative researchers seem to be astonished when in the context of qualitative research concepts like 'internal validity', 'external validity', 'reliability' and 'objectivity' are used. In the conventional paradigm these four concepts were indentified with procedures such as the experimental design, the representative sampling, the test-retest replication and the averaged intersubjective agreement. Because these procedures differ fundamentally from the basic axioms of qualitative research, the astonishment is understandable. If as a qualitative researcher you are convinced that there is no fragmentable reality and there are no simple causal relationships then using an experimental and control group to study the influence of an independent on a dependent variable makes no sense to you. If you think statements free from time and context are impossible you will argue that realities cannot be generalized, nor replicated nor understood by a non-interacting inquirer. You will find sampling, repeated testing and the use of standardized scales useless. In qualitative research there are no 'variables', no 'effects', no 'control' and 'experimental' groups, no 'measurements'.

Lincoln and Guba rejected the concepts of 'internal validity', 'external validity', 'reliability' and 'objectivity' because in their opinion they are inconsistent with the axioms and procedures of qualitative inquiry.

What seems to be forgotten however is that both authors stress the fact that for the quantitative and qualitative researcher the same four methodological questions are appropriate (Lincoln & Guba 1985, page 218):

1) the 'truth' of the findings of an inquiry for the respondents,
2) the degree to which findings may have applicability in other contexts,
3) whether the findings of an inquiry would be consistently repeated if the inquiry were replicated,
4) the degree to which the findings stem from the characteristics of the respondents and not from biases from the inquirer.

To me it seems possible that the concepts 'internal validity', 'external validity', 'reliability' and 'objectivity' can refer to these fundamental questions. The difficulty is that in quantitative research these concepts were defined in a very reductionistic way and identified with the procedures of experimentation, sampling, replication and instrumentation. Lincoln and Guba use the concepts in exactly the same reductionistic and operationalized way quantitative researchers do. In my opinion however these concepts can be still of value in qualitative research if they are described in another way and linked to procedures that fit the qualitative axioms.

Of course one may ask: why hold to these concepts? This question I would like to answer with a personal argument and arguments of parsimony and ease of communication. From the very first thinking about qualitative research it was clear to me that these concepts needed different contents. But I never felt confronted with the impossibility to use them. Also, introducing new concepts that address the same questions for me looks like raising barriers that hinder communication.

The same issue we are confronted with when communicating about music therapy in general. Should we completely develop an own music therapy language or should we integrate in our language concepts that can be understood by different disciplines? For instance, do we need an own music therapy psychopathology and an own theory of psychotherapy, or should we demonstrate that mental disorders as described by other disciplines are expressed through musical experiences, and music therapy is indicated because of musical processes that are able to trigger psychotherapeutical processes that can help to heal mental disorders (Smeijsters, 1993)? In my opinion we need to link the language of music therapy with the language of other helping professions.

The same holds true for qualitative research. We need a common ground that facilitates communication between quantitative and qualitative researchers. I am not saying that in essence these types of research are the same. They are "...mutually exclusive ways of thinking about the world...and cannot be adopted at the same time..." (Bruscia, 1994b, page 9). But when we respect the fundamental differences then we also may ask if there still are some shared methodological questions of inquiry.

When - like Lincoln and Guba point out - there is, we could ask if it would be fruitful to use a language which shows that indeed these questions are shared. What we need to ask next is when and why a quantitative or a qualitative paradigm will be indicated to give answers to these questions. Whether a quantitative or qualitative approach should be used depends on the type of answers we want to give (the purpose of the study) and the attributes of the phenomena under study.

Of course this looks like some sort of a dilemma, because hol-ding to conventional concepts includes the risk that the fun-damental axioms of the qualitative paradigm are lost. However, I believe that using the conventional concepts in a new way can facilitate the communication between researchers and also can respect the fundamental axioms of qualitative research.

Let us have a closer look at the new concepts introduced by Lincoln and Guba and try to understand what they mean.

'Credibility' (in stead of internal validity) means testing if the reconstructions made by the researcher are credible to the constructors of the original multiple realities. In stead of the causal links between fragments of reality the researcher describes complex mutual shapings, inter-relationships between multiple aspects of reality. Here everything influences everything else and each element interacts with all of the others. There is no directionality and it simply happens.

The procedures to increase the probability of credible findings show that the researcher for instance tries to prevent distortions, selectivity and biases. The researcher wants to identify relevant characteristics, those things that really count. This interest resembles the interest of the experimental researcher who wants to know which variables really count.

Further in qualitative research the researcher may investigate the process of 'enabling' which means introducing elements in the context that do not cause changes, but make them possible (the word 'element' is used by Lincoln and Guba). Even if there is no causal link, you might argue that there is some sort of an 'effect' here.

If we look into the goals of qualitative research that are discussed by Bruscia (1994b) you will find 'analysis', meaning the discovery of patterns, recurrencies, categories, types, regularities or themes. Several papers that were presented at the Düsseldorf symposium fall in this category (Langenberg, Frommer & Langenbach, 1994; Amir, 1994).

When, in the way Bruscia illustrates analysis, the researcher for instance looks at relations between nonverbal and musical events, changes in behavior before versus after treatment, relations between verbal expressions of ex-periences and musical improvisations then this of course is no linear causality. But this interest in connections of events, experiences, ma-terials and personal characteristics, this process of linking up, to me looks like the search for connections in quantitative research. Although the idea's about reality differ, a qualitative and quantitative researcher seem to share the same intention when looking for connections.

The challenging sentence of Aigen (1994) that he selects only those incidents that support his interpretations could be misunderstood. There always needs to be a check whether the interpretations made by a researcher are grounded in the data and a check for the chain of evidence the researcher constructed. If there is not, the findings only reflect a personal view of the researcher and not the multiple perspectives of the participants.

Because in qualitative research there is no belief in an independent reality out there, the connections made by the researcher are not verified or falsified by 'reality'. The connections are seen as 're-constructions' that have to make sence for they who made the constructions in the first place.

One could say the reconstructed patterns need to be sound, well-grounded, 'valid' as experienced by the participants. We could say also that they need to be 'internally valid' which means sound for this unique context.

Finally I would like to mention a seemingly paradoxical point. When in qualitative research 'causality' is rejected and at the same time credibility is assured by interaction with participants, than maybe the concept of causality needs to be introduced again because human beings - therapists and clients - co nstruct their realities in terms of causal relationships.

'Transferability' (in stead of external validity) adresses the question if what is researched in one context can be used in another context. Because a context is no 'sample' and every context is different there is no generaliza-tion of findings. Only when there is a degree of similarity between sending and receiving context the results of research can be transferred. Therefor a thick description of the sending context is needed, one of the tasks of the qualitative researcher. Although the basic axioms about reality and the procedures to reach applicability used by the qualitative researcher differ fundamentally from the quantitative procedures of sampling and generalization the concept 'external validity' for me stands for the well-groundedness of findings in another context.

Because qualitative researchers point out there is no stability, they do not strive to repeat a similar inquiry process in the 'same unit'. When thinking holistically there is no similar situation where one experience can be replicated in exactly the same way. Not only human contextes are changing, also the interaction between researcher and participants and thus the design in qualitative research never will be the same. It is impossible to repeat what is a more or less unique process.

In stead of 'reliability' the concept of 'dependability' was introduced to take into account these factors of instability.

It seems to me that by using this new concept something is won but something is lost too.

When it is not possible to repeat history it still is possible to repeat looking at it. The researcher can have different thoughts, feelings or imageries about the same experience at different times. Participants and observers too can have different thoughts, feelings and imageries about the same experience at different times. Doing research needs some sort of 'replication' within and between human minds. The outcome is not 'the truth' but a set of 'multiple perspectives'. Thus 'replication' in qualitative reseach is possible, but it is no replication of the unique treatment but a replication of the descriptions of this uniqueness. There will emerge a never ending 'field of stories' (see Kenny, 1994).

As we saw before qualitative researchers by prolonged enga-gement try to prevent distortions, selectivity and biases. They also try to identify the most characteristic elements. Lincoln and Guba mention the 'testing for misinformation'. This testing happens by repeated observations and the use of multiple perspectives from different participants. For me concepts as 'intra-reliability' and 'inter-reliability' are more satisfying to name these qualitative procedures.

Qualitative researchers argue there can be no 'objectivity', because there is no 'objective reality' and no 'truth'. Realities are seen as subjective con-structed entities. Using the human instrument in stead of standardized measuring instruments assures that in the re-constructions of the researcher the changing context, the meaning of this context, and the subjective perspectives of the participants will be included. No context loaden with sub-jectivities can be understood without a researcher who from the own personal experiences tries to be open and empathic to this subjectivities.
Because 'objectivity' in quantitative research was reduced to the average ex-perience of a number of individuals, in qualitative research 'objectivity' was replaced by 'confirmability'.

Lincoln and Guba conclude that no longer the investigator's characteristics but the characteristics of the data is the issuc. But when the authors find it important that the findings are grounded in the data, and by peer debriefing and auditing inquirer bias about the data is researched, these interests resembles the wish for 'objectivity'. The biasing of data descriptions by preconceived ideas, feelings, theories, and concepts by the researcher need to be excluded.

Rules and Guide Lines in Qualitative Research
In quantitative research because of rules a researcher knows from the beginning what to do, how to proceed. The hypothesis, the instrumentation and the design are developed before research starts and there are no changes during the research process. In qualitative research however there is an 'emergent design' which implicates that there is no hypothesis, there are no measuring instruments and there is no fixed design at the start. If there were, the essence of qualitative research would be lost because qualitative research is a process of interaction between inquirer and context of inquiry. If there is interaction there will be change.

Qualitative researchers in music therapy often categorically hold to the rule that there are no rules in qualitative research. But again I would like to ask: what do we mean by a rule? How do we define the word 'rule'? Is it - like the concepts of 'validity' and 'reliability' - defined in the conventional way?

Then the word 'guide line' - which I introduced in my own qualitative research as outcome - would be better. Because a guide line can be used, but you are not abliged to use it. But if you interpret 'rule' as prerequisite that assures that what you are doing indeed is research and not clinical practice, than it is different. One of the dangers of the qualitative research paradigm is that sometimes everything seems to be research. But as Bruscia (1994b, page 6) points out: "Research is not writing about one's clinical work, making up one's own theory, or sharing one's personal views". If these differences exist we need 'rules' to be sure what is research and what is not. Like the wrong use of subjectivity also the negation of rules can disguise poor scholarship. In qualitative research there are rules too, and denying this is inauthentic (Bruscia, 1994a). Of course not every technique or method to meet the criteria of internal validity (credibility), external validity (transferability), reliability (dependability), objectivity (confirmability) is used everytime. Here the freedom to choose is expressed by the concept 'guide line'. But whatever technique or method is used, we nevertheless need 'rules' such as 'openness', 'interaction' and 'dialectics' to assure we are doing qualitative research.

The Music Therapist as a Researcher
One of the justifications for interaction is given by Lincoln and Guba (1985, page 105) who state that: "Meaningful research is impossible without the full understanding and cooperation of the respondents". Related to therapy

Bruscia (1994b, page 12) says that qualitative research "...is enhanced when the researcher is the subject's therapist or when the researcher actively engages and interacts with the subject". The interaction between researcher and context is part of the qualitative paradigm. Because in therapy the therapist is the one who interacts closest with the client the roles of therapist and researcher can go together. Aigen (1994) when discussing the research of his own clinical practice mingles the question if the therapist should be the researcher with the question if research should be done while treatment is in progress. I agree that combining treatment and research can be of benefit for the client.

But when the therapist and the researcher are the same person we have a problem. This problem can be explained in terms of authenticity (Bruscia, 1994a). Being a therapist is not the same as being a researcher. In therapy the therapist seeks insight for the client's sake, not for the sake of other clients. There can be inauthenticity when someone is not aware of his own perspective. If there can be this authenticity how to handle it in a methodological way?

Because I believe it is very difficult to slip forth and back from one to another role it is much more easy and authentic when there are two persons, one who takes the stance of the therapist, another who takes the responsibility as a researcher. Then the problem of inauthenticity is minimized.

Bruscia's suggestion that the therapist/researcher in an intrasubjective way is responsible for the authenticity of intent to me seems an insufficiant criterium. We know that the awareness of our intent often is distorted. It is possible that a therapist can be as fully aware of this and can go into and out these different roles. But it is a characteristic of research that these processes are controlled a little bit more.

Summary of Conclusions
Qualitative and quantitative research share some fundamental methodological questions. The concepts that address these questions can be the same, but the answers to these questions differ fundamentally because of different paradigms.

Qualitative researchers want to identify relevant characteristics, want to discover patterns, and want to study the process of enabling. The 'chain of evidence' resulting from this needs to be 'internally valid' as experienced by the participants in their unique context. It is also possible that the findings can be 'externally valid', which means that they may be of help in another context. Because a qualitative researcher uses prolonged engagement, repeated descriptions, and multiple per-spectives 'intra-reliability' and 'inter-reliability' prevent distortions, selectivity and biases. Peer debriefing and auditing check for inquirer biases and guarantee 'objectivity'.

In qualitative research some 'rules' give security that the activity is 'research', and not clinical work or theory. 'Rules' also guarantee that the research is 'qualitative'. 'Guide lines' are methodological possibilities that can be used. Because of their freedom to be used the qualitative research can develop out of the unique context and unique interaction.

The music therapist can act as a researcher, and it is important that the experience of the music therapist is part of the research. But because of authenticity it is preferable to use a research team where the music therapist and researcher have separated responsibilities.

The tables give a summary of my line of reasoning in this dialogue. They were used during the presentation of the paper at the Aalborg Conference.

Table 1:	Basic Research Questions
Which phenomena seem to be important over time?	
How to code these phenomena?	
How to connect these phenomena?	
For whom these phenomena seem to be important?	
Which phenomena seem to be important at other places?	

Table 2:	Research Requirements
Procedures:	To select the most important data
Procedures:	To code these data
Procedures:	To re-construct patterns in these data
Procedures:	To exclude personal bias
Procedures:	To explore the universality of findings

Table 3:	Old and New Concepts of Research Integrated
Reliability / Dependability	*Replicating* descriptions of *uniqueness*
Internal validity / Credibility	Making re-constructed *patterns* *credible* to participants
Objectivity / Confirmability	Including *subjective* *multiple perspectives* of participants
External validity / Transferability	Exploring the *usefulness* of findings in *another context*

Table 4:	Old Concepts and Basic Research Questions in Qualitative Research	
Reliability		What is replicated in multiple descriptions over time?
Construct validity		Which (new) words are used to code the multiple descriptions of one phenomenon?
Internal validity		Which credible patterns between phenomena can be constructed?
Objectivity		Are descriptions, codes and patterns grounded in the subjective experiences of the participants?
External validity		Which findings are transferable to other places?

Table 5:	Characteristics of Qualitative Research
NO	**YES**
Universal theory	Naturalistic theory
Causality of isolated variables	Dependency of interrelated phenomena
Experimental manipulation	An ongoing process of change
Standardisation of measurement	The human being as research instrument
Objectivity	Grounded in subjective experiences
Replication of phenomena	Replication of persperctives

Table 6:	Qualitative Procedures

THE RESEARCHER
- uses reports of participants (member check)
- asks independent observers to make observations and interviews experts (peer debriefing)
- repeats his own observations and analyses
- generates and adjusts hypotheses
- constructs patterns and sequencies
- uses several sources, data collecting techniques and theoretical models (triangulation)
- constructs a 'chain of evidence'
- asks independent researchers to check the constructed 'chain of evidence'
- stimulates independent researchers to execute a similar qualitative research study to reflect guide lines (multiple case studies)

Table 7:	Remaining Issues
Subjectivity versus personal bias	
The therapist being his own researcher	
Intersubjectivity versus multi-subjectivity	
Rules versus guide lines	

References

Aigen, K. (in press). The role of values in qualitative music therapy research. In: M. Langenberg, J. Frommer & K. Aigen (eds). Qualitative approaches to music therapy research: Understanding processes and dialogues from the 1st International Symposium. Phoenixville: Barcelona Publishers.

Amir, D. (in press). Experiencing music therapy: meaningful moments in the music therapy process. In: M. Langenberg, J. Frommer & K. Aigen (eds). Qualitative approaches to music therapy research: Understanding processes and dialogues from the 1st International Symposium. Phoenixville: Barcelona Publishers.

Bruscia, K.E. (1995). Differences between quantitative and qualitative research paradigms: Implications for music therapy. In: B.L. Wheeler (ed). Music therapy research. Quantitative and qualitative perspectives. Phoenixville: Barcelona Publishers.

Bruscia, K.E. (1995). Modes of consciousness in Guided Imagery and Music (GIM): A therapist's experience of the guiding process. In: C. Kenny (ed). Listening, playing, creating: Essays on the power of sound. Albany: State University of New York Press.

Bruscia, K.E. (in press). Authenticity issues in qualitative research. In: M. Langenberg, J. Frommer & K. Aigen (eds). Qualitative approaches to music therapy research: Understanding processes and dialogues from the 1st International Symposium. Phoenixville: Barcelona Publishers.

Kenny, K. (in press). The story of the field of play. In: M. Langenberg, J. Frommer & K. Aigen (eds). Qualitative approaches to music therapy research: Understanding processes and dialogues from the 1st International Symposium. Phoenixville: Barcelona Publishers.

Langenberg, M., Frommer, J. & M. Langenbach (in press). Fusion and separation. Experiencing opposites in music, music therapy, and music therapy research. In: M. Langenberg, J. Frommer & K. Aigen (eds). Qualitative approaches to music therapy research: Understanding processes and dialogues from the 1st International Symposium. Phoenixville: Barcelona Publishers.

Lincoln, Y.S, & E.G. Guba (1985). Naturalistic inquiry. Newbury Park: Sage publications.

Smeijsters, H. (1993). Music therapy and psychotherapy. The Arts in Psychotherapy, Vol. 20, 223-229.

Smeijsters, H. (in press). Qualitative single-case research in practice: a necessary, reliable and valid alternative for music therapy research. In: M. Langenberg, J. Frommer & K. Aigen (eds). Qualitative approaches to music therapy research: Understanding processes and dialogues from the 1st International Symposium. Phoenixville: Barcelona Publishers.

Music Therapy in psychiatric rehabilitation program: from deficit to psycho social integration.

Gabriella Giordanella Perilli (I)

Introduction

The main purpose of rehabilitation programs for psychiatric patients is to reduce the consequences of psychosis and avoid cronicity effects. Since there are difficulties in determining at a causal level a correlation between a functional deficit and a brain damage, it seems more useful to consider operational deficit in higher functions (attention, perception, memory), as psycho-pathological events to be treated with a rehabilitative approach, together with medications. In this perspective the rehabilitative process starts focusing on single difficulty, and goes on integrating emotions, thoughts, and verbalisation, at a psychotherapeutic level. The present method, taking in account the genetic, neurologic bases and psychological process regarding musical behaviour, could be of some value in a rehabilitative program which considers operational level of neuropsychological and psycho-social activities in schizophrenic patients, with negative symptoms. The contribution of this work to rehabilitation of schizophrenic patients consists in proposing an integrated methodology, which considers neuropsychological and psycho-social aspects of pathology, together with different functional areas (emotional, cognitive, personal, interpersonal), various levels of awareness (pre-conscious, conscious), knowledge (tacit and explicit), and expressive modalities (verbal, non verbal, musical, non musical). This is not a solution to the rehabilitation problem, but has been proved to be useful to get in touch and to partially disclose some blocked inner processes in schizophrenic people. Theoretical implications concern the opportunity to have a comprehensive framework, like the Lazarus MultiModal Model, to dispose a bio-psycho-social model to read and understand human reality and meaning, psycho pathological events, emotional distress, so to plan a rehabilitative program tailored for each, unique patient.

Planning rehabilitative work

Persons, with chronic schizophrenic disturbances, present positive symptoms together with affective flattening, inattention, alogia, apathy, poor interest, and difficulty with verbal and non verbal communication. Particularly deficit in attention function (selective attention, reaction time) is a significant element found in schizophrenic patients: in fact attention deficit may basically contribute to reduce the whole information processing in this population.

(Green & Walker, 1984; Cutting,1985; Andreasen & Olsen, 1982). Clinical study in this field carried out at the Psychiatric Department of Tor Vergata University in Rome, to which the present author co-operated, pointed out the opportunity to evaluate of fundamental importance correlation between neuropsychological deficit and psycho social adjustment level, since the inabilitant cognitive symptoms may dispose persons to social withdrawal, inactivity, and consequently to a more severe psychic impoverishment. In this perspective it was important to assess patient functions like (1) attention, (2) perception, and (3) memory in order to plan a rehabilitative work considering, first of all, a single deficit as a limit for interacting in the real life, and, in a second time, gradually planning a personality re-integration through a global psychotherapy intervention, including emotion, thoughts, believes, etc.

The present author's opinion was that music therapy in a rehabilitative program could be useful to reduce some negative symptoms, together with anxiety and verbal-non verbal communication difficulty, showed by some schizophrenic patients, assuming those deficit correlated with a poor adaptation of subjective tempo organisation, necessary to be in tune and to interact with own environment. For this reason the present author carried out a study to investigate subjective tempo and subjective time perception in adult with and without psychiatric disorder.The study showed significant differences in some measure and tasks of subjective tempo between the two groups. (Giordanella,1993). Given genetic, neurological and psychological factors that produce individual and group differences, subjective tempo, (operationally defined as the subjective timing or pacing with regard to psychomotor, cognitive, and emotional processes, together with the speed at which a person may apprehend, register, and understand incoming stimuli) has been of considerable interest in clinical situations. Research has shown relationship between subjective tempo and impulsivity (Barratt,1983; Duryea & Glover,1982), endogenous depression (Schwartz,1982; Steinberg & Raith,1985), mania (Cohen,1986), schizophrenia (Limbekne,1981; Liddle & Morris,1981; Stuss & Benson,1988), and anxiety (Barrat,1983). Research has also shown differences in time perception and estimation of objective time duration between psychiatric patients and normal people (Densen,1979; Fraisse,1984).

The entire work, aimed to study a music therapy methodology for rehabilitation of persons with schizophrenic symptoms, included three parts: a) the first began seven years ago and was carried out, as part of a team at Psychiatric Department, Tor Vergata University in Rome, with the aim to organise methods and techniques for neuropsychological rehabilitative purposes for schizophrenic patients. The program was based on the principles of the Lurjia Nebraska Neuropsychological Battery, which includes 14 scales to assess neurological deficits (Cimino, Sabbadini, Ciani,1990; Perilli, Rullo, Saya, Ciani,1990). Whithin such scales there was the rhythmic scale to assess attention and psychomotor situation of patient. In this perspective music therapy intervention was included in the rehabilitative program first of all to restore some basic functions, like attention, perception, and memory, in consideration of the specific information processing behaviour used by human being to process music stimuli, particularly for their psycophysical and structural characteristics. (Giordanella-Perilli, Verucci, Rullo, Ciani,1992; Rullo, Giordanella Perilli, Verucci, 1992; Perilli, Rullo, Saya, 1993). Theoretical premises considered musical behaviour genetically based in human beings, and acoustic musical stimulus being psychologically processed in a specific way, differently from verbal information (Mc Adams,1991; Petsche, Richter, Etlinger & Filz,1994; Peretz & Morais,1994). Consequently musical tasks could provide unique mean to assess and restore impaired cognitive functions, also because musical behaviour is organized by a temporal dimension. The second part of our work, as written above, concerned a basic research to compare adults with and without psychiatric disorders in the subjective tempo area. (Giordanella, 1993). The outcome helped us in planning music therapy methods and techniques founded on the individual temporal organization system. (Giordanella Perilli, 1991). The third part of our study consisted in the application of our music therapy method to other psychiatric patients to verify its clinical outcome and benefit.

The present methodology is an integrated approach divided in four stages: the first and second are considered rehabilitative stages (Contact and Stabilization), the third and fourth are seen as re-constructive stages (Problem-solving and Reconstruction). Each stage includes therapeutic goal, i.e. the first stage has the purpose to establish contact and develop a relationship; the second stage attempts to stabilize client's current adaptive functions and to restore his/her previous levels of operation; the third stage deals with decision making and problem-solving ability; the final stage aims to restructure patient's personality. Whereas the rehabilitative stages provide to re-integrate together the various sensorial system, to stabilize attention, perception, and memory (cognitive functions), to allow patients to experience different emotions and to recognize them, the re-constructive stages aim to allow integration of actual emotional perception with past emotional experience, bringing them at patient's awareness, to deal with disfunction at a pre-conscious level, i.e. irrational thoughts, dysfunctional behaviour to afford life problem, rigid or fragmentary self construct organization, in order to restructure, in a more adaptive way, self identity system. The method provides several rhythmical, musical tasks and experiences for assessment, intervention, and evaluation purposes. In the present music therapy approach for rehabilitative purposes with schizophrenic people, techniques and methods concern cognitive, emotional, personal and interpersonal areas. Tasks, based on the musical stimulus properties allow to assess and evaluate attention function as arousal, brief term memory, attention focusing and interest, which are in relationship with memory process. Together with receptive technique, active techniques are planned to allow patient to receive an immediate motor feed back together with the perceptive one, in order to let him/her learn from musical embodied experience new cognitive schema and motor behaviour. Tasks, concerning evaluation of musical piece characteristics, consider the ongoing links between perceptive system and affective-emotional state of patient, elicited by musical excerpt. Those tasks focus on structural properties of music, which require patient to use a selective attention ability, an effort to focus, and a longer attention span. In verbally describing musical pieces, patient has to use apperceptive function, which recognize percept by giving it a meaning through a double integration, one between actual different sensorial systems perception, the other as an associative integration of present perceptions and previous experience. Tasks and experiences concerned receptive and active music therapy, are proposed with a progressive complexity, based always on patients needs, resources, characteristics, and actual situation. In this regards the role of the music therapist has to be flexible, open to here and now dynamics, to allow the ongoing therapeutic process, providing a secure relationship context, both musical and interpersonal.

In a study carried out at the chair of Psychiatric Clinic of Tor Vergata, University in Rome with 18 schizophrenic patients, a number of significant correlation were noted when correlating the neuropsychological performance with the negative symptomatology. In particular it was observed a highly significative correlation (P .005) between the global evaluation scale of the Scale for the Assessment of Negative Symptoms (SANS) (Andreasen & Olsen, 1982), and the rhythm scale of Lurjia Nebraska Neuropsychological Battery (Golden, Purisch, Hammeke, 1985) (Cimino, Cantelmi, Bersani, Ciani, 1994).

Clinical case studies reported changes both in musical behaviour and in psychiatric rating scales, SANS and PASS, the Positive and Negative Syndrome Scale (Kay, Fiszbein, Opler, 1987), together with score in Lurjia Nebraska Neuropsychological Battery after a music therapy individual structured intervention, carried out with out patients, for two years at that Psychiatric Clinic, Tor Vergata University in Rome (Verucci, San Martino, Giordanella Perilli & Spalletta, 1994).

The third part of our study regarded the application of our music therapy integrated approach to groups of schizophrenic people.

To realize whether musical tasks and experiences described in the previous paragraph, may play a significant role in the rehabilitation of schizophrenic patients, two pilot studies will be described. Specifically, the first experiment examines whether some negative symptoms, showed by schizophrenic people, like affective flattening, lack of interest, anxiety, asociability, and inattention can become significantly less severe over a series of twice a week, group music therapy sessions, within a three-months period; evidence was also sought whether, as a consequence, the patients' standard psychiatric ratings, measured independently, were significantly modified (Cavicchio, Pecoriello, Giordanella Perilli, Roncone, & Casacchia, 1994). The second experiment, with the purpose of including or not music therapy in a day hospital unit, to reduce the consequences of psychosis and to avoid chronicity effects, would examine whether and how music behaviour, showed by psychiatric patients could significantly improve, attending over one year weekly music therapy group sessions; changes in dysfunctional behaviour could be clinically observed, as dependent variables, being considered the most relevant outcome by administration board for including or not music therapy in the rehabilitative program.

Experiment 1

Method

Participants: Twelve in patients (five women and seven men, mean age = 43.5), of the Psychiatric Clinic, University of L'Aquila, Italy, attended at this study for three months.

The subjects were informed about music therapy intervention, and only if interested, they participated as volunteers. They were included considering ages 18-60, and clinical diagnosis (schizophrenic disturbs, psychotic non schizophrenic disturbs, bipolar disturbs). According to DSMIII-R (APA,1987), six patients were diagnosed with schizophrenic disturbances, four with major depressive symptoms, two with bipolar disturbances, in a depressive phase. The duration of illness was of 10.08 (4.87) years. All patients were taking medication. An independent consultant psychiatrist administered the Brief Psychiatric Rating Scale (BPRS) (Overall & Gorham, 1962) to assess patients psychopathological conditions. An independent nurse administered the Nurses Observation Scale for Inpatient Evaluation (NOSIE-30) (Honigfeld,1976), adapted and validated for Italian psychiatric patients (Stratta,1992), to assess overt behaviour observed in psychiatric inpatients, e.g. social ability, social interest, psychotic overt behaviour, etc. The two Scales were administered before and at the end of the music therapy treatment period, to evaluate whether the patients' psychiatric symptoms were significantly modified.

A Questionnaire, regarding musical experience, background and preferences, was filled in by each participants during the initial session. Those information were used both to plan activity and to evaluate modification in musical behaviour, at the end of the music therapy treatment.

Music Therapy Treatment Sessions. The Music Therapy Sessions were conducted by two non-medical workers specialized in psychiatric and psychosocial rehabilitation, with three year music therapy training, supervised by a music therapist. Each group session lasted one hour and took place twice a week in a large, nice room, provided with an unidirectional mirror to allow video registration of session. The room was equipped with chair for each participant, a sheet- board, ORFF instruments, a guitar, flutes, a key-board, a stereo equipment to reproduce and to record audio tapes, musical tapes, sheets and pencils. Due to psychopatological situation and hospital organization, the participants, during the treatment period, attended to music therapy with an average of 7 (s.d. 2.1) sessions for each subject. The treatment was at a reha- bilitation level, considering the here and now emotional state and thoughts of patients, elicited or associated to actual musical experience.

The sessions were planned to gradually improve patients' cognitive, emotional, personal and interpersonal adaptive behaviour.

Music Therapy techniques and tasks. In the cognitive area, the tasks concerned recognizing similarities and differences in acoustic-musical patterns, to produce and reproduce rhythmic patterns, following different prompts, both using body parts and instruments. In the emotional area, tasks and experiences were planned to recognize different emotions linked first to musical event, and to express them in an adaptive and social way. The subjects were required to verbally described musical pieces by a semantic differentiated scale (i.d. slow-fast), together with personal emotion elicited while listening to that musical piece. Tasks to improve personal and interpersonal area, were planned to modify positively self image, to increase verbal communication and allow social interaction. The patients were required to write three-four personal characteristics and to express them through a rhythmic or melodic improvisation. The musical expression was considered as a positive reinforce to support a more acceptable self image, and a help to establish social inte-ractions. Moreover, during that experience, other characteristics emerged, not yet considered by the patients (e.g. active, interested, able to take decision). Another technique consisted in the musical dialogue, using untuned or tuned instruments, between a subject and the therapist, or between two participants.

Data scoring. Four independent raters judged participants' musical and non musical behaviour during music therapy sessions, by observing through the mirror and, later on, by watching video recorded sessions. Each rater followed a grid to take note of technique, level of attention, motivation, participation and interaction shown by participants, exploratory behaviour towards musical instruments, ability to express emotion in a congruent way, kind of feeling, etc. Interrater agreement was very high.

Results. The observation grid was disposed as a phenomenological tool, and did not consider a point scale, so it is possible to present results concerning musical behaviour only in a descriptive way.

Modification in musical behaviour. An element very interesting was the gradual, observable change noted in patients' musical behaviour. At the beginning, all patients refused any kind of contact with musical instruments, together with non verbal communication to express themselves, i.d. through singing a song. During four sessions, the most of patients (80%) did not show any exploratory behaviour, in fact they used only the first instrument chosen. First of all, the participants were allowed to experience and to explore instruments in any way, so to become accustomed with them, feeling secure to use them without anxiety for being judged by the therapist or peers. During three sessions, the patients interacted only with the music therapist. Through rhythmic tasks they succeeded to interact as a group. By listening to musical piece suggested by each participants, verbal communication and social interaction were improved by discussing personal reason, preference in choosing a piece for group listening. Improvising to express feeling, elicited by a musical piece, was very appropriate for the participants to get in touch and become aware of different emotions. The subjects reached a more adequate contact with external environment by evaluating temporal characteristics of musical pieces, together with their objective length. Through musical dialogue, changes in musical behaviour were evident, regarding less rigid rhythmic patterns, dynamics, integration with partner's improvisation. Improvising to depict some personal characteristics, patients became aware of unknown part of self (e.g. active, satisfied, pleased). At the end of music therapy sessions, all patients showed a good approach with instruments. Often sessions were concluded playing or singing all together. During the last session, two participants, who have been arguing very badly in the clinic, played friendly together overcoming their conflict. Comparing the two different situations, allowed the participants to understand each own responsibility for common goal, and what behavior could be more convenient to live in a satisfying social way.

Self report of participants for Music therapy experience. All 12 participants verbally expressed their appraisal and enjoyment for the music therapy sessions, listing the advantages to pass time in a more interesting and constructive way; they defined session as "a moment when it is possible to feel relax, to pay attention to music and not to own problems and disturbing thoughts". Nine out of twelve showed particular satisfaction since they succeeded to express through music their "frozen" feeling and emotion; the same persons were very satisfied because "through music experience it was easier to establish interpersonal contact with other people".

Changes in Psychiatric Scores. Table 1 shows significant differences between the first and final rating for BPRS and NOSIE ($p = .05$). There is a reduction for total score and for sub items in both scales, after the music therapy treatment period.

TABLE 1
Within-group Comparison Between First and Final Psychiatric Ratings

	First rating	Final rating
B.P.R.S.	48.1 (9.7)	28.4 (6.7)*
Anxiety	3.6 (1.3)	2.0 (0.6)*
Emotional Inhibition	3.1 (1.7)	1.9 (0.6)*
Thought disorder	3.0 (1.7)	1.6 (0.7)*
Tension	3.4 (1.0)	1.7 (0.4)*
Depression	3.4 (2.3)	1.4 (0.6)*
Slow motor behavior	3.5 (1.6)	2.2 (0.8)*
Unusual thought	3.5 (2.6)	1.7 (0.8)*
N.O.S.I.E.		
Social Ability	7.5 (3.7)	3.5 (2.4)*
Social Interest	13.6 (5.1)	6.8 (4.9)*
Self care	7.9 (4.4)	3.2 (3.1)*
Irritability	9.9 (5.7)	4.1 (3.9)*
Overt psychotic behavior	4.5 (4.9)	1.4 (1.6)*
Slow motor behavior	7.2 (3.6)	2.6 (1.8)*

* t test. $p < 0.05$

Discussion.

The results of Experiment 1 indicate that although the schizophrenic group was too small and not matched with a control group to provide statistically reliable data, they may clinically support the opportunity to follow the proposed music therapy method for rehabilitation of negative symptoms shown by schizophrenic and depressive patients. Satisfaction, positive feeling, better social interactions, expression of emotions, relaxed state as told by participants in their self reports were observed by medical and non medical staff, outside the music therapy setting, during daily time, toward other patients and staff. For this reason this kind of music therapy treatment seems worthwhile during hospitalization, to help patients to live that experience in a more acceptable way, to allow patients to begin or to continue a psychotherapy intervention. At a behavioral and psycho pathological level, the patient group showed a reduction in the scores of the two psychiatric scales, showing at the same time an improvement in their condition as inpatients and a better compliance to drug treatment. This experience does not confirm the hypothesis regarding a "paradoxical effect on dissociate and positive symptoms", as described in a study concerning the first period in which nine schizophrenic patients were treated by music therapy intervention (Galvano,1989). The limits of our study concern the absence of a control group and the length of the treatment period. Quite interesting are the tasks and measures regarding subjective tempo to assess and evaluate attention and perception in schizophrenic patients, but it is not yet available a standardized scale. The satisfaction expressed verbally and non verbally by the participants is a soft parameter to evaluate the outcome of the treatment, but it represents an important variable to determine the quality of psychiatric intervention, especially because it is told as a personal experience by schizophrenic and depressive people, who lost feeling of satisfaction and pleasure.

Experiment 2

Method

Participants: Sixteen day hospital attendees took part in the study, four women and 12 men. The participants lived in the same area, in Rome. All subjects were screened and diagnosed as suffering from chronic schizophrenia by their psychiatrists, according to DSMIII-R (APA, 1987). That psychiatric unit was staffed by psychiatrists, psychologists, psychiatric nurses, and social worker. Patients could attend at a program of group and individual activities for rehabilitative purpose, including verbal psychotherapy, recreational activities, which could aid the patient's return to work, whenever possible and suitable for him/her. The age average was 35.5 (9.5), with a duration of illness of 11.6 (5.9) years. All patients were taking medication.

Music Therapy intervention. This experiment began three years ago, but here there will be described the outcome concerning one year period, presenting data collected with musical tasks. Music Therapy sessions were conducted by the present author, while a medical or non medical assistant observed and took note of relevant events happening during session. The setting consisted in a large room, provided with chairs and ORFF instruments, a guitar, flutes, triangles, a key-board, a stereo equipment to reproduce and to record part of musical experiences, musical tapes, pencils, and sheets. Each weekly session lasted an hour and includes 5-6 participants, matched basically taking in account their functional level, in order to plan tasks and experience tailored to the needs and resources of each patients within the group.

Music Therapy techniques and tasks. The methods and techniques were the same used for Experiment 1, except that some patients were ready, after ten months, to work at a deeper level, for example to musically express early recollection, to experience a structured guided imagery and music technique, to compose a group song as expression of their therapeutic process.

Data collection. Some tasks were provided to collect data at the beginning and after seven months. During five-six sessions, patients participated, individually or in group to receptive and active tasks planned to assess and, after a period, to evaluate some cognitive, emotional, personal, and interpersonal functions.

67

Methods of Assessment.

- Task 1: Reproduction (three or four times) of four rhythmic patterns, with different number of events and duration. The total score is maximum 28.
- Task 2: Recognition of differences and similarities in melodic contour and pitch between melodic patterns, including eight events each. The total score is maximum 10.
- Task 3: Description of musical pieces. The total score is maximum 4.
- Task 4: Feeling expression (sad, angry, happy) Vocally. The total score is maximum 9.
- Instrumentally. The total score is maximum 9.
- Task 5: Polarities improvisation. Alone. The total score is maximum 3. With a partner. The total score is maximum 3.

TABLE 2
Within-group Comparison Between First and Second Music Ratings

	First Rating	Second Rating
Rhythmic Patterns		
Reproduction	12.9 (5.4)	18.6 (6.8)*
Similarity and		
Difference Recognition	4.1 (3.9)	5.5 (3.5)
Musical pieces		
description	1.4 (1.2)	2.5 (1.4)*
Feeling Expression		
Vocally	4.3 (1.0)	5.4 (1.0)*
Strumentally	4.1 (2.6)	6.4 (2.0)*
Polarities Improvisation		
Alone	1.1 (0.5)	2.1 (0.6)*
With a partner	1.0 (0.2)	2.0 (1.0)*

*t test, p < 0.05

Results

Changes in tasks scores. Table 2 shows that the participants in music therapy sessions showed significant differences between the first music rating and that administered after a 7-months period (p =.05), for four out of five tasks. Reproduction of rhythmic patterns improved probably for a learning effect, since specific rhythmic exercises were executed during group sessions. Selective attention seems to be impaired to recognize more than one characteristics of melodic stimulus. The description of musical pieces showed an increasement in the amount of words used, together with association of personal feelings and recollection of past experiences. As far as feeling expression is concerned, it improved especially regarding instrumental improvisation, and a better differentiation between different feelings. Polarities to depict situations (i.e. two different seasons), or two personal characteristics, seemed more easily to be performed alone than with a partner.

Discussion. The changes in scores presented have to be matched with clinical observation made by psychiatrists regarding psychopathologic symptoms. In fact it was possible to note a higher level of activation in the majority of patients, mimic and verbal expression of pleasure and satisfaction for music therapy experience, an improvement in attention also in tasks outside music therapy session, an improvement in quantity and quality of social interaction between the patients and between the patients and normal people outside the day hospital, a reduction in anxiety, intrusive thoughts, and obsessive behavior, more time spent in leisure time and in a relaxed state, expressed willing to work, more participation to social activities. From a musical perspective, there were dramatic changes in how the most of patients lived music and music experiences: from a superficial to a deep involvement. Also their musical production began disorganized and became more congruent and integrated. The data regarding musical production were only phenomenologically examined through the recorded tapes, and represented a meaningful information of effectiveness of the proposed methodology, in order to tailor it to the unique personal organization.

Conclusion. The experience showed some interesting results, especially from a phenomenological and clinical point of view, in fact music therapy was included in the rehabilitation program in two psychiatric units. There are limits in evaluating the proposed method due to the fact that there were no control group, and a complete set of data for the experiment to support clinical evidence showed in the rehabilitation of schizophrenic patients. A more consistent study is in progress to define the method and instrument necessary to its validation. Notwhitstanding it appears that patients' quality of life was really improved and changed from "cold" to "warm", as a patient told us. The main purpose of rehabilitation program for psychiatric patients is to reduce the consequences of psychosis and avoid cronicity effects. Since there are difficulties in determining at a causal level a correlation between a functional deficit and a brain damage, it seems more useful to consider operational deficit in higher functions (attention, perception, memory), as psycho pathological events to be treated with a rehabilitative approach, together with medications. In this perspective the rehabilitative process starts focusing on single difficulty, and goes on integrating emotions, thoughts, and verbalization, at a psychotherapeutic level. The present method, taking in account the genetic, neurologic bases and psychological process regarding musical behavior, could be of some value in a rehabilitative program which considers operational level of neuropsychological and psychosocial activities in schizophrenic patients, with negative symptoms. This understanding is supported by literature which reported that musical activities of various kinds benefit adult psychiatric patients (Cassidy, 1976; Verdeau-Pailles 1981; Unkefer,1991; Bruscia, 1987, 1991; Nordoff & Robbins, 1977; Lecourt, 1987; Pavlicevic,Trevarthen, Duncan,1994), and from the temptative data of the two experiments, illustrating outcome at neuropsychological and psychological levels: stimulation of sensorial/emotional responses, and modification in affective states; increasing in attention, perception, and motor behavior; improvement in social interaction; reduction in anxious state; improvement in cognitive organization and strategy; increasing and articulation of self concept system.

The present author's theoretical and pragmatic approach is supported also by many authors who, following cognitive theoretical perspective, regard useful to dispose specific sensorial/affective non verbal techniques, together with verbal ones, to modify an emotional state and allow cognitive, behavioural change, considering that the emotional and cognitive processes are partially independent and interactive between each others, at different levels of awareness (Rachman, 1980; 1981; 1984; Beck, 1976; Meichembaum, 1977; Wolpe, 1978; Lang, 1977; Ellis, 1962; Lazarus, 1976). The contribution of this work to rehabilitation of schizophrenic patients consists in proposing an integrated methodology, which considers neuropsychological and psychosocial aspects of pathology, together with different functional area (emotional, cognitive, personal, interpersonal), various levels of awareness (pre-conscious, conscious), knowledge (tacit, and explicit), and expressive modalities (verbal, non verbal, musical, non musical). (Unfortunately this article has only space for the description of the psychosocial methodolody; eds.).

This is not a solution to the rehabilitation problem, but it has been proved to be useful to get in touch and to partially disclose some blocked inner processes in schizophrenic people. Considering a not well balanced functionment within brain hemispheres (left brain hyperfunction and right brain lower function) in schizophrenic people, it could be reasonable to suppose that different tasks and experiences in music domain may give opportunity to patients to learn again more adaptive emotional and cognitive schema, in order to re-organize in a more integrated way some impaired brain functions. Research studies about what is really effective in psychotherapeutic interventions point out that such interventions need 1) to build a therapeutic relationship (roles, empathic resonance, mutual affirmation); 2) some specific techniques addressed to specific patients; 3) to be focused on patient's emotional processes; 4) to introduce patients to take an active, cooperative, and responsible role to their therapeutic work; 5) to be long enough in order to allow patients to learn more adaptive thoughts, emotions, and behavior to be used outside therapeutic setting, in the daily life. The above elements constitute basic characteristics in many music therapy approaches. From a research point of view, it could be relevant to take into account such previous characteristics regarding the efficacy of intervention, and to plan on them research study. The outcome could represent a valid help to define the specificity of music therapy and to compare music therapy efficacy with that of other kind of therapies.

References

American Psychiatric Association. (1987). *Diagnostic and Statistical Manual of Mental Disorders*, III ed., Revised (DSM-III-R). Washington, DC: American Psychiatric Association
Andreasen, N., & Olsen, S.A. (1982). Positive and negative symptoms. Archives of General Psychiatry, 39, 789.
Barratt, E. S.(1983). The biological basis of impulsiveness: The significance of timing and rhythm disorders. Personality and individual differences, 4, 387-391.
Beck, A. (1976). Cognitive Therapy. New York: International Universities Press.
Bruscia, K.E. (1987). Improvisational Models of Music Therapy. Springfield: C. Thomas.
Bruscia, K.E. (1991). Case studies in music therapy. Phoenixville: Barcelona Publishers.
Cassidy, M. D. (1976). The influence of a music therapy activity upon peer acceptance, group cohesiveness, and interpersonal relationships of adult psychiatric patients. Journal of Music Therapy, 13, 66-76.
Cavicchio, A., Pecoriello, B., Giordanella Perilli, G., Roncone, R., & Casacchia, M. (1994 June). *Intervento breve di musicoterapia con pazienti psichiatrici ricoverati in un reparto di degenza* (Brief music therapy treatment with psychiatric inpatients). First Italian Congress of Music therapy. Ercolano. (in press).
Cimino, M., Sabbadini, M., & Ciani, N. (1990). Riabilitazione neuropsicologica del paziente psicotico. In M. Casacchia & R. Roncone (Eds.), II National Congress of Italian Association for Psycho social Rehabilitation: Riabilitazione Psicosociale in Psichiatria. Ruoli, Metodi, Strutture e Validazioni (Psycho social rehabilitation in psichiatria. Roles, methods, structure, and validity) (pp. 181-184). Naples: Idelson.
Cimino, M., Cantelmi, T., Bersani, G., Ciani, N. (1994). Clinical and neuropsychological correlates of size of the cerebral ventricles in schizophrenic patients. Analytic Psychotherapy and Psychopathology, 13, 1: 73-82.
Cohen, J. M. (1986). Rhythm and tempo in mania. Music Therapy, 6 A (1), 13-29.
Cutting, J. (1985). The psychology of schizophrenia. Edinburgh: Churchill Livingstone.
Densen, M.E. (1979). Time perception and schizophrenia. Perception and Motor skills, 44, 436-438.
Duryea, E. & Glover, J. A. (1982). A review of the research on reflection and impulsivity in children. Genetic Psychology Monographs, 106 (2), 207-237.
Ellis, A. (1962). Reason and emotion in psychotherapy. Secaucus, N.J.: Lyle Stuart.
Fraisse, P. (1984). Perception and estimation of time. Annual Review of Psychology, 3, 1-36.
Galvano, C. G. (1989). La musicoterapia nel trattamento riabilitativo integrato del disturbo psichiatrico: uno studio clinico longitudinale (The music therapy in a rehabilitative integrated treatment for psychiatric disturbs: a longitudinal clinic study). XXXVII National Congress of Italian Society of Psychiatria. Rome: Edizioni Internazionali.

Giordanella, G. (1993). Organizzazioni temporali nella strutturazione dei processi cognitivi in soggetti normali e soggetti con disturbi psichiatrici (Temporal organisations to structure cognitive process in normal and psychiatric people). Doctoral dissertation, Università Pontificia Salesiana, Rome, Italy.

Giordanella Perilli, G. (1991). Integrated music therapy with a schizophrenic woman. In K.E. Bruscia (Ed.). Case studies in music therapy. Phoenixville: Barcelona Publishers.

Giordanella Perilli, G., Verucci, M., Rullo, S., Ciani, N. (1992). L'approccio musicoterapeutico col paziente psicotico in training riabilitativo: analisi dei protocolli operativi (Music therapy approach with psychotic patient in rehabilitative training: analysis of operational methods). Analytic Psychotherapy and Psychopathology, 11, 4: 57-59.

Golden, C.J., Purisch, A.D., & Hammeke, T.A. (1985). Luria Nebraska Neuropsychological Battery: Forms I and II Manual. Los Angeles: Western Psychological Services.

Green, M., & Walker, E. (1984). Susceptibility to backward masking in positive versus negative symptoms in schizophrenia. American Journal of Psychiatry, 141, 1273-1275.

Kay, S.R., Fiszbein, A., & Opler, L.A. (1987). The Positive and Negative Syndrome Scale (PANSS) for schizophrenia. Schizophrenia Bulletin, 13, 261-276.

Lang, P. (1977). Imagery in therapy. Behavior Therapy, 8, 862- 886.

Lazarus, A.A. (1976). Multimodal Behavior Therapy. New York: Springer.

Lecourt, E. (1980). La pratique de la musicothérapie. Paris :Les Editions E S F.

Lecourt, E. (1987). Recherche exploratoire sur la psychopathologie du vecu sonore a l'hopital psychiatrique. La Revue de Musicotherapie, 8 (1), 1-10.

Lidlle, P. F., & Morris, D. L. (1991). Schizophrenia syndromes and frontal lobe performance. British Journal of Psychiatry, 158, 340-345.

Limbekne, I. P. (1981). The psychological tempo: Data on movement tempo and on time perception. Magyar Pszichologiai Szemle, 38 (5), 495-504.

Mc Adams, S. (1991). Musica: una scienza della mente? In C. Boschi (Ed.). Musica e Scienza. Il margine sottile (Music and Science. The thin edge). Rome: ISMEZ.

Meichembaum, D. (1977). Cognitive-Behavior Modification: An integrative approach. New York: Plenum Press.

Nordoff, P., & Robbins, C. (1977). Creative music therapy. New York: John Day.

Overall, J.E., & Gorham, D. (1962). Brief psychiatric rating scale. Psychological Reports, 10, 799-812.

Pavlicevic, M., Trevarthen, C., & Duncan, J. (1994). Improvisational music therapy and the rehabilitation of person suffering from chronic schizophrenia. Journal of Music Therapy, XXXI (2), 86-104.

Peretz, I, & Morais, J. (1994). Specificity for music. In C. Faienza. Music, speech and the developing brain: The case of modularity of mind. Milan: Angelo Guerini & Associati.

Perilli, G., Rullo, S., Saya, A., & Ciani, N. (1990). Riabilitazione neuropsicologica con la musicoterapia (Neuropsychological rehabilitation with music therapy). In M. Casacchia, & R: Roncone, R. (Eds.). II National Congress of Italian Society for Psycho social Rehabilitation: Riabilitazione psicosociale in psichiatria. Ruoli, Metodi, Strutture e Validazioni (Psycho social rehabilitation in psychiatry. Roles, methods, structures, and validity). (pp. 815-817). Naples: Idelson.

Perilli, G., Rullo, S., & Saya, A. (1993).I deficit neuropsicologici nella schizofrenia: un progetto di riabilitazione con la musicoterapia (Neuropsychological deficit in schizophrenia: a rehabilitative project with music therapy). Analytic Psychotherapy and Psychopathology, 12, 3, 209-215.

Petsche, H., Richter, P., Etlinger, S.C., & Filz, O. (1994). EEG facilities for the study of brain processes elicited by music and language. In C: Faienza. Music, speech, and the developing brain: The case of the modularity of mind. Milan: Angelo Guerini & Associati.

Rachman, S. (1980). Emotional processing. Behavior Research and Therapy, 18, 51-60.

Rachman, S. (1981). The primacy of affect: Some theoretical implications. Behavior Research and Therapy, 19, 279-290.

Rachman, S. (1984). A reassessment of the "primacy of affect". Cognitive Therapy and Research, 8, 579-584.

Rullo, S:, Perilli, G., & Verucci, M. (1992). Dal sintomo alla narrazione: il ruolo della musicoterapia nella storia clinica di uno psicotico (From symptom to story telling: the role of music therapy in the psychotic patient clinic history). Analytic Psychotherapy and Psychopathology, 11, 4, 69-71.

Schwartz, M., Friedman, R.J., Lindsay, P., & Narrol, H. (1982). The relationship between conceptual tempo and depressive children. Journal of Consulting and Clinical Psychology, 50, 4, 488- 490.

Steinberg, R:, & Raith, L. (1985). Music psychopathology: Musical tempo and psychiatric disease. Psychopathology, 18, 254-264.

Stratta, P. (1992 May). Nurses Observation Scale for Inpatients Evaluation: a validity study of the Italian version. Abstract Book World Psychiatric Association, Regional Symposium, Palermo .

Stuss, D.T., & Benson, D.F. (1986). The frontal lobes. New York: McGraw Hill.

Unkefer, R.F. (Ed.). Music therapy in the treatment of adults with mental disorders: Theoretical bases and clinical interventions. New York: Schirmen Books.

Verdeau-Paillès, J. (1981). Le bilan psycho-musical et la personnalité. Courlay: J.M. Fuzeau S.A

Verucci, M., San Martino, L., Giordanella Perilli, G., & Spalletta, G. (1994 June). Musicoterapia in un paziente con disturbo delirante (Music therapy with a patient suffering from delusion disturb). First Italian Congress of Music therapy. Ercolano.(in press).

Wolpe, J., The practice of Behaviour Therapy. New York: Pergamon Press.

* The original Appendices, presented at the Conference, can be ordered from the editors.

Musical Voice -
Treatment & Speech Therapy with Deaf Children

Claus Bang (DK)

Music is Communication

All our pupils at the Aalborg School might be characterised as having communication impairment in the sense that language limitations of a motoric, sensory or emotional character are understod as an obstacle to communication and function in society.

Music can establish contact without language, and through music therapy we find unused potentials in other communicative paths that assist with developing language. Since music produces a means of communication of a predominantly emotional character (non-verbal or pre-verbal communication), it is of importance and has great application exactly where verbal communication is not used because the spoken language is not understood. To the contact impaired persons, who are most often receptive to music, music will become the theme through which communication can take place. Communication may be described as verbal, emotional and is motor interactive. When verbal and motor communication do not function sufficiently, the emotional expression must be tried in order to reach the mind. As an emotional form of communication, as an unambiguous means of communication, music can replace the ambiguous verbal communication.

As a form of communication music is one of the possibilities of human interaction. As is the case in the development of social psychology, music therapy demonstrates unmistakable tendencies to understand music as an emotional way of communication, as a means of contact, the therapeutic application of music there is a possibility of making the treatment include interaction disturbances, or through communication, to tackle communicative disorders.

To all people, but in particular to the communication impaired, to hear music and to make music means communication. He, who is actively making music, can by means of the music, communicate with himself and thus reestablish his identity with his own body. Passive receptive music therapy, when the client is exclusively listening to music, may also turn out to be effective, as it offers the client a possibility to turn his attention to the music as a theme, and possibly create an object relationship.

Using the traditional terminology of music therapy, music offers the client some of the following therapeutic active resources, namely to listen, to be creative, to participate. Through music the handicapped person will have an opportunity of gathering experiences from the musical structure, experiences of self-organization and experiences of relating to others.

Music is a unique source and intermediary as to order energy, ability establishing contacts, actualizing self-knowledge, and not in the least, establishing or re-establishing human relationships.

Music appeals to the human being as a whole and influences the total personality in a way different from other forms of speech and language therapy. The integrating and emotional effect of music diminishes the abstract which often accompanies man in many of the traditional situations of learning language.

The language retarded person can only learn language through verbal action. But, the language retarded person can also learn to learn through musical action. Music is a language for all people. In the severest cases when it is not possible to learn through the language, music as a special human resource for communication is indispensable. Through music, an interactive development can be initiated for every human being.

Music - a Way to Speech and Language

Music and speech are based on perception and interpretation of sound starting with an auditory experience. In music therapy as well as in speech therapy, we are engaged in the auditory processes and the production and perception of sound. In both kinds of therapy we try to assess the pupils or clients reaction to sounds and all the factors involved in the developmental process. The auditory perception comprises the ability to distinguish between different sounds, their pitch, timbre, intensity or duration, all the characteristics which contribute to the meaning of sound. Music and speech concern ability to remember and to imitate sounds.

Sounds which have not yet been integrated into musical patterns as melody or rhythm or in verbal patterns as language, already contain elements of intensity, duration, pitch and intonation. The four characteristic elements can be perceived in spite of a severely reduced function of the brain.

Speech therapy can start with sounds that have not yet been structured into meaningful patterns. In treatment we shall then have to analyse the character of the sound produced and perceived, and engage ourselves in gradual process through which man transforms sounds in a meaningful language produced by his own body by means of physical movements which he is able to control, co-ordinate and use consciously. Any deficiency or blocking of the auditory system or of the ability to move is therefore a hindrance for the acquisition of language.

The resemblance between the construction of a music language and of a verbal language makes music a very important aid in speech therapy. Music language is first and foremost referred to as the perceptual and mental processes, such as hearing, memory and imitation of sounds heard, together with motor control of the necessary physical movements. When we speak an amalgamation of the elements attended by symbols of speech and music is taking place. During perception of speech and music the process is leading along the path in common to the sensory fields of projection and to the various centres processing information. Music activity and active listening to music can produce functions supporting the acquisition of language, of attention and perception, the transfer of movement to sound and of sound to movement, such as an experience of the unity of language, music and movement.

Musical Speech Therapy for the Hearing Impaired

The development of man is accompanied by sound, which is such a highly integrated part of the environment that very often we are not consciously perceiving these sounds. What we call silence is only a relative conception.Consciously or unconsciously, we learn from our birth the surrounding sounds. Our normal means of communication is with linguistic sounds, which we first perceive and later imitate. To those with normal hearing sound is an auditory perception, but the sound waves, which are produced by a vibrating sound source and are transmitted to us through the air, can reach us in other ways. They can be felt through the skin and the bones in parts of the body, in addition to the ears. This sound perception cannot be compared with what we hear, but it enables the deaf person to be in contact with the surrounding world of sounds.

To the deaf person music is thus primarily a series of vibrations, which are perceived and transported to the brain along other lines than the auditory organ. None the less, these vibrations can carry rhythms, sounds and melodic sequences, and cause reactions in the deaf person leading to activities of great value to him. The rhythms and tones, so to speak, are experienced from within as vibrations connected with the auditory input (kinaesthetically and auditorily rather than visually) gives rise to a spontaneous desire of the hearing-impaired person to transform the rhythmical-musical influence perceived into his Crown forms of expression, such as movements, mimicry, speech and singing.

Of the many human activities, speech is presumably the most rhythmical and musical. At the same time, speech and language are the most valuable instruments for communication and memory. Therefore working with hearing-impaired children's speech and language is most essential. One of the additional handicaps in the case of hearing impairment is that the control of the voice is lost completely or partially, often resulting in monotonous or forced, strained and squeaking voices.

This is to a high extent hampering these pupils in their communication with those who are able to hear. The rhythm of speech is a rhythmic movement of the speech organs, such as respiration, voice and articulatory movements of the mouth, together with the sounds from the larynx. We hear the speech movements, and thus hearing is a sensory-motor-process. Practising music and movement will train the auditory sensory-motor functions and the memory of such sequences and their use. Consequently, musical activities are indirectly training the basic functions of speech and language.

Music and language offer so many points of resemblance that the basic elements of music can be employed as a means of teaching the hearing-impaired and other handicapped groups to break the verbal monotony, to speak rhythmically and melodically, thus developing and improving communication with the normal hearing.

The crux of the music therapy programme at the Aalborg School is therefore the speech training and language stimulation through music, the musical speech therapy, which is started when the pupils are two or three years old, and which is then integrated in the daily teaching of articulation and speech by co-operation between parents, advisers, teachers, speech therapists and the music therapist. By this form of therapy we try to improve the voice levels and the voice qualities of the pupils, at the same time systematically teaching the accentuation in intensity, duration, pitch and intonation by utilising the pupil's residual hearing by means of hearing aids, the ability of sound perception in the whole body, and the contact-vibration sense, particularly in the limbs.

Tone Bars in Practice and in Research

In musical speech therapy a great number of special musical instruments are used, such as the Sonor Tone Bars, the frequencies of which are from 64 to 380 Hz, a range where the greatest part of the deaf have some residual hearing. This means that the residual hearing to a certain degree can be activated and utilised through work with the tone bars, which possess very specific acoustic-vibratory qualities. Since 1972, we have concentrated the use of tone bars in musical speech therapy because of the remarkably good vocal responses from our hearing impaired and multiply handicapped pupils to this sound stimuli. The Danish Research Council for the Humanities has with grants, during the years of 1973-1976 supported my reseach project *"Physiological Sound Functions, Perception and Reproduction of Sound in Profoundly Deaf and Normal Hearing Children Exploring the Use of Tone Bars in Sound Analysis and Musical Speech Therapy."*

The purpose of the project is an examination of the voice material of profoundly deaf and normally hearing children, aged 5-15, and an analysis of the effect of musical speech therapy with Sonor tone bars on the qualities of these pupil's voices and vocal function. The analysis includes tone, intensity, time of tonation, frequencies, intonation, compression, modulation, learning the half-glottal stop, reduction of nasality, etc. Further the intention of the project is to determine if the improvement of deaf children's speech and language, as a result of this tone bar therapy, will cause an increased comprehension of those surrounding the deaf and consequently improve the possibilities of communication in society.

At the Aalborg School, I have tape-recorded the spontaneous voices of 30 deaf pupils and 30 children with normal hearing, aged 5-15, and their vocal responses, using the BA-sound, applied to 26 different tone bars in a series of different test-positions, each of them showing different paths of perception. At the Institute of Phonetics at the University of Copenhagen, I have transformed the tape-recordings to curve material on the sonagraph and mingograph equipment. The curves have been measured for data processing and examined statistically in co-operation with assistant professor Allan Dresling of the Institute for Electronic Systems, Aalborg University.

In the following areas concrete improvement in voice and speech through the therapy with Sonor Tone Bars have been proved:

1. *Pitch and frequency span, its regulation in the spontaneous voice.*
2. *Intonation, compression, intensity of the spontaneous voice.*
3. *Sonority of vowels, motivation for structured articulation.*
4. *Voice malfunctions caused by stress, changes at puberty, etc.*
5. *Accentuation in intensity, duration and pitch. Elements of Prosody.*

On the basis of the analysed materials, two mathematic models of calculation have been developed for a qualitative evaluation of vocal improvement of the responding and the spontaneous voices. The purpose has been to make a comparison between the voice qualities before and after the training with the tone bars, and on this basis to define pedagogic and therapeutic guidelines and methodical instructions concerning the use of tone bars in the professional treatment of voice disorders and speech trasining of hearing impaired pupils. Concurrently, with this work, experimental measurements have been carried out in co-operation with assistant professor M.A. Børge Frøkjær-Jensen from the Audiologopedic Research Group at the University of Copenhagen, on the electronic instrument, which he has developed, measuring improvement of voices by a spectral analysis of the voice. Further, Allan Dresling, supported by the Danish Natural Science Research Council, is at present developing a general model of data analysis for automatic processing of data from the electronic measuring instrument used for voice analysis.

In order to determine the value of the tone bar therapy as part of the speech and language treatment of mentally retarded, motoricly disabled and multiply handicapped (e.g. deafblind and psychotic-autistic pupils) the project is also designed to develop training programmes for the use of the tone bars with these handicaps. In the normal school too, there is a marked need for the use of the tone bar method when working with voice improvement. For the pupils with hoarse, noisy or monotonous voices the tone bar therapy has shown considerable improvement of the vocal tone and modulation.

We feel that the use of the tone bar therapy has broadened to even more fields, such as the fact that special education has started new research of the physiological sound functions. Based on the experiences which have been achieved, the committee for deciding articulation and voice treatment methods for hearing-impaired in the Nordic countries and in several other European countries have decided to introduce training programmes using the Sonor tone bars. Through the close co-operation of the teaching and treatment teams organised concerning musical voice treatment and speech therapy, we can, as a result of intensive training, achieve an improvement of the handicapped person's possibility of perceiving and reproducing the rhythm and melody of speech and of language, the result which will mean better modulation, an increased mastering and understanding of language and thus, development of handicapped pupils' potential for communication.

Music thinking and the experiencing body

Ruth Eckhoff (N)

Introduction

Music thinking is a multi-disciplinary field relating to many aspects of theoretical and practical musical activity. Within many of these fields of science there is a growing awareness of the linkages between music and the role of the body in the perspective of active experience. Interest in this topic has grown considerably during the last decades.

Within *modern developmental psychology* and baby research, several theories using musical concepts have emerged. The work of Daniel Stern and Colwyn Trevarthen will be used as examples here. The somewhat older *French school of phenomenology* has made important contributions to this theme, and especially Gabriel Marcel who was also a musician, composer, and music philosopher. *Social anthropological theories of music* describe and discuss the close connections between music and dance or movement in so-called "primitive" cultures. Or as Charles Keil is an example of, they may study musical subcultures in the western countries.

Modern studies of popular music exemplified by Richard Middleton and Barbara Bradby point out a body perspective as a core concept when trying to understand phenomena of listening and making music. I will also mention theories that combine music and body thinking within the following fields: *music pedagogy,* (Swanwick, Orff, Dalcroze) and within *music psychology* (Meyer). These theories share a mutual concern for bodily participation in musical activity. They point out the importance of letting oneself be moved and touched by music, of bodily human *being-togetherness* in the world of music. My impression is that these ideas signify the emergence of a new paradigm.

To limit my topic I have decided to leave out some relevant and interesting areas; one is body perspectives in the western history of music thinking from the Greek antique up to our time, another is body perspectives in eastern "high" culture music traditions, a third would be music and meditation, a fourth might be the role of the body in foreign so-called "primitive" cultures.

During the last decades there has been an enormous focus on the body in western societies. In the same period music industry and music mass communications have expanded tremendously. One may ask what the connections are between these phenomena. This big question cannot be answered in detail within this lecture. Both in music and body culture huge paradoxes exist. The body is cultivated in many not-experiencing ways like in body building, in commercials, in piercing, in cosmethical surgery and so on. Eating disorders increase, so does prostitution, pornography and sex industries. At the same time a lot of body therapies and new age pnenomena are becoming very popular, probably to counteract the unhealthy body cultures. In western countries a lot of different musical cultures and subcultures exist. The body socialisation is an important part of any music culture and the differences are striking. Trends in some music cultures may bring people closer to their body experiences, like much of the rhythmical music. Others may have body alienation as an effect, for example death metal music. Many of the theories to be discussed in this lecture result from an interest in describing under which circumstances connections between musical and body activity can promote health. Music therapy itself can be seen in this historical line.

Motion is a core concept that link the two areas, music and body together. Its origin is surely bodily, but it is enormously important in music thinking. Emotion *(e-movere)* comes from the same root. It means to be moved. Through strengthening the ability to experience our bodies, we will also learn to be in closer contact with our emotions. This will lead to a richer musical experience in listening, dancing, singing and playing.

Some perspectives on the experiencing body and intersubjectivity
Before looking more closely at the most important theories combining music thinking and a body perspective, I shall clarify the basic philosphical and antropological perspectives relating to the concept of *"the experiencing body"*. This concept focuses on how we sense and perceive our body from within.

Our body is perceptive, memorative and expressive. The totality of perception is stored in our body memory, in what we can call our *body self.* The body self is the foundation from which feelings, thoughts and other complex expressive capacities emerge (Petzold 1992). It is also the origin of musical expression and other kinds of human artistic creation (Frohne-Hagemann 1995).

The French phenomenological school of philosophy (1945-1960), represented by Gabriel Marcel, Maurice Merleau-Ponty and Paul Ricoeur, has created an influential anthropology that gathers the human being instead of splitting it into body and soul or matter and spirit, according to the Cartesian dualism. They were all inspired by Martin Buber, who launched the idea of intersubjectivity (Buber 1923). Their philosophy enlarged the role of the body to encompass qualitative aspects of living, responding and perceiving.

Gabriel Marcel defines intersubjectivity in a philosophical way (Marcel 1978; i Petzold 1980). His definition is a precursor to the concept of intersubjectivity that we find in modern infant research and interaction theories.

The definition has three parts:

* An involvement in the other person in a way so that the
  interest in the other is not objective or functional,
  but deeply personal.
* Personality, which means that I always speak directly
  to a person and not above him. I do not treat the other
  but I try to touch him and let myself be touched by
  him.
* Being together, in a way so that real contact is the
  base of the mutual touch from person to person. Such a
  togetherness makes possible a contact that is not
  distorted by projections and transference.

Contact is experienced with the total body organ of awareness according to Marcel (1978, 2; in Petzold 1980). He is also preoccupied with the general distinction between *being* and *having* and uses the body as an example. He points out that we need both the subjective and the objective way of relating to our bodies. The subjective way can loosely be expressed in the sentence: "I am my body". Marcel calls this *the phenomenal body* (Marcel 1935; in Randi Berg 1969 or in Petzold 1980). He is aware that we are of course our bodies but also something more than our bodies. However, when we say "I have a body" we objectify ourselves. Gabriel Marcel calls this *the object body*. The german Hilarion Petzold, who founded the school of Integrative Therapy, from which I am educated, would probably say: "I am my bodyself, my ego and my identity (Petzold 1991).

These two ways, the subjective and the objective may be generalized to how we relate to other persons, to the world. They are grasped differently. The subject way must be lived through a total awareness, that means ontologically. The object way is to understand through the intellect, by naming and classifying, separating and dividing, as in science. Once you do this you are detaching yourself from the phenomenon under study. Marcel says that there are certain aspects of life that cannot be explained through science, he wants these to be reserved for what he calls mystery or the meta-problematic sphere. These aspects are to be found in love, encounter, religion, art, nature etc. The sense of being cannot be understood intellectually, it is attained by going into or uniting yourself with existing things, by heart, by being caught or absorbed by the phenomenon itself. Poetically you could describe it as letting oneself be floating in time, much like the way one may drift away listening to music. Such thoughts seem to be more common in the western world nowadays than they were when Marcel wrote this (1935). Many of you will notice the similarity with, for example, the gestalt therapy focus on staying in *the-here-and-now*. It is also close to the aims of meditation, martial arts and so on, ideas which to a large extent originate in the eastern philosophies.

Merleau-Ponty (1945) introduced in his book "The phenomenology of perception" three very important concepts: *the body subject, the incarnated body, and intercorporality.* The body subject is identical with the person as such. The body is animated, incarnated or filled with soul. Many people and especially psychiatric patients often feel disembodied, you can get the feeling of a lifeless or poorly incarnated being. The concept of intercorporality is derived from intersubjectivity by addressing the bodily aspect of being together. Intersubjectivity is to a large extent learned through a mutual body socialisation, a microclimate of body sensations, movement, postures, touch, eye contact. All of these are important ingredients or qualities in nonverbal interaction or communication.

Paul Ricoeur dealt with the temporal *being-in-the-world* (Ricoeur 1971 and 1983; in Petzold 1992). Human beings co-exist with other human beings in *co-respondence*, in a common *field-of-experience.* This co-existence begins and ends with the body.

Music, the body, intersubjectivity and coexistence

Now to return to music thinking: Gabriel Marcel is deeply involved with music, which is fundamental to his existence. Music reinforces his sense of streaming presence, it increases the feeling of existence. To him, music is carrying truth in the sense of a certain reality, not telling the only truth, but something truly existing. Music is non-ambiguous, it sympathizes with reality. Therefore he feels a resistance towards making it an object of analysis and reflection. So much is said between the lines in music that cannot be grasped by the cathegories of thinking. So he nourishes and reproduces himself from inside by singing, playing and composing. This gives him a feeling of deep essence, much like the experience of contact encountering beloved persons. This is what he wants to express in his compositions.

It is the living body subject who experiences the co-existence with music in this way, I would say. The body sensations are the base of all experience, also the musical type. Marcel writes about music experience and about body experience in different documents, but both types of experience are for him strongly connected with being alive, being present, being in time. He must have been aware of the relation between the two, even if I have not found this explicitly formulated. It would be interesting to read his musical diary, which is in French only, to learn whether this includes his body perspective (Marcel 1980; in Kjerschow 1993).

One critical commentary should be made at this point. When speaking of music, Marcel implies the western classical tradition. He is himself part of the western European "liebhaber"-culture that cultivates universal and general philosophical reflections on MUSIC. This kind of reflection is part of the love of music. This can be seen for example in the following quotation from Gabriel Marcel: "Music was too active in the movement of my thought to be the object or content of my thinking" (Marcel 1980; in Kjerschow 1993). Whether Marcel was himself aware of the context from which he operates, I do not know precisely.

Music is always perceived in a cultural context and many music cultures do not have a tradition to reflect philosophically on musical issues.

"Musical" theories of infant development

As mentioned before, intersubjectivity is a core concept in both the French school of phenomenology and within modern theories of infant development, the so-called interaction theories. They have some common features of interest to this subject. Firstly, some interaction theories use concepts which stem from, or are closely connected to, music thinking. It is interesting that a kind of music thinking can be found in the field of general developmental psychology. Secondly, interaction theories focus intensively on the development of body sensations and experiences. I will give some examples.

Daniel Stern came up with the idea of *affect attunement*, which means that the mother tunes herself emotionally to the body of the child. Attunement or to tune are words coming from music language. The purpose of the mothers attunement is to contain and share the totality of the childs psychophysical presence and experience. The baby is exposed to a huge amount of impressions, but its nervous system is still immature and unable to handle all this information. Therefore the mother has to interpret the stimuli and organize them in a way so that the child can safely relate to them. The affect attunement is necessary to ensure a "good enough" dialogue between the mother and the child. The mother matches the form and movements of the child's global reactions, by regulating the level and the contour of the intensity, the pulse, rhythm and duration of her voice, movements, gaze and facial expression. In this way the mother provides a frame for the child, she answers its emotional expression and gives a musical form to its expression. In this way the child is mirrored and thereby confirmed.

Vitality affects are sensations of everything streaming in us, all that is increasing or decreasing, they are musical forms in time. Such vitality affects may have different degrees of intensity, from the very discrete to the very strong sensations (Daniel Stern, 1991). Winnicott has a parallel to this in his concept "the censor being", it is essential for the child's vitality to have a constant sensation of being or existing (Wrangsjö 1995).

Traditionally, psychoanalytic literature has been preoccupied with studying affects in the sense of the relatively strong states that are structuring memory the most. Discrete affects have not been focused. Traumatic emotions are the much too strong, shocking states that the individual handles with the help of defence mechanisms (repression, splitting, anaesthesia etc.) The defence mechanisms are psychophysical and become inscribed in the body or embodied. The bodily sensitivity is thus reduced, resulting in a lack of awareness of the weaker vitality affects. In consequence, the child experiences islands of sensation, not an ever ongoing feeling of life. Stern's contribution is a more dynamic and continous explanation of affective states. His description is truly musical and founded in the perspective of the experiencing body.

Colwyn Trewarthen, a biologist well-known to music therapists, has developed another theory on mother-infant interaction, focusing on a dynamic music thinking. Microfilm has been taken of both the mother and the child shortly after birth, showing that they take turns in a kind of pre-verbal dialogue like equal partners. The mother uses a baby language ("motherese") with rhytmical and melodical features and with a pulse to which they both relate. They change initiative, the one is making sounds while the other is actively listening, like musicians taking turns improvising music. The child may even adjusts his body language after the dynamics of the mother's voice. Trevarthen sees this as musical interaction forms or structural precursors, called protoconversation and eventually developing into mature forms of dialogue.

The two researchers differ in some ways and especially in the way they define intersubjectivity. To Trevarthen intersubjectivity is a biologically programmed capacity. This capacity is inborn and made to ensure that the child gets what it needs. Stern is a psychoanalyst and his focus is on emotional sharing. The child has to go through two forms of relatedness or stages of self development before it, around 7 months of age, has the capacity to relate intersubjectively and be aware of the emotional sharing. The earlier stages are *the emerging self* and *the subjective self*. To have a sense of a subjective self is a necessity to the child before being able to relate intersubjectively. In the earlier stages the mother provides the needed structure to ensure interaction, according to Stern.

Still, what the two researchers have in common is of greater interest to my topic. Stern and Trevarthen describe the development of mother - child interaction. They do it to a large extent in musical terms and from a perspective of body sensations.

All human beings share the experience of lying in the mothers womb. But every mother has her unique body, unique movements and unique forms of vitality affects. The foetus is exposed to massive sound stimuli from her body; her voice, her heartbeat, the "whizz" from the veins, rumbling from the guts and so on. Through this the child has aquired an immediate knowledge of his mother. According to Petzold the foetus can read the vitality contours in the physiology of the mother, but it cannot differentiate whether the mother is for example angry or sexually aroused (Petzold 1995). Anyhow, in the interaction between the foetus and the mother we can find some of the origins of the close connections between music and body experience.

Musical gesture, the role of the body in music making and music listening

Theories of musical gesture seem to be important to my topic. Works by Meyer, Swanwick, Middleton will be examined. Common for all theories of musical gesture is the idea of a close connection between bodily expression and musical phrasing.

Leonard B. Meyer put forward his theory as early as 1956 in his book "Emotion and meaning in music". There he mentioned physical experience as an aspect of music listening and used the word *musical gesture*. Meyer was a phenomenologist, musicologist and practicing psychologist. He also used the notion *embodied meaning,* which sees the music as a body carrying a certain non-referential meaning. The concept *sound term* corresponds to musical gesture and refers to a meaningful musical phrase in a context.

The music listener adjusts himself *ideo-motoric* before listening to music. Meyer calls this the *preparatory set.* The listener responds psychophysically to the music on the background of his expectations, and whether they are fulfilled in the actual course of the music. The psychic or the physical component of these responses cannot be analyzed separately. Meyer postulates that muscles per se cannot perceive, the bodily reaction results from mental grouping in gestalts, that rhythm is understood mentally and that the mental processes rank before body processes. This wiew is highly controversial in recent times (unfortunately there is no time to discuss this thoroughly here). Anyhow, Meyer contributed to an upgrading of the bodily aspect of music listening. His points of view were considered radical in the 1950's.

Swanwick, a professor of music pedagogy, takes up the idea of musical gesture. He sees them as meaningful human expression, but gives no precise definition (Swanwick 1988). He critizises the early nineteenth century research on music physiology, which emphasizes polygraphical measurements and thus eschews the experiencial aspect. Swanwick reviews and discusses the older theories connecting music thinking and physiological perspectives. He concludes that the analytical perspective of most of the theories is too narrow, too static and only being described in visual terms. He sees musical structures as meaningful connections, more or less efficient, between different musical gestures. Swanwick prefers a dynamic description using expressive words from music or body language, e.g. movement, flow weight, size, and direction.

In trying to find a theory of musical gesture, Richard Middleton is in the front line with his research on popular music. He thinks that we perceive music as processes, these processes have forms analogous to physical gestures. Musical gesture originates from even deeper layers in human beings, kinesthetic patterns, cognitive maps and affective movements. Middleton refers to other theoricians supporting this kind of thought. Lévi-Strauss has a theory of correspondences between musical and somatic structures. Blacking has the idea that musical processes are linked to somatic states and rhytms, and Barthes the idea of musical processes as *somathemes* or figures and forms of the body (for references to Lévi-Strauss, Blacking and Barthes; see Middleton 1990). Middleton points out that the culturally specific gestures are rooted in the human biology. Here he cites Maróthy in his decription of the so-called periodicity zones of the body (Maróthy 1974, 1983; in Middleton 1993). Periodicity zones are areas working rhythmically or periodically, like lungs, heart, feet, fingers, speech organ, ear drum, eye (light waves), ultra-sound perception, electrochemical neural circuits,etc. According to Middleton, Maróthy draws a spectrum of regular nerve impulses on the one hand to direct bodily movements on the other hand. All the different components combine and overlap in numerous ways. From within this spectrum musical gestures may arise.

At least it may be concluded here that there are several theories from different fields of science trying to describe more or less similar phenomena, by linking body processes to musical expression.

The consequence of this would be to emphasize the importance of bodily awareness and body experience in music education and in the training of musicians. In music education there are schools with a clear body perspective, such as the Orff-tradition, the Jaques-Dalcroze method, the Steiner eurhythmics and modern rhythmic-education (refer to Swanwick, 1988). Such a tradition seems to be more developed in Sweden and Denmark than in Norway. Denmark seems to be in the front with all the rhythmical evening schools where music, movement or dance is taught, a fact which has to do with an upgrading of rhytmical music in these countries.

Rhythmical music and bodily participation

Rhythmical music is a central field of study for socialanthropologists and popular music researchers. The former study rhythmical music in foreign cultures as well as musical subcultures in the western countries from social anthropological perspectives. The latter study different forms of western popular music. The interest in rhythmical music and especially rock music is for both groups clearly body-oriented. The importance of rock music in western cultures can be understood as an effort to bring people back to their bodies, as a kind of revolt against the esthetics of western classical music. According to the Freudian heritage, classical esthetics put forward the virtue of deferred gratification of needs and sublimation. The audience is expected to sit still (and not cough), be patient and focus their attention to long spans of musical form. The relieving of tension may come after having grasped the music horizontally. This listening experience is a higher social class phenomenon.

People from the working class are generally more close to their bodies, through which they provide their income, than people from the higher classes. However, the economical exploitation of the working body often leads to body alienation. Even if the worker trusts his body as an instrument, he may have lost the awareness of body experience.

The earlier mentioned popular music researcher Richard Middleton is also well known for new methods of analyzing popular music, texts and music. He wants to restore older gesture- or kinesthetically oriented participating models of analysis, and create new methods. Such forms of analysis has for a long periode been overshadowed by statically oriented, structure-analytical models. Middleton asserts the importance of using both types of analysis. As an example he mentions social anthropological studies of foreign cultures, where filming of music and dance is used in analysis. By comparing the two sets of data, namely the musical

sound and the movements of the bodies, the musical structures are better understood (Middleton 1993).

The feminist perspective on popular music is also interesting in the context
of rhythmical music. Barbara Bradby has studied differences between male and
female ways of participating in popular music (Bradby 1993). She shows how
males deal with culture, language and technology, while females represent
emotionality, body and sexuality. Men own the studios and use modern
technology to manipulate the female body and her voice, and they assert
themselves through music journalism. When looking at the different ways of
using the voice, the tendency is for males to be rapping and females to be singing
in a soul way. Men talk and women sing, and men are oriented towards rhythm,
while women are oriented towards melody. As an example of weird ways of
putting together symbols in relation to sampling and technological manipulation,
she mentions a music video from the group Black Box. The voice being heard
belongs to a ripe, motherly, black soul-singing women, while the body dancing on
the screen belongs to a young woman exhibiting a unisex image. The voice of the
older, black woman is valued above that of the white, young women. At the same
time the young female's body is worth looking at, while the older woman's body
is considered less attractive.

The music social anthropologist, Charles Keil, has with his theory of
participatory discrepancies, contributed thouroughly to the understanding of
rhythmical music and its relation to the body (Keil 1966, 1994). He critizises
Meyer for generalizing his theory too much. Keil points out that Meyer's theory
of embodied meaning is only relevant to western composed art music with its
focus on syntactics. It is not relevant for rhythmical music in the western
countries or non-western music cultures. Instead he generates the concept
engendered feeling to describe more process-oriented or improvised musical
forms.

Typical to rhythmical music is what we call *groove* or *swing,* different
types of *vital drives*. These are built up in unique and highly specialized ways.
There exists intricate relations between a regular pulse and the repetetive rhythm
patterns. In addition, the individual musicians perform microvariations that
cannot be measured. These variations may go against the pulse, they may be *"lay
back"* (delayed) or *"on top"* (too early).

Details of such vital drives cannot be written in scores, they must be
experienced bodily and mentally by the participants. Rhythmical music cannot be
analyzed in a static or syntactic way, the result would be to objectify the music or
disconnect oneself from the living musical reality. Evidently, Keil's ideas are
close to Marcel's distincion between being and having. Descriptions of rhythmical
music must take into account the immediate, the motoric gestures, the horizontal
accumulation of tension, the *here-and-now*, to quote Fritz Perls. In this music the
gratification of needs is connected to the immediate bodily experience, you are
invited to find *"the inner child"*, have fun and break borders. "Don't worry, be
happy", Bobby McFerrin sings.

Conclusion

I have shown linkages between music thinking and *the experiencing body* in different fields of science, inside musicology and outside. I regard these connections to have important bearings to music therapists. When reading theories of music therapy, I noticed that the body perspective largely is absent. To me, this observation is alarming. Keil, the music social anthropologist, once said: "If music is so closely associated with bodily effort, why not build a bodily aesthetic adequate to the task" (Keil 1966).

I will end this lecture by emphazising the importance of developing theoretical tools and practical strategies concerning a body perspective in music therapy. Music therapy students should be trained to become aware of their bodies, to be bodily present towards their clients. They should be after-socialized in a culture of musical intercorporality or *corpo-musical correspondence* (Frohne-Hagemann 1995) and they must be taught the corresponding meta-theory. In my opinion, music therapy theory and practice that lack perspectives of the experiencing body are failing.

References:

Berg, Randi. *Alternativ til det absurde, en studie i G. Marcels filosofi*. Ide og tanke-serien. 1969. Tanum, Norge.

Bradby, Barbara. Sampling sexuality: gender, technology and the body in dance music. *in popular music 1993. 12/2*. Cambridge University Press.

Buber, Martin. *Jeg og du*. 1923 Inzel Verlag Leipzig. Cappelens upopulære. Cappelen 1992.

Johns, Unni. "Gjensidighet i improvisert musikalsk samspill sett i lys av teorien om tidlig mor-barn interaksjon". *Psykologisk inst. UiO*. 1991 Norge.

Keil, Charles. Motion and feeling through music. *in The Journal of Aestetics and art critisism. 1966 Vol. 24. No. 3. 337-349*.

Keil, Charles. The theory of participatory discrepancies: A progress report. in Charles Keil and Steven Feld. *Music Grooves 1994*. Chicago University Press, Chicago.

Kjerschow, Peder Christian. *Tenkningen som deltakelse*. 1993. Solum, Norge.

Merleau-Ponty, Maurice. *Phenomenology of perception*. 1966 Routledge & Kegan Paul, London. 1945 Paris.

Middleton, Richard. Popular music analysis and musicology. Bridging the gap. *in popular music, 1993 12/2*. Cambridge University Press.

Middleton, Richard. Studying popular music. Chapters 6 and 7. 1990. Open University Press. Philadelphia.

Petzold, Hilarion. Det terapeutiske forhold i integrativ terapi. Artikkel oversatt og utgitt av Norsk Forening for Integrativ Terapi (* NFIT), Oslo. 1980 Junfermann, Paderborn.

Petzold, Hilarion. Integrative body and movement- therapy, a multi-modal approach to the "body subjekt". Artikkel 1992.
* NFIT, Oslo.

Petzold, Hilarion. *Integrative Bewegungs- und Leibtherapie* i 2 bind. 1988 Junfermann, Paderborn.

Petzold, Hilarion. "Vitenskapstreet" som forklarings- og erkjennelsesmodell for teori og praksis i Integrativ terapi. 1994. * NFIT Oslo. 1991 Düsseldorf.

Petzold, Hilarion. Lectures at Kinge Pension, 1995. Norway.

Stern, Daniel. *Barnets interpersonelle univers*. 1991. Hans Reitzels forlag, København.

Swanwick Keith. Music, mind and education. 1988. Routledge, New York.

Trevarthen, Colwyn. "Intersubjective exchange and transfer of understanding in infancy" *in British journal of educational psychology, 48 (feb.) 106.* 1978 Edinburgh.
Trevarthen, Colwyn. "Infants trying to talk: How a child invites communication from the human world." in Søderberg, R. *(Editor) Childrens creative communication.* 4th. International Congress for the study of child language. 1989 Lund University Press.
Wrangsjö, Björn. När själven möts uppstår musik. Daniel Sterns själv teori. *in Nordic Journal of Music Therapy. 1994. 3 (2).*

* NFIT is Norsk Forening for Integrativ Terapi (Norwegian Association of Integrative Therapy). Address: NFIT, POB. 9397 Vålerenga, N-0610 Oslo, Norway.

Music Therapy in Mental Health, with Specific Reference to Work with Older People, and the Role of the Muliti-Disciplinary Team

Helen Odell Miller (GB)

Introduction

In this keynote address, I will attempt to open up some issues pertinent to music therapy as practised in the field of mental health. I was first asked to do this in order to highlight an often neglected area of work in the literature - that of music therapy with older people. I will not be providing a comprehensive guide to music therapy in the field of mental health throughout the world, but more a short overview, leading to a specific discussion about older people, using our service in Cambridge to provide clinical material. Mental Health encompasses a wide range of issues, but I am concentrating on the severe forms of psychiatric illness.These include schizophrenia, manic depression, depression, anxiety states and psychosis, in addition to problems of old age such as dementia.Here, we will be primarily concerned with older adults suffering from severe mental health problems, whose dependancy means they are cared for, and reliant upon a multidisciplinary team, which could include Therapists, Doctors, Social workers, Psychologists, Family members related to the patient and volunteers. I am not suggesting that Music Therapy is any less effective with those who are less psychologically dependant,but I am of the belief that in this economic climate we may need to prioritise and highlight the people for whom Music Therapy may be more effective than other therapies.To enable the treatment to be effective it is important to have the support of the multidisciplinary team and to understand the role of other carers.I will particularly highlight the often neglected area of music therapy with those suffering from dementia.

Let us look generally at some issues of definition and theory in Music Therapy. During the last decade, there has been a world-wide attempt to try to understand its different definitions and theoretical concepts, summarised in Maranto (1993). In this book Music Therapy: International Perspectives there are extensive lists defining approaches to music therapy used all over the world. An underlying division exists between those who feel Music Therapy must develop its own theories arising from Music Therapy practice, and those who feel more strongly that Music Therapy would be more effective and more easily defined if it were based upon already existing theories, predominantly those derived from psychoanalysis. For example Lecourt (1988) in France has developed a particular approach based on Freudian and post Freudian psychoanalytic concepts and her work is an example of the music fitting into an already existing psychoanalytic framework. Likewise, John (1992) in his article "Towards Music Psychotherapy" in the Journal of British Music Therapy also implies that a clear theoretical framework governing practice would be desirable, and goes some way to clarifying and explaining the function of music in therapy in relation to psychoanalysis. Specifically, he writes about the function of music in conscious and unconscious processes, preferring to describe his work as Music Psychotherapy. - He writes:

"It seems that when playing music, feelings are often represented without necessarily being consciously felt. I am convinced from clinical experience that when this "preconscious phenomenon" is used in therapy it can be a way of both regulating and controlling the flow of affect, and preparing consciousness to receive and tolerate affect. This process of music being literally a medium through which unconscious material can bypass repression and become conscious in words forms the basis of music psychotherapy".

These two examples may be a far cry from the primary healing function ascribed to music making in the approach of Nordoff Robbins (1977) or from the approach of Alvin (1991) in the early stages of Music Therapy in the UK. Here, the musical impact on the clients in therapy is considered of prime importance, rather than the understanding of unconscious process as derived from psychoanalysis within the relationship between therapist, patient and music. I want to say here that I shall be using references to other peoples work in order to highlight points I want to make, rather than referring to all the relevant literature. Much exellent work is going on in this field which will not be mentioned. Elsewhere in Europe, Music Therapy in Mental Health with adults is covered in the literature in many different ways. Kortegaard (1992) and di Franco (1992), both show influences from psychoanalysis, and del Campo in Maranto (1993), shows a humanist approach.. Raijmaakers (1992) covers a similar subject to that asked of me today and highlights the importance of the role of music therapy in assessment and diagnosis, within the multi-disciplinary team for elderly patients in The Hague. Towse, (1995) highlights the importance of a psychoanalytical framework, working with older people with functional disorders but interestingly for a British music therapist, emphasises the importance of listening to live and recorded music, feeling that improvisation may not always be appropriate here. Sessions take the form of a group discussion after listening, with the music therapist taking a supportive analytic role. In the same book (Wigram,Saperston and West 1995) I discuss an opposing view, arising out of my work with people who are in advanced stages of dealing with dementia, and for whom interacting through music is often the only means of contact with the outside world, (Odell-Miller pp 84 - 85, 1995). For those with organic problems such as dementia, it is well recognised that use of instrumental improvisation is often the only useful method of containment, expression, interaction and resolution, and this will be one of the central themes in this paper.

Other music therapists have made contributions to the theoretical debate about music therapy which are relevant here. In summary, Priestly (1975, 1977,1994) developed Analytical Music Therapy, Heal (1989) coined the term "Analytically Informed Music Therapy" and Elaine Streeter has discussed musical counter-transference to quote a few examples. Bruscia (1987) describes different approaches in his book Improvisational Models of Music Therapy and more developments have occurred since it was published. Many other Music Therapists have acknowledged influences from psychoanalysis too numerous tolist comprehensively here. Among these are Rogers (1992) Towse (1991) and Woodcock (1987).

Hanser and Claire (1995) are among others from outside Europe who describe work with the elderly mentally ill fitting into humanistic and developmental frameworks, but this work cannot be described in detail here. At this point, I want to share something of my dilemma in preparing for this keynote address. I was asked originally to concentrate upon the older age group, many of whom still live in residential settings, despite improvements in community care provision. Having read literature and written more recently about the younger age group with whom I also work, with manic depression, and schizophrenia (Bruscia 1989) (Odell-Miller1995), I seemed more compelled to speak about these younger people. Why should this be, especially when many music therapists are providing services to older people, particularly with dementia, and music is often the only way in to helping them on a therapeutic level? The introduction to this paper concentrated on an examination of particularly psychoanalytic influences on music therapy in mental health. Here I want to suggest that the psychoanalytical concept of countertransference in particular has much to offer in understanding both the direct relationship between therapist and patient, but also the processes within staff members and staff teams as a response to the work. Perhaps the nature of the difficulties of such work was influencing my avoidance. i.e a prevalence of deaths, physical frailty ,and difficulty in engaging in the therapy.as shown in the examples of referral reasons and outcome of music therapy treatment.

So it is possible that my own resistance to focussing on the older population is part of my own countertransference to the work although consciously it is an area which has given me much job satisfaction.

Having pondered all these questions, I feel it is all the more important to stay with this theme of older people, for whom music is particularly significant. I want to think about issues such as why the work with older people is often seen as less glamorous or more draining by health care professionals.To do this we must see how analytical concepts such as transference and countertransference have an important role to pay in understanding the work. Another fundamental question is:

How can music therapists work within a multidisciplary team?
When clients are extremely dependent on many different agencies, including

family, carers, institutions and services, the multidisciplinary team becomes an essential component in the work, which at best provides excellent care, and at worst could inhibit the work of the music therapist. Music Therapists are dependant on the team for the patient to benefit from therapy both for practical things such as taking the patient to therapy and for supporting the idea that therapy will be useful for the patient . The following discussion tries to address these issues, looking first at residential settings, and later at work in the community. Within both settings, it is assumed that there is a clear referral procedure, and for this to be effective, literature needs to be provided for the multidisciplianry team.and an assessment procedure must be in operation .

Let us first consider a factor I have called the disturbance in the institution and the darker side. Working within the multidisciplinary team in a residential setting particularly is important,and much of the time this is a positive experience. However it is important to see what part the Music Therapist can play when things are not working so well.

During my 17 years experience as a Music Therapist in psychiatric residential settings, an overwhelming factor has often been the atmosphere of hopelessness and despair. As a result, it is not uncommon to find staff reacting defensively to this with hostile attitudes, conflict and forgetfulness; undermining their therapeutic endeavours. The conflict can be between those who believe in something hopeful for the patient (which is usually only possible after acknowledging their own negative feelings about caring for these people), and those who have lost all sense of hope for the people in their care. It is important for the Music Therapist to understand these phenomenon, in order to work in a multidisciplinary setting, and know that there may be unconscious feelings amongst staff arising from looking after confused people all day, which if not understood, could get in the way of the Music Therapy process. Regular liaison is essential for things to work for the benefit of the residents. It helps to understand that perhaps the reason why others forget to bring the patient to her Music Therapy sessions although she has been coming for 20 weeks at the same time on the same day each week, may be as a result of becoming unconsciously forgetful or confused like the residents.

Music Therapy for these residential groups of people is particularly important because the verbal elements usually found in ordinary fluent speech and language are often missing. Those with psychosis often express themselves in unconnected language, and have a deep disturbance not always accessible in ordinary ways of relating, and those who are confused or 'demented' often express themselves in unconnected regressed speech.

In the video you will see later the importance of instrumental improvisation, vocalising and the developing of an improvised way of relating which offers something the clients can relate to. The therapeutic environment and relationship are as important as the music in this work, and good liaison, support and supervision essential. The Music Therapist can take many approaches, and introduce a variety of types of alternatives from intensive individual Music Therapy, to Tea Dances, and more 'Open' sessions. Within all this, we have found that a psychodynamic and sometimes psychoanalytic approach to the work is useful. Even if the client has little insight him/herself, it can be important and helpful for the therapist to try to understand unconscious processes which may be happening, even if it is inappropriate to reflect these verbally to the client. This helps understand not only the client, but what I have called the disturbance in the institution..

Personally, I have found it most useful to constantly reflect upon and draw upon many different theoretical perspectives, and out of this to build theories of Music Therapy .

With the elderly, loss of memory and the onset of dementia may seem to make a psychoanalytic approach redundant. My experience is that this is not so. Working with very damaged people places enormous demands on the therapist such that she needs to understand unconscious processes which may be going on. This is in order to work with disturbed people in a long-term setting where change may be little and infrequent. Indeed there may be no motivation for change for continuing care residents, who may have resigned themselves to never being discharged to community life. Depression may be enormous, and this coupled with the confused or psychotic expression of some patients requires staying power by the therapist. .

Cohen (1952) when talking about long term psychoanalysis writes in a way which is relevant for the Music Therapist in a long term residential setting with clinically ill people.
" .... *it seems that the patient applies great pressure to the analyst in a variety of non-verbal ways to behave like the significant adults in the patient's earlier life. It is not merely a matter of the patients' seeing the analyst as like his father, but of actually manipulating the relationship in such a way as to elicit the same kind of behaviour from the analyst.*"

Let us turn now specifically to some music therapy examples in our service for the elderly.

I recall an example showing the clinical processes which can be intensely difficult, described by a colleague, Carol O'Connor. She is a Music Therapist working full-time with elderly confused people, and wrote the following in a case presentation. She was working with a lady who was very distressed; with a history of schizophrenia and possible frontal lobe dementia in addition:

"Dorothy arrived at the last assessment session smiling, touching my arm affectionately and saying, "Hello dear". She sat on the piano stool and pulled the metallophone near to her. She started to play it in the most extraordinary delicate manner with her nails, making it sound like a balalaika. She did this very gently and quite sensuously for some time, then she slowly

started to take the notes she had been playing apart and to dismantle the instrument very carefully. The playing had an unusually powerful effect on me, and I began to feel unaccountably nauseous". The patient later actually vomited during the session, and the therapist felt that the music had represented a dismantling of the mind also, which had to somehow be held by the therapist, hence the Music Therapist beginning to experience the nausea. This was a particularly intense experience in individual Music Therapy, but I mention it here as I think the pain and despair of some older people can be usefully acknowledged in therapy in order to enable patients to hear their suffering. This can be difficult and distressing for the therapist, and supervision with other like-minded people is essential. We encourage all therapists to have individual case-work supervision, and we also have a Jungian analyst supervising a group of Arts Therapists which is an excellent challenging educational supportive and enriching experience. As well as the individual therapist acting as a container for what is unbearable, the multi-disciplinary team can also serve this containing function.

The Tea Dance, for example, which we shall see later in a video excerpt, acts as a support for staff and clients alike. Art Therapists, Physiotherapists, Occupational Therapists and Music Therapists are all involved. It is a fortnightly event as much like normal life as possible, where there is entertainment, socialising, dancing and tea and people can participate as much or as little as they choose. It is not a formal therapy, and everyone understands this. As Music Therapists we see our role as completely different to that within a therapy session, but our skills and training are shared and we enjoy a change of environment as much as staff and clients enjoy coming. This event is important in helping the team deal with the darker side of the work, and indeed has improved relationships with nursing staff. Writing about the work has also kept motivation alive . Music therapy is practised and understood on many different levels, as we can see ranging from outcome based research projects (Hanser and Clair1995; Odell-Miller1995), to a psychoanalytically informed way of understanding the work. A constant feature within this, is the musical skill, and improvisational nature of the work, providing a special dimension often difficult to explain in words.However,it is important to provide summaries and data for colleagues most essentially to encourage clinical understanding of the therapy, and to ensure future funding, as the tables of referral and outcome show. Now, in order to gain a fuller understanding of what happens in a group, and individual sessions I will outline two cases.

Example of Group Work
Connie was an 88 year old lady with Alzheimer's disease in advanced stages. She had little recognisable speech, but her personality seemed to reveal itself through vocalisation and gesture on the ward. She lived on a continuing care

ward, and had no family or relatives close to her, having lost her husband ten years previously. During her earlier life she had been a teacher and raised three children. She wandered aimlessly around the ward when engaged in any specific activity, and was referred to music therapy by the consultant specifically to a group. Reasons given on the referral form were 'to provide a place for her to interact with others through a non-verbal medium, and to provide a place for her to express herself in a secure setting. She attended the weekly music therapy group for 4 years, during which time she deteriorated physically, but seemed to maintain a sense of self, and a will to socialise and interact. These phenomenon were particularly prevalent during music therapy sessions. On the ward she often shouted at others, seemingly in anger and frustration, and occasionally hit out at others. As the referral was to a group already in existence, and she had little ways of entering into discussion, or showing insight, assessment took place in the group over a period of four weeks. During the assessment time, Connie was able to make use of instruments, and vocalise in a way which led to her interacting with others, and wanting to communicate. She vocalised using "da da da, ma ma ma," and other sounds, often in the tonality of the group improvisation, and often beat the drum loudly exhibiting an excited chuckle, and wide eyed smile. In quieter moments, she settled and listened, sometimes with tears in her eyes when minor harmonies, or reflective songs were improvised. She occasionally wandered around, but often purposefully, as if towards me at the piano, or towards other group members, pointing and moving rhythmically with the musical pulse. As a result of these sessions, she continued in the group, and became an established member over the next four years.

Summary of the sessions (Details of this approach are in (Odell 1995 pp 99): Connie always seemed excited on arrival at the sessions, and recognised everyone as if saying hello, through her disjointed vocalising. Group sessions last for 45 minutes, and instruments used are tuned and untuned percussion, including Gongs, Drums, Tambours, Cymbal, Maracas, Metallophone, Kalimba, Bass Xylophone, Recorder, Guitar and voice.

During the first part of the session, I usually allow space for each person to acknowledge their presence. Connie used this space as a chance to express her individuality by using an instrument (usually Metallophone or Maracas - her choice) whilst vocalising. I would improvise with her, and gradually a rapport built up through this interaction. Connie developed a way of following me around the group, by gesturing or pointing rhythmically or even by walking around. She would often greet others, which was a major aim of the group overall - to enable contact between members to take place.

The middle part of the group was centred around building improvisations between the whole group or in threes or pairs, where interaction and expression seemed more intense and perhaps allowed more in-depth feelings to be shared verbally and musically. For example Connie would sometimes hum, or beat in a particular way and I would musically develop this. This could lead to others joining in, or remain as a dialogue between two members.

Over the years Connie developed a preference for the Bass Metallophone, and would share this with another member, Mary. They were increasingly interested in making music together, using the 'white note' scale, with a feeling of interaction and dialogue. I would support from the piano or with the recorder, if it seemed important to be close to them. I would describe this as the therapist taking a containing role, within which other members could join in. Sometimes I would play firm harmonic rhythmic chords in the bass whilst another member improvised in a free way, perhaps aggressively drumming at irregular intervals, to give another example.

I identified during Connie's therapy, that she needed to express herself loudly at times and that this would often be followed by a quieter period of reflection, when she would sometimes be tearful. This was seen as useful for her in that it seemed cathartic. I do not feel that catharsis itself is necessarily enough, but what I would try to do was show support and understanding by reflecting to her musically or verbally how she might be feeling. She, and others seemed to find this useful, after a group improvisation.

In the final part of the session it is important to enable things to close in a way which helps members sense an ending, to prepare them for going back out of the therapy session. Connie became more aware of the ending during her years in therapy, and would often settle and sit as if contemplating saying goodbye. Occasionally song material was improvised around a theme of ending and goodbye, perhaps putting Connie and others in touch with their own experiences of endings, grief, and death. However, with Connie it was not possible to be certain, only to sense that she often seemed to want to express profound emotion, developing into hugging, kissing and clinging onto Mary, her neighbour, or a helper in the group. She would then be able to settle again, and leave peacefully as if the group had 'contained' these feelings. I would be aware of a need to slow down, or speed up the musical and rhythmic pulse according to the mood of the group.

Connie, whilst physically deteriorating through the effects of Alzheimer's disease, was able to experience an emotionally expressive place within which her final years could be contained most importantly on a non-verbal level. She related with others both in an excited exuberant way, and seemed to value the consistent relationship with others provided by the group. I could understand perhaps something of what she was experiencing, and often felt she was 'clinging' to a familiar nurturing relationship reminiscent of other relationships she may have experienced. My countertransference response was to be a nurturing figure but Ineeded to allow her freedom to break away from a symbiotic relationship .The multidisciplinary team supported the therapy, but it was noticeble that they would often respond to her as a child,and I felt at times that in the music I may have been tempted to do this too.

She moved wards three times in four years, and as she had no family visiting her, she had generally a bereft, isolated existence. The group provided a stable space within which she could be herself, and deal with these last years of her life. She remained involved and engaged until shortly before her death, despite her physical frailty.

We have seen so far a variety of approaches taken with the older person, and will now look at an example of work in the community setting where the multidisciplinary team is functioning well, with a 60yr old man called *Martin* suffering from a form of presenile dementia. The work we shall look at is a specifically music therapy orientated approach, where the relationship, and building of this, has been intense. It has been very important to reflect upon the nature of it. Sometimes it has seemed that the client has been able to receive transference interpretations, such as "you seem to be relating to me as if I'm your pupil", but the work fits into a humanistic approach (informed by psychoanalytic thinking) particularly because in this instance the work takes place in the family home, and realistic day to day issues are of paramount importance e.g. how his wife is, and how she has made space for the sessions.Countertransference in this work is intensely significant as we shall see- the music is extremely rewarding, but.the relationship is often fraught, with Martin struggling to maintain his facultuies.

The function of the multidisciplinary team has been of primary importance for Martin, who is suffering from a particular form of dementia called Simultanagnosia. This is a disorder where there are problems in the functioning of the higher visual perceptions of the brain. Areas which integrate the visual field are failing, which means that Martin can see one thing, but not many things at once i.e. his field of vision is affected. He first presented with a right parietal syndrome meaning that his non-verbal memory was impaired i.e. the construction of his visual-spacial memory was affected, and he could not distinguish shapes, or remember other visual aspects, whilst his verbal language and cognitive functioning were in tact. His musical memory remained unimpaired, although he could no longer read music. His life and work had been in the musical field, and particularly in improvisation and composing. Thus his ability to improvise is still not very much impaired, and he is able to return to a musical phrase or section of music used at the beginning of a piece, at the end.

He was first referred by the psychiatrist, who had a clearly defined area of work of music therapy in mind," to help him work through some of the emotional implications of his diagnosis" . In later letters, once the therapy had been underway for several months, the psychiatrist wrote that he seemed often depressed, with almost "too much insight into his condition" - but also that - "Although he has considerable difficulty expressing himself he did explain to me that he found weekly music therapy visits very helpful, and his wife has commented that he seems brighter after these sessions". This is an ideal investment of music therapy, rather than one of sabotage mentioned earlier, when the ward team forgot to send the patient to therapy; as all those in the team including his wife believe in the importance of therapy. Two other key people are the Community Psychiatric Nurse, who visits weekly to help with practical coping strategies and to provide support to Martin and his wife, and the Psychologist, whose intervention has been aimed at "trying to help the couple understand his neuro-psychological strengths and weaknesses."

After nine months of music therapy, he is now quite cognitively impaired, and sometimes cannot identify his wife. He has a good relationship with her and is affectionate but recently occasionally aggressive as a result of frustration. In contrast, his recognition of me perhaps shows the power of the musical 'rapport' in maintaining some sense of orientation. Here the notion of countertransference is crucial in helping to understand his bewildering transference towards me. He treats me as if I am a partner, child, pupil, nurturer, and fellow musician..This is significant because he was a lecturer in music. Thus his capacity to remain orientated relies upon me finding another way of relating to him without taking these transference roles on. He is developing more of a rapport with me musically and often says - "I feel this is so good for me - its just there, music is here - you touch it and you get it." He also has recently began to improvise on his own between sessions, something which he had no inclination to do when we first met because he was afraid of the piano. " It comes up to hit me" . It seems that this fear has subsided, the more our work develops, and that through improvising, he has recognised a way of expressing himself, and also it is an area in which he feels expert and confident. The role of the other team members has freed him up to have music therapy for himself and his wife has always respected the privacy of this, enabling proper boundaries to exist although the work takes place in the home.

I feel the sessions are achieving what we set out to hope for, because of the involvement of the whole team.

To finish this presentation, we will hear some excerpts of sessions which his wife has given permission to be played in order to further understanding in this field.

In summary many music therapists are finding within a psychoanalytical approach, that music sometimes becomes less central, and words prevail. However, as these examples show, the music remains central, but psychoanalytic concepts are useful in helping the music therapist think, and understand more about the work and its team context. This enables music therapists to remain hopeful in a field where otherwise the overwhelming emotion could be one of despair.

References

Alvin, J   1991   *Music Therapy* Oxford University Press.

Bruscia, K   1987   *Improvisational Models of Music Therapy.* Springfield, Illinois Charles C Thomas.

Cohen, M.B.   1952   Countertransference and Anxiety. In. Psychiatry 10, 143.1. 1.

del Campo, P.   1993   Music Therapy in Spain. In. Maranto, C. : *MusicTherapy: International Perspectives* .Jeffrey Books U.S.A.

di Franco, G.   1992   A Methodological Approach in the Mental Health Field In: *Music Therapy in Health and Education* .Ed. Heal, M., Wigram, T. Jessic Kingsley Pub.

Hanser, S & Clair, A   1995   Retrieving the Losses of Alzheimer's Disease for Patients and Care-givers with the Aid of Music. In: *'The Art and Science of Music Therapy - A Handbook'* Ed. Wigram et al Harwood Academic Publishers, Switzerland

Heal, M   1989   In Tune with the Mind. In. D. Brandon (ed.), *Mutual Respect: therapeutic approaches toworking with people who have learning difficulties.* Surbiton : Good Impressions.

John, D   1992   Towards Music Psychotherapy.In Journal of British Mucic Therapy 6 (1) , 10-13 .

Kortegaard, H   1992   Music Therapy in the Psychodynamic Treatment of Schizophrenia In. *Music Therapy in Health and Education.* Ed.Heal, M., Wigram,T. Jessica Kingsley Pub.

Lecourt,E   1988   *La Musicotherapie.* Paris: PUF. (col.Nodules)

Maranto, C   1993   *Music Therapy: International Perspectives.* Jeffrey Books.

Nordoff, P and Robbins, C   1977   *Creative Music Therapy.* New York,: John Day

Odell-Miller, H   1995   Approaches to Music Therapy in Psychiatry with Specific Emphasis upon a Research Project with the Elderly Mentally Ill In. *'The Art and Science of Music Therapy - A Handbook'* Ed.Wigram et al Harwood Academic Publishers, Switzerland

Priestly, M   1975   *Music Therapy in Action.* London. Constable.

Priestley, M   1977   Music, Freud and Recidivism. British Journal of Music Therapy 8, (3), 10-14.

Priestley, M   1994   *Essays on Analytical Music Therapy* .Barcelona Pub. U.S.A.

Raijmaekers, J   1992   Music Therapy's Share in the Diagnosis of Psychogeriatric Patients in TheHague. Paper presented at the European Congress of Music Therapy , Cambridge.

Rogers, P   1992   Issues in Working with Sexually Abused Clients in MusicTherapy . In Journal of British Music Therapy. 6, (2), 15-16.

Streeter, E   1995   Talking and Playing : The DynamicRelationship within Music Therapy. In: Journal of the Institute of Psychotherapy and Counselling.Vol. 3 p.1- 11.

Towse, E   1991   Relationships in Music Therapy : do music therapy techniques discourage the emergence of transference? In British Journal of Psychotherapy, 7 (4): 323-330.

Towse, E   1995   Listening and Accepting. In *'The Art and Science of Music Therapy - A Handbook'* Ed. Wigram et al Harwood Academic Publishers, Switzerland

West, R Wigram, A Saperston, B   1994   *The Art and Science of Music Therapy. A Handbook.* Harwood Academic Pub. Switzerland

Woodcock,   1987   Towards Group Analytic Music Therapy. Journal of British Music Therapy.

The integration of Group-Music Therapy in Multi-Disciplinary Teams

Almut Pioch and Albert Berman (NL)

1. Introduction

The developments in the field of psychiatry are moving fast. Not so very long ago the main question was: what medicine does the patient need? After this there was a period in which people were fighting about the question: which psychotherapy is the best: client centered, behaviouristic or perhaps psychoanalytical treatment? Nowadays a psychiatrist or head of a clinic may ask himself too: *which nonverbal therapies are important* to offer to the patient? There are so many possibilities. Do I choose drama therapy, so that my patients can play after situations of their childhood to process them? Do I choose for instance art therapy to create meaningful pieces of expression? Should I take psycho-motoric therapy, to stimulate body functions? Or do I choose music therapy, and why would I? Is a combination of those therapies necessary, or is one enough? The psychiatrist would like to have a *therapy-offer* up to the measures of the capacities of the patients, goal orientated, not to much and if possible during a short period. The psychiatrist in the nineties will be aware of the limited financial means, so he will especcially think about *grouptherapy.* Beside to this he will ask himself: how do I organise this, in what way do I compile the groups? How will I get enough information about what's happening in those therapies? When he has made his choice, he will soon be surrounded by therapists of a divorce background; he has a multi-disciplinary team.

We are two of those therapists, who work in such a multidisciplinary team, in adultpsychiatry, within a clinic for supportive and reconstructive psychotherapy. This implicates that we are treating patients with severe personality disorders and neurotic problems. They stay for about one till two years in the clinic or in day treatment.

In our lecture we will try to make the choices easier for our hypothetical psychiatrist, by answering a couple of questions. That's the task we music therapists stand for these days. The questions are:

1) What does group-music therapy add to a multidisciplinary treatment?
2) In which organisational setting can group-music therapy develop an
   optimum function?

Question 1. can be looked at in many ways. We have choosen to mention some contributions group-music therapy adds to a multidisciplinary treatment, by looking at the way *how music works in a group*. Giving an answer to question 2. we compare two organisational models for group-music therapy. Of course there are more possibilities and mixtures of models thinkable. What we especcially want is to encourage *a discussion* about the place of music therapy within organisations. We hope that these situations are recognizable too for music therapists who don't work within the field of psychiatry.

2. What does group-music therapy add to a multidisciplinary treatment?

We want to start with the effect of making music in a group. Therefore we begin with a few short music-fragments from one long improvisation. The players in this improvisation departed from the themes "power" and "love". It took twenty minutes in total. The players knew each other for a while and listened to each other carefully. They tried to change along with the music.

What we heard is essential for musical communication, *the players relate to each other expressively and receptively at the same time.* In each moment everyone contributes to a common product and is influenced by the others. This simultaneity of sending and receiving makes that the players atune themselves to the others. The aspect that no explicit content is communicated makes that the emphasis is more on the *affective contact on the basis of empathy.* This is different in the verbal communicaton where just one after the other talks and where because of the explicit content tuning in stands less central. This emotional contact which each other leads to a strong group-cohesion and makes that patients experience it as a real "group"-therapy. The group-cohesion - or the feeling of belonging together as a group - is very important for an effective group-treatment because it forms the basis for therapeutic group-processes. In this way group-music-therapy offers a specific contribution, which affects also other situations when the group is meeting each other.

The *common musical product* to which everyone contributes can be experienced as esthetical. This gives satisfaction or even a "kick". But it doesn't come always to this feeling of mutual relatedness. The experience of "sitting on your own island" or obstuckting each other is no exception. *The problems in the functioning of the group become more obvious* in music-therapy than in other forms of therapy. That's because you can hear interactional problems so clearly when you make music together. When this happens the therapist kan influence the group-process by directives for the improvisation, by choosing instruments or by giving play-roles to individuals. Or she can let it go until the bombshell's is being dropped.

This leads us to the the second music example. A part of a punksong, which a group has made about their anger. The staf had let them down during their vacation. We can hear the ambivalence about the psychologist in the lyrics: *Anita in her private room takes you by the hand*, they sing. - We probably all share the experience that *music and feeling are closely related.*

The *symbolic and veiled manner of musical expression* is responsible that it is possible to adress different emotions. Group-music therapy delivers a contribution in activating and stimulating emotions. So it is in this punkversion, where the music provides a save frame for expression of the anger, which saves it from feelings of shame and guilt. *Aggression gets a function , so music provides containment.* Expression of this feelings without anxious or even with pleasure leads to integration of this feelings.

Another group of feelings that can be expressed especially in music is *warmth, intimacy and fusion with the whole.* This has to do with the before mentioned *simultaneity in musical communication.* The feeling of being part of a whole kan probably be experienced more strongly in music than in other forms of expression. An other example deals with this. - We listened to a young woman, who sat for years still, listening in the church, a very severe church were there was no place for expression of emotion. Here its the first time that she exposed herself. She uses the holding surrounding of the group, which she belongs to for several months. It was happening spontaneously and the group felt that they had to give her the space to come up to the fore in this way.

Patients with personality-disorders usualy have problems with relating to others. According to different theories these problems are caused by an incomplete seperation and individuation during childhood and by this a badly developed autonomy and identity. Therefore these patients experience contact as a threat of their weak autonomy. So they cut the contact as soon as it gets more close and intimate.

In the last example we heard pretty close intimate music. But it was not broken. Contact in musical improvisations is so safe because it *happens in the context of play* and it is limited in time to the play. It is possible to stop out of it at any time or to change it in a more seperated mannner of contact. In this way music can contribute to the *consolidation of autonomy.*

In addition the communicative character of music offers the possibility to *try different roles:* like taking the lead, follow others, rivalary, make contact or break it or place yourself in the spotlight. Group-music therapy offers possibilities to experiment and train these roles, but people don't perceive it as a trainings situation, because of the play situation of making music. By *developing an own style, preferences for certain roles or instruments* somebody can work on the development of the own identity. In group music therapy all this is being worked out in relation to others which leads to the experience of being an own person, different from the others.

Let us listen to the last music-example. A song about the water catastrophe in Holland. The group uses this theme for playing with humoristic and morbid fantasies. It has taken them 20 minutes to compose this song.

Sometimes a special life-event, phase or even a trauma can be linked to a certain piece of music. Because music can strongly be connected to feelings, this certain piece of music can trigger the feelings of this event. Sometimes patients communicate their feelings to the group by having them listen to the music and sharing the feelings about it. Especcially if emotions has been dissociated it can function as an important supplement to the work on a theme in verbal therapy and can lead to acceptation and integration.

There are probably more issues where music therapy can make valuable specific contributions. We now want to keep it on these four contributions to a multidisciplinary treatment:

1) Facilitation of group-cohesion and the influence on the group-process
2) Activating and expressing of emotions
3) Consolidation of individuation and autonomy
4) Sharing emotions of life-events

The psychiatrist who wants to create a therapy-program for his department, has now got a picture of the possible contribution of group music therapy. If he finds the former mentioned elements are interesting, he will perhaps decide to put group music therapy into the program. How can an *optimum use* of music therapy be reached? It will be a goal that patients within group-music therapy can work on their individual treatment and do experience the therapy as a meaningful part. The question is, how does a group have to be compiled? Which form of deliberation does the music therapist have to attend? In short we could say: a couple of choices have to be made. But upon what do these choices have to be based? We're reaching here the point of *treatment-philosophy*. We would like to make a distinction between *individual-orientated* and *group-orientated* treatment-philosophies. Of course more distinctions are thinkable, but we limit ourselves to this starting- point.

Within an individual treatment-philosophy group-music therapy will be put into service of the individual treatment, the music therapist is purely fixed on that focus. Within a group treatment-philosophy the groupdynamics will be an important factor and this needs a lot of attention and tuning in of the music therapist.

We first want to start with the most often occurring model: the individually oriented treatment-philosophy. Hereby we will discuss the composition of groups, the place of music therapy within the team, problems and disadvantages.

3. Indicated group-music therapy

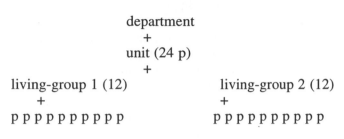

As we can see in this diagram the music therapist composes his music therapy group from different living groups. The psychiatrist or psychologist will have to decide *if* music therapy is the best treatment possible, in other words: is group music therapy *indicated* to this person? The music therapist can help him by letting the patient go through an *observation program.* Together they can draw up a clear individual treatmentgoal. At a treatment deliberation, in which the music therapist now and then participates when his patient is discussed, they can evaluate if the goal is reached. That's a very well-ordered way of working. We now want to look at question 2: can group-music therapy in this organisational setting develop an optimum function.

First, what are the consequences for the group?
The group is compiled from loose individuals of various living groups. A couple of patients will be glad to be released from their maybe suffocating group life on the ward. They can show a totally new behaviour in a totally new group. Others will have problems with the fact they don't know each other well. A strong side of group music therapy is, as we said the stimulation of group-cohesion. The music therapist can enlarge cohesion through musical interaction, but this cannot work on in other situations, because other therapies are also indicated for evryone individually. We think, group-therapeutic elements can not come to their full development as good as in groups who know each other well. The group has less *holding capacity.* An example: a patient going through a hard time, maybe having suicidal thoughts and who is very depressive, will not come to the music therapy session without the support of group members. In groups who follow a fixed program, groupmembers say: go with us, you're one of us, and maybe you will feel better after the session. It seems to be, that less holding of the group implicates a bigger chance of staying away or increasing resistance. In our

opinion the level of practising in a group will be difficult to exceed, we can't go very deep with this kind of group.

What are the consequences for the place of the music therapist in the team?

When only for a few patients in a department music therapy is indicated, the music therapist just has to be at deliberations when the patients are subject of a treatment deliberation. That's only now and then, so difficult to organise. Because music therapy groups are compiled of various living groups, is it impossible to attend all treatment deliberations, otherwise the therapist doesn't have time anymore for therapies. However, it will be important to keep tuning in about indication, goals, way of working and results. Otherwise the music therapist doesn't work multidisciplinarily, but *isolated.* When group music therapy doesn't get enough support of the teams, when the music therapist almost isn't seen on the unit, will that too have it's effect on the patients. The expectation and hope that music therapy has an important contribution to make to the treatment is an important non-specific factor and will not be propagated by the team when music therapy is isolated. The chance music therapy is indicated for patients may diminish, and that it doesn't meet with the demands of the unit. We know many examples of music therapy collegues who couldn't keep a good contact with the rest of their institution and even sometimes lost a part of the jobs. The departments couldn't see anymore what happened at music therapy. Working with indicated group music therapy therefore asks a permanent effort of the music therapist to keep the contact going on. And that isn't easy.

We conclude that indicated music therapy, from an individual treatment-philosophy, is an option to which we can make a few side remarks. The other option for the psychiatrist who wants to make place for group-music therapy in his therapy offer, is bringing it as a part of a group-orientated treatment-philosophy, we call it integrated into multi-disciplinary teams. First we would like to explain what this means.

4. Integrated group-music therapy

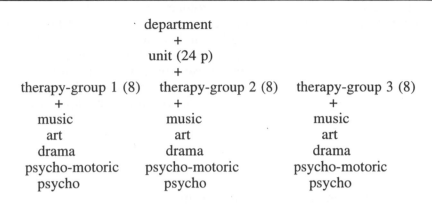

department
+
unit (24 p)
+

therapy-group 1 (8)	therapy-group 2 (8)	therapy-group 3 (8)
+	+	+
music	music	music
art	art	art
drama	drama	drama
psycho-motoric	psycho-motoric	psycho-motoric
psycho	psycho	psycho

Here we see how a group orientated treatment-philosophy can be worked out in a treatment program. Of course it's an example, in no way a definite choice. How we *should* make a choice for which therapy, we will discuss at the end of our lecture. There has to be chosen, otherwise the program will be to much filled up.

In this model a *therapy-group is indicated* for the patient, and in this way he has to go to a group of therapies. Patients are placed into one of the groups. This happens in cooperation with the therapists, after for instance a *period of introduction* and observation in one of the therapy-groups. To achieve this there is an aim at a *comparable level of functioning,* say no patients with a week ego-strengh are put together with patients who have much more ego-strengh. Because of this the group will get a *homogeneous character.* In this group it's important patients know about each others problematics and goals. We can reach this by working with *contracts or working-goals* who are shared in the group.

The whole week a therapy-group follows a *fixed, compulsory program,* like mentioned above, plus depending on the structure of the unit, sociotherapy, labour therapy etc. Next to this there can be the possibility to have *individually indicated therapies,* but very limited, for the therapy-group program fills the biggest part of the week. The therapy-groups have to differ in measure how deep they go. We will give an example, from therapy-groups with patients suffering of severe personality disorders.

One therapy-group could consist of patients with a dependent personality disorder, combined with maybe a depressive syndrom, after loss of important others. The emphasis within the therapies can lie on taking responsibilities, activation and sharing of emotions. Group-*music* therapy can contribute to this by evoking emotions, and stimulating experimentation with stronger roles within music playing.

Another therapy-group could be a group for patients with borderline personality disorder, who have great problems with intimacy, and are experiencing strong emotions all the time, with which they don't know what to do. They can stand more confrontation and want to know who they really are. Group therapies can be aimed at the strenghtening of autonomy and control over feelings. Group-*music* therapy can stimulate expression of feelings into music making, giving them a steady form, taking away the fear of losing control. Patients can develop their own style within music, experiencing their autonomy.

We now will have a look at our second question again: can group-music therapy develop an optimum function in this organisational setting?

First again: the consequenses for the group

Because patients very soon know each other thoroughly, they go through a lot together, we're experiencing group music therapy becomes a very intensive therapy. On the one hand a lot of conflicts can come up and people may have trouble carrying the tension. On the other hand very vulnerable themes can be touched in integrated group-music therapy, like intimacy, as we heard in one of our music examples. We percieve group-processes become more heated, every time a lot happens. Patients know from each other what they want to reach (because of contracts and working points) and address one another clearly about how motivated they are, when there's doubt about that. They know they need each other to learn and to grow. When *group-cohesion and holding* do increase, the group is able to guide patients with a lot of resistance through a difficult phase. Behind the resistance often is hidden a great fear of not being able to control emotions, like aggression. After a period of time the patient notices that his aggression is taken up by the group-music making. It gets a functional form and maybe even is fun. Beside to this we notice that a *bond between various therapies* can be developed. They can tune into each other. For instance we can take the case of a female patient who has a great fear of being rejected. In a session of group-music therapy she becomes aware that she's more able than before to be intimite with other patients during an improvisation. After that she attends *psycho-motoric therapy* and she feels she can come physically closer to the others, she can trust them more during confidence tasks. In *drama therapy* for the first time she dares to play a nasty role, and hears from her group-me mbers it was okay she did that. Maybe after that, the same week, the patient works on a piece of clay in *art therapy* together with someone she always avoided in the group. Verbally she can connect between these experiences and her past in *psychotherapy* and maybe she can conquer her fear of rejection.

Second point was: what are the consequences for the place of the music therapist in the team?

When music therapy is integrated part of a fixed program, the music therapist has to attend *all* treatment deliberations of a unit. The unit-timetabel takes this into account. Beside there must be a regular exchange about groupdyna-mics, for instance about problems in handling a group and in times when there are crises. As we can expect, this all costs a lot of time. Fortunately there too are positive effects to this. The possibility therapies are tuned in with each other will grow. Because of all these moments of contact at the unit the music therapist will get a permanent place in the multi-disciplinary team, what brings along the positive feeling *all stand together for one goal.* If the team is able to be open about what's happening within the therapies, the chance therapies are splitted, what means the therapists are playing off against each other will diminish. What's more, the music therapist who stands in the middle of a team can exert an influence on the policy of the unit, like in deciding on the level of confrontation of support which is desired in treating a certain problematic and target-group.

We feel some side remarks to integrated group-music therapy will be necessary. As positive as we scetch it, it may not always be in practice. The fact music therapy is a *compulsory part* of the group-program will have its consequenses. Sometimes the music therapist will have to work with patients or even a group with a lot of resistance against music therapy. The positive side to this we told before. But it can be *quite heavy,* certainly when one patient infects the whole group with the effect the whole group is not motivated. The music therapist has to stand very strongly in his shoes not to think it's terrible and wrong what he does, it will sooner or later pass by. Also than it's important to have the *full support* of the team, the knowledge about the level of confrontation these patients can stand and the fact that in some other therapies maybe the same problem is occurring with this group. Sometimes we see a patient is placed in the wrong group, the approach is too confrontating or too supportive. After placing him in another group, the therapies can have a more positive effect. In a small amount of cases group-mu sic therapy can *not contribute* much to the individual treatment, that's a part of the reality. In general people are *enthousiastic* about integrated group-treat ment and they can feel every therapy has to make its own specific contribution.

Another side remark can be made about the music therapist, who has to limit himself to be connected with *a few units* or departments, and can not work for all patient categories anymore. Otherwise it will be impossible to attend all necessary deliberations, and he will not be part of the team. Some music therapists will find this attractive, others don't. We feel it's gratifying to be able to specialise ourselves into the problematics of a few categories.

Through this we are better able to make a treatment offer that's up to the measures of the capacities of the patients.

5. Conclusion

To our way of thinking a *group-orientated treatment-philosophy,* in which a music therapist works *integrated within a multi-disciplinary team* is a fruitful model. Group music therapy can take a good shape and we feel it is certainly an alternative next to working with indicated therapy, the other model we discussed. Naturally other thoughts about models can be worked out, and maybe there's a synthesis possible of the mentioned opposites. It would be wonderful when more ideas about an optimum organisational model for group music therapy would be developed. A discussion is very urgent. Within music therapy there has been very little attention to this subject. Music therapy seemed to take place within a vacuum, or a laboratory, with no or little influence of other factors involved. The idea of isolation, what we seem to notice in quite a few places, has been too little productive. Policy-mak ers couldn't get enough information about the specific contribution of music therapy in a team with other therapies, it seemed to be music therapy was the solution for everything. We would like to leave that idea.

Finally we once again address ourselves to the imaginative psychiatrist, who wondered which nonverbal therapy he should put into a therapy offer for his patients who suffered from personality disorders. Of course we think music therapy is indispensable and we have made some remarks about it. Beside we want to plead for the other *creative arts therapies* as well: drama therapy, art therapy and also the nonverbal psycho-motoric therapy. Why are we doing this? We think personality disorders, early traumas and neurotic problematics come up and can be worked on in all ways a person can express himself: not only by talking, but in movement, visions, sounds, play, etcetera. All sensory perceptions, brain functions and body functions are involved. In that sense we could say the nonverbal and verbal therapies together *cover the psyche* of a patient. Each therapy has its own specific contribution to make and can not replace another. When a psychiatrist or policy maker of a clinic follows that idea with us, then there will be no concurrency and we can join in coopera- tion fruitfully. This way the optimum integration of group music therapy within a multidisciplinary team can become reality.

Music Therapy with High Functioning Autistic Clients: A Case Study

by Helle Nystrup Lund (DK)

Introduction

The material for this presentation has been gained from my first clinical experience with music therapy during my practicum period at the Psychiatric Hospital in Aalborg in the Fall of 1994, and from my final thesis, which I finished May 1995. The case material is from a therapy process with two highfunctioning autistic clients. I will focus on one client, Peter.

It must be taken into consideration that when speaking of autism, it is in the light of the experience with two high functioning young men with autism.

Method and preconceptions

In the therapeutic process with two high functioning autistic clients I have experienced that my role of initiating contact and change in the therapy has seemed to be more dominant than with other client groups. Since my influence on the therapy to an extent seemed to determine the process of events, it became important to reflect on "what made me do what I did".

In the situation in therapy it often seems that the approach or method is based on intuition. But when analyzing the therapy, preconceptions which have determined the way to approach the client may be revealed. If we as therapists become conscious of our preconceptions of the client and the therapy process, we will also know how these preconceptions influence and structure the way we look at the client and approach him in therapy. Paying conscious attention to our preconceptions about our clients can help us to realize if, or when, they hinder the best therapeutic treatment. Also, the conscious attention to preconceptions may help to change or expand an approach.

"Givens"

When paying attention to the factors determining or having influence on the approach, it becomes appropriate to introduce the term "given". Dr. Kenneth Bruscia uses the term *"musical given"* for the conscious or unconscious choices made by the therapist, which determine the frame of freedom and structure given to the client in the musical improvisation in therapy. An example of a musical given is the playrule. (a playrule can be; to only play on the black keys on the piano, or to express happiness). The formulation of the playrule makes a frame for the musical improvisation. The concept of givens may also be used in a broad sense, meaning all the factors determining the way the therapy is carried out, from metatheoretical considerations to specific psychological theories and the setting in clinical work. As the playrule focuses the improvisation, so does a philosophy of life focus the view on human beings.

Now, I will try to give an account of some of the givens that I have found important to be aware of when working with two high functioning autistic clients in therapy.

In the case with the clients Mike and Peter, two autistic clients who were in therapy for a period of 6 months, an important question that occured to me when evaluating the therapy, was - why did I carry out the therapy, when these two people seemed to wish to be left alone?

To answer this question I found I had to turn to basic humanistic beliefs that I recognize;

- *every human has a natural strive for personal growth*
- *every human wish to be seen and loved as he is*
- *every human has a wish to communicate, to enter a social context.*

These three points are my preconception of whoever I am meeting and working with in therapy. I believe those are human qualities fundamental to all human beings. I believe that these qualities may be distorted or hindered in their expression (f.ex. in handicaps), but they can not be eliminated. These basic philosophies that I believe in, make a foundation for my approach to other people and function as points of reference when meeting my autistic clients in therapy. So when I meet my autistic clients in therapy, I believe that they have a fundamental wish to communicate with me even if the situation seems to indicate the opposite.

Although the three basic beliefs are abstract and so independent of the individuals possibility to express these needs/wishes, I still include the potential for expression.

Besides these humanistic concepts, existentialistic thought has showed to be important for the way I approach my clients in therapy. I believe that a part of psychosis is a choice, although it is an unconscious choice. The individual choice, and specifically the conscious choice is a significant point in existentialism. I believe my autistic clients should be given the possibility of making a conscious choice of communication or withdrawal, since the choice of withdrawal from the world has seemed to be unconscious. Because I believe that sharing thoughts and feelings enrichens peoples lives (from my own experience), I take care to make the best conditions for making the choice of contact.

Generally speaking, philosophical standpoints have general influence on a therapeutic approach. Theoretical standpoints have more concrete influence on the therapeutic approach in therapy, and of the therapists understanding of the therapy process. The understanding of a clinical situation reflects theoretical and philosophical standpoints.

My theoretical orientation in the object relations theory and the early mother/child communication/relationship, makes a natural focus on the client therapist relationship in therapy, which is clearly reflected in my perception of a situation in therapy. My education as a music therapist gives me a natural focus on psychological issues in therapy.

Introduction to video example:
Now I will show an example of a musical improvisation from therapy and then discuss my theoretical understanding of the situation and how my philosophy of life is reflected in this example.

The example will show the first 3 minutes of a 20 minutes long musical improvisation from the tenth session with Peter. Peter is 28 years old, lives in a protected home, and comes to therapy with Mike (the other client in the group of two) once a week. Peter has almost no facial expression. Untill this point of time he has only smiled a few times very briefly and he has seemed to be overwhelmed and scared by it. He has some language but doesnt use it.

There are two musical layers - instrumental; we are both playing xylophone, and vocal; we are singing a song (in Danish). I am encouraging him in singing to relate to me - the song lyrics are "I would like to play with you, would you like to play with me? Yes, I would like to play with you". The lyrics change over the same melodic theme but "play with you" is replaced by "smile with you" and "look at you". Peter does not respond to my instrumental initiatives, but answers my questions, most of the time out of the musical context.

My understanding of the situation
Peter is exploring the smile. He is both exploring the physical sensation of a smile and the connection to the feeling of joy. When he has smiled for some time the feeling becomes overwhelming and he withdraws to seriousness or an emotionless expression. He is experiencing the switch between an outrovert and introvert attention/focus. Sometimes his smile is sincere and filled with joy and a few times his smile is just the physical manifestation without feelings connected to it. He is also shifting between smiling to me and smiling to himself. By returning his smile with a sincere and direct smile consisting of feelings of happiness, joy, recognition and appreciation, I am stimulating Peters awareness of feelings of joy and happiness in himself, as I am showing my recognition and appreciation of his expression. At the same time I am/my smile is containing Peters projected unbearable feelings. The music is functioning as the intermediate space whereinto the unbearable feelings are projected out to be taken in by me. The music makes a containing frame for the emotional expression.

I am filled with joy and laughter; a combination of my own joy and the received projection of an unbearable strong feeling of happiness and joy, that I try to contain and control. I am so overwhelmed with joy that I have difficulty controlling it, but at this moment I find it important to contain and not express these feelings, since Peter is not ready to contain them himself, and a strong or uncontrolled emotional expression will scare him.

Matching Peters mood changes from a smile filled with emotion to an emotionless expression, is quite difficult. I am forcing unnatural fast shifts between very different psychological and emotional attitudes. On one psychological level I am matching Peters rapid mood changes, on another psychological level I am stable and calm as a safe base in contrast to the confused emotions. This is seen in my steady playing and singing and my physical calmness.

In the music the development of contact is also taking place in the verbal dialogue/vocal duet. The verbal communication in the music is conscious and structured. It is a communication to which Peter can relate in a conscious and concrete way.

How does the understanding of the situation show a significant theoretical standpoint?

In this session I believe Peter is experiencing an emerging awareness of the connection between the feeling of joy and the physical sensation/manifestation of a smile. He is also experiencing interpersonal communication in the exchange of a smile and in the vocal dialogue. Peters lack of or confusion of emotional expression is not believed to be suppressed by defense mechanisms. Defense mechanisms are not believed to be the primary reason for lack of or confusion of emotional expression.

My perception of the situation can be considered in relation to the theory of autism seeing autism as a reaction to neurological defiencies. But if a neurological deficiency is causing the "missing link" between physical and emotional expression, the possibility of learning or achieving awareness of the connection between physical and emotional expression, should be excluded or limited. In my perception Peter is actually going through a process of learning how to recognize own and others' feelings and to gain understanding of the communication of feelings. In this learning process the therapy functions as a practise place.

This leads to the conclusion that it is possible through practise to counteract a neurological weakness to a certain extent. For Peter, a high-functioning person with autism, the neurological weakness is believed to be mild, which leaves better possibilities for learning. Even though Peter have learning disabilities, he still has potential to learn, even if it is only possible under special circumstances, like music therapy. - The analysis of this situation shows that although my general focus has been psychological considering the client therapist relation in the context of the object relations theory, I also consider neurological aspects. I have found that it is possible and helpful to approach what seems also to be a neurological problem psychologically.

How does the philosophy of life influence my
intervention method and understanding of the situation?

Previously when speaking of existentialism I have stated how an approach should be encouraging the client to make the positive and conscious choice of contact. I believe this is reflected in the direct way of approaching Peter. In the example Peter is confronted with my wish to play with him and smile to him, he is encouraged to make the choice of contact in words and music. There is coherence between intervention method and philosophy of life.

I have stated that I believe Peter is actually learning the meaning of emotions and learning how to communicate emotions. A definition of "learning" is necessary to find coherence or contradiction to the philosophy of life. There are two possibilities; a) I am teaching Peter to connect emotion to physical expression by demonstrating how it is done. I am showing him the meaning of communication. Metaphorically speaking I am planting a seed. Peter is taking in something new from me, something that wasn't there before. OR b) Peter is discovering the connection between emotion and physical expression and the meaning of communication within himself *as if* it wasn't there before. In this case my role is to stimulate an awareness of latent qualities already existing within himself. Metaphorically speaking I am watering a seed, so it can grow.

Returning to the fundamental beliefs of humanism, the statement that every human has a wish to communicate shows my position in this matter. According to my philosophy of life, I believe Peter has the potential, or the seed within himself. My role is then to stimulate and encourage a development of latent potential. Now, turning to my philosophy of life I do get the "right" answer. But I am not perfectly convinced that my philosophy of life has explained the reality in the situation.

My conviction in my philosophy of life is not so strong that it overrules my doubt of what actually happens in the concrete situation.

Since the interpretation of the situation is ambiguous, my philosophy of life is the only point of reference. Still, the possibility of questioning it should be present. This is an example of a situation where philosophy of life has crucial influence on the understanding of the situation.

For me it has been important to realize how my philosophical and theoretical standpoints has influence on the way I see the client, and the risk that my philosophy of life and theoretical orientation can prevent me from seeing important aspects of a concrete situation in therapy. When I am unsure of how to interpret a situation, and I have a need for an explanation, my philosophy of life may determine how I choose to interpret the situation, rather than the situation itself.

This has also made me realize how it sometimes is better not to try to explain or understand a situation fully. Being open to more possibilities, leaves space for the client to reveal what is the reality.

When dealing with situations like this, I find it important at the same time to hold on to convincement and curiosity. Curiosity gives possibility and motivation for new thinking, and convincement a starting point.

Women Patients in Forensic Psychiatry - The Forgotten Ones?

Katie Santos (GB)

Introduction

This paper seeks to clarify some of the myths and perceptions that people have of female mentally disordered offenders; their problems and difficulties, and the therapeutic approach that I have been using in music therapy with some of these women.

The title of this paper suggests that women are forgotten. On reflection I realised that most people are unaware that I work with women, therefore how can they be forgotten? This made me look closely at attitudes and perceptions, would we prefer to conveniently forget female offenders? If so, why? Is the truth too difficult to bear?

The system of placing mentally disordered offenders in Special Hospitals, or Secure Units, is complex and vast, and as such needs a document on its own. Because of this I am not going to describe the system in yhis context.

As I stated previously, one of the reasons for writing this paper came about from the reaction I get when I mentioned that I work with women. For some reason people perceive 'offenders' as men, and find it hard to acknowledge that women can commit equally horrific crimes. Interestingly enough a higher percentage of women (33%) than men (23%) are admitted to a special hospital with the diagnosis of psychopathic disorder (Poitier 1992); and although a lower percentage of women (45%) than men (74%) are on restriction orders, women are less likely to be discharged (Stevenson 1989).

Attitudes to women who commit offences are often a mixture of confusion, fear, and horror. As Dr. Gillian Mezey, a senior registrar at Broadmoor Hospital in 1990 states, "If a woman commits an offence which is regarded as incompatible with her female status she has committed a double transgression. She has transgressed against the code of what it is to be feminine - docile, passive, and gentle - and she has transgressed against the criminal law."

She may either be regarded as doubly bad, doubly evil, and put into prison for a long time, or, if she is not bad, therefore she must be very, very mad, and in need of psychiatric treatment in high security."

Hilary Allen in her book 'Justice Unbalanced' (Allen 1988) shows that the majority of men diagnosed as psychopaths are sent to prison; whilst the women are dealt with psychiatrically. From this it is easy to deduce that women are treated differently from their male counterparts, and that different attitudes and values are used when sentencing women.

What is considered acceptable or understandable behaviour in men, is not acceptable in women. Drinking, fighting, unstable relationships, drug taking - all these things are unacceptable to society, because they are not the way women are meant to behave. All these factors may support a diagnosis of mental disorder, and may mean that a woman ends up in a maximum security hospital, often with an indeterminate sentence.

Whilst researching for this paper I became aware of the many difficulties that women have within the forensic setting, some of which I have already mentioned. However, one of the central issues that has been brought to the fore is that of mixed wards.

At present I am working in two forensic units, the first being Broadmoor Hospital, which is a high security facility for mentally disordered offenders; the second being a regional secure unit, which is a medium security facility. There are huge differences between these two settings with regards to the environment for women. In the large hospital women are on separate wards. This means that the only contact they have with men is at work and social functions, or with male nurses and other professionals on the ward. In the secure unit there is a great difference; the wards are mixed, and, depending on admissions, there can be either one woman to sixteen men, or, more usual, three or four women in a group of fourteen men. Obviously a lot of women find this very difficult. Often they have come from a female prison, and are used to an all female environment. A lot of the women have been subjected to abuse, physical and mental, from men, or have had very destructive relationships with men. Being thrust into this mixed environment, from their 'safe' environment in prison, causes an immense amount of anxiety. Another issue that is raised is the fact that bedroom doors are unlocked, and, although the patients have their own keys, they still feel very uncontained and unsafe.

It is this problem of creating a safe environment for these uncontained, unsafe women that I would like to focus on. To illustrate this I would like to share some work that I have been doing at the secure unit. Nine months ago myself and the principal psychologist felt that ther was a need for a group, soley for women, which would enable them to deal with problems particular to women, and provide them with support for each other. As I have explained the wards are mixed, and consequently so are most of the groups that take place. The aims of the group are as follows:

- To enable the women to express themselves throught the medium of music therapy.
- To provide an opportunity for exploration and expression of feelings and emotions.

- To encourage the women to look at, and explore relationships between themselves and others.
- To provide an opportunity to discuss underlying conflicts within a safe setting, with the support of other female patients.

The sessions are once a week for an hour, and are open to any women who are staying in the unit. Consequently the group does change fairly regularly due to people leaving the unit. For the purposes of this paper I will focus on two patients, one of whom has attended the group since the onset, and the other who joined in session five.

SHARON

Sharon is 31 years old, and is diagnosed as suffering from mental illness. She is one of three children. Sharon's behavioural problems began at the age of 13, she would regularly truant from school, and was caught stealing; at the age of 15 she began setting fires. At 16 years old Sharon gave birth to her first child, and subsequently had two more children by different men. These two children were formally adopted. Sharonthen had a fourth child by the eldest childs father. In 1989 the social services became concerned about the children's welfare, and 1991 her eldest daughter was put into care. By 1992 Sharon's mental state had deteriorated significantly, and she was convinced that the Mafia were going to kill her and her youngest daughter. In 1993 Sharon had become markedly more paranoid, was having aural hallucinations, and due to these killed her daughter and then set fire to the flat.

Sharon was admitted to the unit shortly after her offence, and presented as someone who was fragile and uncommunicative. There was little or no eye contact, and she would answer quetions monosyllabically. Since her admission there has been one incident of fire setting, and no incidents of physical or verbal aggression. However, she has been seen to be sexually inappropriate with male patients, and this continues to be a problem.

When Sharon first attended music therapy she was withdrawn, quiet, making no eye contact, and her verbal interaction was very limited. She would often choose to play the metallaphone, looking down constantly, and rarely contributing to any discussion that followed the music. Musically she was inhibited, staying with the one instrument, unwilling to try any different sounds. Her playing was fairly repetitive and monotonous, often playing scales up and down the metallaphone. The mood of the others in the group appeared not to affect her, although occasionally she would laugh inappropriately. However, she was always keen to attend, and would often ask whether the session was happening that week.

Session 5 was, what I consider to be, a very important sessions for Sharon. At the beginning of the session all the women were very tense, as one of the group announced she was leaving the unit. This brought about a lot of conflicting feelings within the group, and particularly for the patient concerned. The group decided to play music for this patient which was very evocative and emotionally intense. Whilst playing this piece Sharon still appeared very withdrawn and unresponsive. After playing everyone was sitting quietly when a spider crawled across the floor. The group became concerned over the fate of this spider, wanting to put it somewhere safe. At this point Sharon stood up, walked over and stamped on the spider. After she had done this she smiled at everyone then sat down. The effect of this on the group was dramatic, people sat in stunned silence for a few minutes, then I suggested we played some music, and asked if anyone wanted to think of a title for a piece (expecting something connected death or killing). The title suggested was ' The quiet one', followed by the comment "it's the quiet ones you have to watch".

During this piece Sharon played the metallaphone with much more vigour and enthusiasm than usual, although she still remained with her head and gaze down. Towards the end of the music Sharon began systematically 'destroying' the metallaphone by knocking the bars off one by one. At the end of the piece the group was silent for several minutes, Sharon remained still and quiet. It was suggested to her that maybe the music was about her, she looked up and nodded.

Gradually, in subsequent sessions, Sharon has begun to change. She has begun to experiment on new instruments, almost playfully, in a very childlike manner, trying to shock us by playing the cymbal suddenly, moving rapidly between the instruments. As her confidence grows musically, she is becoming more open in other ways. She has begun to talk about numerous topics, including pregnancy, childbirth, and firesetting. One of her more interesting comments was made only recently, and is of particular significance to the difficulties women have in the secure unit. It had been noted that Sharon was becoming very flirtatious with the male patients on the ward, again in quite a childlike way. During a music therapy session we were exploring the issue of suicide (which a lot of our women attempt). Sharon became very animated, and disclosed that she had attempted suicide before, but "hadn't done it right", with pills and alcohol. She then explained that she didn't think she would be able to do it another way, but was sleeping with as many men in the unit as possible in the hope that she would contract A.I.D.S. Obviuosly within the unit there is the rule that sexual relatrionships are not to take place, but it is inevitable that people will find a way to break the rules. This potentially dangerous situation, for Sharon, is only possible due to the fact that she is on a mixed ward. As a result of this disclosure it has been possible for us to begin to explore issues around her index offence and low self esteem. Sharon has begun to trust the women's group, and is beginning to allow us to help her with her difficulties.

ELSA
Elsa is a 21 year old woman, she is diagnosed as having a borderline

personality disorder. Elsa is the eldest of four children, and has an extremely difficult family background. Elsa was regularly sexually and physically abused from the age of six. At the age of eight Elsa began cutting herself, and at nine she began to set fires. She was placed into care from the age of thirteen antil she was sixteen., due to her 'uncontrollable behaviour'. Elsa worked sporadically for two years, but then began committing a variety of crimes including theft, burglary, and arson.

Elsa's psychosexual history is shaped by her abusive childhood. She had one heterosexual relationship when 14 years old, but her subsequent relationships have been with women. These relationships tended to be fairly sadomasochistic; Elsa has found that cutting holds little pleasure sexually for her, but does derive pleasure from cutting her sexual partner.

Elsa was admitted from prison, having committed arson. Whilst in prison Elsa had become suicidal, and also admitted to auditory hallucinations urging her to harm herself, and set fires.

On first meeting Elsa she presented as an amenable, friendly woman, although there was an underlying hostility evident. She joined the music therapy group in her first week, and was willing to participate, displaying musical understanding and sensitivity. She then revealed that the only lesson she had enjoyed at school was music, and that she was quite a proficient flautist. From the first I felt that there was an immediate bond between us, Elsa's musicality provided a link, and as I began to know and understand her more, I realised that she presented a huge challenge to me.

Within the group Elsa began to dominate the sessions. She would introduce subjects quite freely, as long as they were not too personal, and create music and themes for others in the group. However, if topics that she found too challenging were introduced, she found it hard to stay with them, and would literally walk out of the room. Often she would make surreptitious threats about breaking windows or 'kicking off' as she called it. On the ward Elsa's behaviour deteriorated; she smashed windows and would use the glass to cut herself, and would keep the cigarette lighter, if it was given to her. Often these acts would result in her having to be restrained, which then would reinforce her own belief that she was 'bad and not worh anything'.

It became clear that although Elsa was beginning to form important relationships, i.e. myself, the psychologist, and her primary nurse; she was finding it extremely threatening and difficult to cope with. Within music therapy this was manifesting itself in an almost playful way, for example., Elsa would put her hand to my throat threatening to strangle me, or talk about wishing to kill me; all this was said whilst smiling and laughing.

One of the major issues for Elsa was her history of abuse. She was, and still is, reluctant to talk about it, but being in a mixed ward was causing her considerable anxiety.Due to her inability to discuss these matters her behaviour became very destructive, and she felt unwilling to trust anyone. In the music therapy group Elsa began testing to see if I could contain her anger and negativity. She regularly refused to attend sessions if I asked her to come, but would 'change her mind' if the psychologist asked. She would then wait to see if I would react to this rejection in any way. This finally reached the point where Elsa refused to speak or look at me. I felt that she needed reassurance that however 'bad' she was I would still keep coming back. For two weeks she refused to acknowledge my presence, until she finally agreed to attend the group.

On entering the music therapy room Elsa began by saying she wanted to kill me, I suggested we played some music. Elsa refused, but said she would listen. The other patient in the group played briefly, then asked to go to the toilet, the psychologist went with her. Elsa immediately suggested we played, and proceeded to try and 'kill' me with her music.

Elsa chose to play the drums and cymbal, I was playing the piano, but could not be heard. I then moved onto the drums as well. The music was incredibly violent and uncontrolled, I attempted to contain these feelings that Elsa was displaying. Half way through this the others returned and joined in, by the end of the piece we were all exhausted. Elsa was shocked, she had clearly not expected me to be able to control and contain her music and feelings. She began to talk rapidly about how difficult it was being close to people and trusting them, and how she would always try and get rid of them by being as 'bad' as possible.

After this session Elsa's attitude towards me changed, and she obviously felt safe enough to disclose snippets of information. Only recently she has admitted that she was very concerned about a male patient who was, and had been for some time, sexually harassing her. This had reached a point where she wasn't sleeping at night in case he came into her room. Obviously this unwanted attention was evoking strong memories of her childhood, and she was becoming convinced that there would be a repitition of the abuse. We are at present working with Elsa to encourage her to assert herself in more positive ways, and to help her feel more in control of her life.

Conclusion

Women are in the minority in the forensic system; they encounter prejudice both from inside and outside the system. These women, as I have stated, are usually vulnerable, uncomtained, and unsafe. I feel that more provision needs to made for the specific problems that women encounter.

In setting up the music therapy group I feel that I have provided a small respite for these women once a week. The group never ceases to amaze me in the amount of support and feeling that these women have for each other. I hope that the future will bring more understanding about this group of patients, and the realisation that although integration is good, sometimes segregation can be equally beneficial.

The forgotten ones need to be remembered, the unnoticed need to be heard.

NOTE : The views presented in this paper are those of the author and do no necessarily reflect those of the S.H.S.A.

Reference:

Allen, H. (1988) *Justice Unbalanced*, Open University Press. London

Music and Art in Cancer Care - a Group Therapy Approach

Anne Olofsson (S)

Introduction

Main focus of this presentation will be on clinical work, describing group therapy experiences and sharing reflections on this work. But first I will give a brief introduction to the Psychosocial Unit and a short background to the therapeutic needs confronting the music therapist.

The Psychosocial Unit

Radiumhemmet is the oncology department of Karolinska Sjukhuset, a university hospital in Stockholm, treating adult cancer patients, for short or long periods of time, both in-patients and out-patients.

In the early 70´s, a Psychosocial Unit was created, to study and handle psychological and social problems caused by cancer, not only to patients but also to relatives and staff. Services include education and training programmes, developmental work and research, information about psychosocial work to other oncology units in the region and international cooperation. Clinical patient work includes individual support and councelling as well as rehabilitation group programmes.

The unit is staffed by a multi-disciplinary team of about 10 pers. (Psychiatrist, psychologists, nurses and administrative staff). I was appointed to the unit in 1988. Two years later, I was joined by a nurse, training in expressive arts therapy. We now work as a team, supporting each other in representing artistic and non-verbal therapies - unfamiliar in the strict medical world.
Exploring the worlds of music therapy and expressive arts therapy, we work across boundaries, highly appreciating the possibilities to integrate different modalities, which, we feel, affects the therapeutic work in a broadening and deepening way.

Encountering Cancer

Some of you have faced cancer, personally or in your close environment, and are thus familiar with the fact that encountering a life threatening disease evokes existential questions as well as psychological and emotional reactions. It touches deep into the personality and previous traumatic experiences may reappear.

More than 50% of today´s patients are cured, and modern cancer treatment offers many patients several years of living with cronic illness and a sense of well-being, despite the fact that the illness cannot be cured.

However, life may be marked by side effects of treatment, by general weekness and symptoms caused by the illness or by psychological reactions, as anxiety or depression. Often these reactions are temporary, but they may be permanent or even increase.

Progression of the disease despite treatment, implies confrontation with difficult and unwanted symptoms, but most of all with a tangible life threat. Most cancer patients have to face a series of losses and have to accept increasing dependency and live in constant uncertainty.

Dealing with all this takes time. It is a process towards healing and personal growth, but which, particularely in an initial state, may be very hard to accept and to express.

It is a general assumption that interventions which adress the healthy parts and powers of a person (as interventions supporting an understanding of the situation), may help increase patients´ quality of life.

Sometimes problems motivate individual therapeutic support, but we know that to patients with moderate problems, participation in group activities can be very beneficial - improving psychosocial adjustment and psychological adaptation. To patients in advanced stages of the illness, participation in support groups have indicated improved quality of life and of survival.

Creative therapy group

The creative therapy group takes 6-8 patients and meets 6 times on a weekly basis for 2 hrs sessions. Groups vary concerning diagnosis, phase of illness, age and gender but what they all have in common, is that they have chosen themselves to be a member of this group. The music therapist and expressive arts therapist are group leaders.

A main objective of this activity is getting closer to life issues and to promote coping, creating a neutral, safe and holding space for the individual to work on her situation and issues, to promote self-understanding and encourage a feeling of wholeness. Many group members are experienced cancer patients, well-informed and familiar with existential questions. Still, the group is vulnerable and under constant stress. To create a safe and holding space, a clear structure, intuition, trust and courage are nescessary ingredients.

The short time span does not allow much in-depth work, but still holds important processes. I picture the six weeks as a crescendo - diminuendo: broadening - widening - deepening - narrowing - surfacing - tying ends together. Every session has it´s theme and a rough plan, but is only created in the moment.

I will describe the group more closely through the process of a patient.

Case study

Esther, a 49 yrs old woman, a non-academic with administrative work. She is positive, cheerful, talkative and very social. She has plain looks, is ambitious about her physichal condition and very much an out-door person. She is married

130

and mother of a 20 yrs old daughter. Esther was treated for a breast cancer about 5 yrs ago. After mastectomy and post-treatment, she could return to normal life.

3 1/2 yrs later, she developed lung and later bone metastases, underwent chemotherapy but with limited success. At the time she starts our group, further progress of the illness is discovered and she is again undergoing chemotherapy. Esther has longed to join the group, consisting of 6 women and two therapists.

#1 In her opening statement, "why I am here", Esther talks about her own illness with little emotion but is moved by listening to the others. She has a playful attitude and jokes about her unability to paint, but is very eager to try.

Esther´s motif is a *ship,* sailing on the blue see. The ship is a universal and archetypical symbol, often representing the journey through life or the transition from life to death.

Closing the first session, participants are asked to reflect on today´s experience and note the first word that comes to them. Each person says her word, at the same time accompaning it with body movement. The group, standing in circle, reflects back by doing the same. Esther expresses *"emptiness",* her body slack, drooping shoulders and head.

#2 Esther describes a busy last week. Despite working almost full time <u>and</u> doing the housework, she denies any sense of fatigue. She talks a lot, interrupts and prefers general subjects, avoiding any emotional material.

Benjamin Brittens´ "Simple Symphony/Saraband" accompanies a guided imagery excercise, leading past the meadow, path, house and going back. Using oil pastels, Esther paints *"Spring Promenade".* In a corner is placed a house, only half of it is in the picture, half of a door and of a window. The house is surrounded by a flowry garden. Vivid, powerful lines and dazzling colours. A path leads through the painting, water in the distance.

The picture mirrors Esther - a social and colourful person who really shows very little of herself.

#3 One of the group members complaints about life´s unjustice. Immediately Esther expresses indignation and insists that her illness has enriched her life.
Today´s main task is clay-work. Whilst Daniel Kobialka´s version of the Pachelbel Canon fills the room, busy hands softens the clay, which is slowly given the shape of an animal. Each animal is given a name and is then presented to the group.

Esther has made two animals. One is *"Sleepy",* her old dog, placed in a resting position. He´s a sporting dog, very active, runs fast and far every day, but afterwards he is exhausted and needs a good rest. He keeps a strict feeding schedule and prefers meat only. He is a persistent, stubborn character and has a favourite corner in every room.

The other animal is *"Hans",* an alligator, who lies waiting in the swamp. Esther says:

You can hold a baby one if you tie it´s jaws, but I suppose only the "indians" can hold the big ones. It´s eyes are placed low, on the sides of it´s head and it has breathing holes on it´s head. You cannot protect yourself against it, really.

Esther starts telling her story with a giggle, but suddenly a blazing blush colours her skin. She speaks more slowly and seems to hear what she is actually saying and connecting on an emotional level. The group is very moved by the whole situation, knowing that Esther has given a very clear portrait of herself as well as of her disease.

#4Esther briskly talks about physical excercise and outdoor life during the past week-end, hours of biking and long walks. Describes how she matches her present chemotherapy with full-time work and domestic responsabilities. When another group member airs concern about her present weekness, Esther comments:

Oh, I´m sure it´s just the weather!

Discussion continues, uncovering joint difficulties and mutual fears as well as secret hopes and dreams. Slowly Esther expresses feebleness, admitting she was completely exhausted after the long biking tour, but still had to cook for the family and, by the way, her husband expects her to do a lot in the house. She likes to feel competent and hates falling asleep in front of the TV.

Blushing, her lips trembling and with tears in the eyes, she says she cannot cry. Esther then tells the group about the trauma when her baby daughter fell seriously ill and how Esther somehow convinced herself that this was life´s big struggle, that nothing worse would ever happen. *And then I got this...*, she says.

The sound of ocean waves accompanies a guided relaxation. Afterwords, group members are asked to say a few words about their present feeling or thought. Esther says *community/togetherness*.

#5The group explores a collection of musical instruments and engages in creative music making. Esther tries the xylophone, but prefers a set of bongos. Her index fingers firmly bouncing the rhythm of a childrens' rigmarole ooooO - ooooO - ooooO - o o o O. According to the traditional words, she is counting herself out : *"then you shall die"*.

Coda

Esther continued to approach death through symbolic language, using varying modalities. She said she was puzzled by a sense of deepened self-understanding, that she could feel but was unable to verbalize.

After completion of the therapy group, Esther phoned us a couple of times *"just to say hello"*. The chemotherapy worked well for a period and Esther enjoyed a couple of good months, but late summer she had another relapse. Mid August she died in the ambulance on her way to hospital

Conclusion

We have experienced how patients, on a deep, symbolic level have been able to approach issues of vital importance. Issues that were too frightening to bring up in a family conversation. The symbolic shape - clay figure, poem, picture, melody... offers possibilities to approach difficult material and gradually come to understanding and insight.

Referring to empiric data, based on subjective observations and individual patient´s comments about their experience, we find some quality-of-life factors that seem to be of special importance to the group members, and I will give you *Esther´s comments* on

- social factors   *"togetherness, identification, support, sharing, friendships "*
- physical experience   *"learning that the body still can enjoy pleasures of movement or relaxation"*
- emotional experience *"excitement of experiencing new and creative ways of expression"*

It is very positive to meet others in a similar life situation,
to know there are others fighting low odds
I liked being part of a group, I felt support and encouragement.
It has provided new ideas and inspiration.
And made me realize that I can allow myself to feel tired and down.

And about

- music   *"relieving, relaxing, strengthening"*
- painting and clay-work   *"Felt good to be creative, I need more time for that"*
- body movement   *"Wonderful to move, it helps my brain rest"*
- writing   *"Surprising! I had no idea that I had so much knowledge, opinions,*
                                                      so much to express!"

- group discussion, sharing   *"I never thought I would get so much out of that! "*
- guided imagery   *"I would have loved to do more, I discovered a new land*
                                                      where one can go at any time"

Frank - "The Wounded Angel" - A Case Study

Kimmo Lehtonen (SF)

Introduction

Frank came to individual music therapy, because as a musician he thought that it was expressive music therapy that would suit him. He could thus in therapy do the kind of things that were best suited for him.

Music therapy developed both with the help of common playing sessions as well as the conversation and listening of records connected with them. Frank had come to therapy after having noticed that his own "zest for life" had dried up. In the case of Frank this was to bc seen for instance in the fact that when acting as a gig musician he had according to his own words drifted into a "considerable amount of messing about", which manifested itself as a heavy consumption of alcohol. A couple of times Frank had also taken narcotic trips, which he said he wasn't yet especially fond of. A couple of times Frank had been involved in the cases in connection of which he had fallen into most various situations under the influence of the forgetful state of intoxication. He had awoken in the strange lady's bed, in his neighbour's car etc. This kind of uncontrollable and chaotic situations and the simultaneously increasing depression had awakened Frank to realize that something should be done to his several problems, which he according to his own words had for long been able to handle and control by making music.

A very essential reason for Frank's "awakening" was also the fact that he had a five-year-old son, whom he according to his own words wished "a little better fate than he had had himself".

The Process

The music therapy process started in very positive signs. The therapist's and Frank's worlds were very much "alike" and at the beginning the topics of the conversation were for instance different guitar models, amplifiers etc. Frank seemed to be willing to stay on the superficial level. In the common playing moments there prevailed a more brotherly than competitive atmosphere. In the playing moments we were learning common pieces and "changing riffies", as Frank expressed the matter using musician slang. The action continued this way in the therapy moments taking place once a week for nearly two months, till Frank got a surprising fit of rage starting to hit strongly the amplifier with his guitar.

The situation was followed by the following conversation heated in tone:

135

The therapist:
> "Holy hell, don't you dare to break that amplifier"!

Frank:
> "Holy fucking God damned Devil. Satan it doesn't give the right
> sounds...(continues after a while)...I`ve had enough of working with
> these fucking things. Whether you're at work or having leisure or if
> you go to therapy, it's always the same damned scraping facing you
> there. To hell with my life..."

The therapist: (takes the bass off)
> "Do you mean to say that this music business is not the right way to
> make therapy? Would you like to talk and explain some of the problems
> you mentioned"?

Frank:(very silently and submissively)
> "I don't know, it always happens to me this way. Whenever I would like
> to talk and explain my affairs it goes the same way. I am such plastic
> finger,who only keeps on playing and playing..."

The therapist:
> "Yap, this is a strange point. You know well that you got angry with
> that amplifier when it didn't give you the kind of sounds that would
> please you. One could naturally think that you are so much inside this
> music that it is like your voice. You kind of speak and address with
> your playing. Could that be the case"?

Frank:
> "Well, I guess so. When still a small kid I was thinking that music is the
> best thing that I know and what I can do. At the same time it was like a
> ticket of admission out of all the dullness of everyday life. I said to
> myself: boy you should strive to be another Clap (Eric Clapton) and
> then at latest it will relieve mybeing (laughing sadly and bitterly). Fuck
> my emanations are well all over. I didn't become a Clap, but I became
> a rock gelding of thousand gigs. Well, damn it, I can't say it any better.
> It is always the same thing also in this therapy, the musician's best
> friend is another musician and what do they talk about: music".

After the episode there started out of common agreement a verbal stage in
therapy, in connection of which was played Frank's favourite music, mainly
rock-, jazz- and blues music. The matters had got a verbal form, which Frank
associated strongly with music. The images aroused by music and the dreams
coming up through the influence of music started to govern the process. It
belonged to Frank's habits to wander around in his past with the help of

associative memories aroused by music while the present-day events stayed at the background.

In the connection of music Frank's enormous richness in imagination started to come out, through which musical forms got the form of different images and simultaneous emotional experiences connected with them. The difficult problematic situation of Frank's early childhood started quickly to become activated. Under the influence of the temporary regression aroused by music the questions of the early childhood got new dimensions. The matters started to take shape often through certain kind of dreams, whose thematic material Frank was handling like musical material.

Frank:

"Yesterday I was listening to Peter Gabriel's music somewhere on the borderline between sleeping and waking and I thus saw a very real-like dream. In our dark kitchen there appeared an old man dressed in black mantle just like in "The Seven Seals" (a film of Ingmar Bergman, which was very close to Frank). The man gave me a small picture, in which there was...(starts crying and can't talk anything for a little while)...the painting of Hugo Simberg "Wounded Angel". Somehow I then outlined that I am just that angel, who has been in some way seriously hurt".

The therapist:

"That must have some important meaning; how does Hugo Simberg have anything to do with your background? Do you like especially Simberg's paintings"?

Frank :

"I remember how we always went with grandma to the old church in Tampere where there were those stunning frescos of Simberg. I could have been sitting there any length of time possible. On one hand they fascinated me somuch that I was itching and on the other hand they somehow frightened me deeply. I was looking at the "Garden of Death" in the dim church while the organs were roaring in the loft. I still remember even that smell when I was squeezing collection money in my sweaty palm. (starts crying again).

In her excellent book "Hugo Simberg - the Painter of Dreams" Riikka Stewen (1989) describes the frescos in St. John's church in Tampere. According to her Simberg wrote to his brother from Ruovesi that he wanted to paint everything that makes man cry in his inner self. Maybe the church of St. John became the place where his wish was secretly realized. (Picture: p. 146).

Stewen (1989) continues dealing especially with the mystery of "wounded angel" saying among other things the following: The most enigmatic of the shapes, angel, also arouses images, where lightness and heaviness are joined together. The wings have an innate ability to lift what is heavy where the family of gods lives, said Socrates to Faidros when describing with the help of myth the essence of soul. The drama of the wounded angel could be linked with the destinies of soul. It doesn't reveal what has happened, in the picture one can only see the deadened echoes of tragedy, light reflections of a heavy incident. The mystery of the wounded angel is after all an oblivion; lightness and heaviness, remembrance and oblivion, beauty and getting wounded. In the symbolism of the "Wounded Angel" many people would like to see reflections of Simberg's long period of illness from the autumn of 1902 to the spring of the following year. But isn't the illness oblivion of one's own self, loss of identity - nobody's land of transitional rites and symbolic death like puberty. (Stewen 1989, 123-125-126).

Frank's dream brought in a lightning-like way forth the traumatic life of Frank's childhood brought up by grandma and grandpa, his father's tragic early death and the mother, who wanted to live a life of her own remembering her son only through hasty visits, which involved a tremendous amount of doughnuts, sweets and lemonade. Deeply moved Frank tells that he still in adulthood soothes himself by eating and drinking huge amounts of food and beer. The matter came out again through the association aroused by music. One of Frank's favourite pieces, the record of Allman Brothers Band, "Eat the Peach", aroused associations on one hand through the dead members of the band and on the other through the name of the record:

Frank:

"Well, Eat the Peach...I didn't eat peaches,but doughnuts when mother came visiting me.Once my mother had on her coming bought doughnuts from the market hall. As usual there were an awful lot of them. Mother was always holding me for a while in her arms and stroking my hair. I remember that mother always smelt good...It was that 4711. Once I asked her what that smell really was...I was always thinking that I truly have a pretty and fine mother. I was such an overweight cat- faced poor thing myself. When mother brought those doughnuts, I started to devour them furiously. Mother was talking with grandma while I was eating all the time pushing the doughnut into my mouth with both hands now and then sipping red lemonade out of the patentcork bottle...

Then mother went away again. I remember that crystal bright blue feeling (Frank often described his emotional feelings by using analogies to colours and materials),*but somehow an outside feeling. When the nightcame I vomitted every single crumb of doughnut and drop of lemonade into grandma's bed...I still remember how the grandma kept on saying, oh you poor little boy, oh you poor little boy..."*(starts crying again).

The emotional states tuned by music changed easily into narrative associations, through which the earlier cathartic emotional states experienced through music started to articulate themselves and to get a concrete and narrative form. The members of the Allman Brothers Band, who had died accidentally, also aroused strong emotions and personal experiences of identification:

Frank:

> *"I don't know what was those guys' distress.* (Duane Allman and Barry Oakley who both died with one year's interval in motorbike accidents nearly on the same spot). (Frank considered the cases were caused by the self-destructive drive). *When still a small kid I was thinking a lot of death. I was imagining how I am lying in the coffin and the people beside it are crying. I was thinking that this is the way I'm going to revenge people and show them how wrong they have treated me...Earlier also when I was playing on stage I tried to look sad and absent-minded so that some woman would have noticed it... It can be that my wife noticed it somehow, she came up to me and started to make a fuss taking care of me. You could say that at the beginning she was like a mother to me, who was looking after my things...put on something warm Frank, don't drink or eat too much, stop that smoking...Okay, I have sometimes said that I got at the same time a wife and a life-insurance combined".*

Frank states that he has never been able to talk about his affairs, but music has for him always been the expression channel of difficult emotions, in the connection of which he has never had to explain anything, only to express and experience:

Frank:

> *"Well, my trademark is formed into a more and more cuttingly sharp, in a certain way crunching guitar sound and a long sustaining sound. Somebody has sometimes asked me how I can be so relaxed although my guitar is howling like in death pain...I have answered this by saying that maybe I'm howling from inside...I must admit that in some successful jam sessions I get the kind of feeling that there is a cold wind blowing inside me. This is connected with a certain kind of outside feeling from which I have always suffered.*
>
> *The world and the people are in a kind of closed acquarium, which I'm trying to pierce with this cutting voice of mine. I'm trying to shout but yet nobody seems to listen...*
>
> *Now I remember that Federico Garcia Lorca's poem "The guitar", which greatly influenced me. My guitar is yelling and howling such*

childhood crying, which can no longer be understood in adulthood...The
crying of a lonely and rejected child...(can no longer continue talking...)

(...After a while in a changed voice,) *fuck this self-pity, I am really like*
a blind orphan boy tumbled over a circular saw".

In the case of Frank the meaning of music as a transitional object was especially emphasized. Music was for him the world, into which even when small he had moved his difficult emotions and which also before the starting of therapy was for him nearly the only symbolic channel of request for help.

The cutting "guitar sounds" told about strong psychic distress. However, they were not interpreted this way, on the contrary they were considered an indication of great artistic talent and playing skill. The signs, which Frank was sending unconsciously and partly consciously, could however not be interpreted in the right way. It was only through the verbal treatment having become activated in music therapy that the non-verbal meanings bound to music could be dissolved through a confidential discussion.

The central "healing" element in the therapy process was formed the "healing grief" linked with music and the "sad" events brought out , which were not lived through and which had essentially shaded Frank's life. Frank, who had grown up in the care of his grandma, had even as a small kid adopted the role of a "good-natured child without any problems". At the same time he had been fairly far forced to withdraw from normal intercourse with the chaps of his age:

Frank:
"Our granny always said that our Frank would never do such or such a
thing. Our Frank doesn't go playing out in the yard, because there is
always only teasing and mischief. Our Frank won't become a vagabond
like his father, who left his family and died of booze. Our Frank will
become something great. Our Frank will be a real master in that
factory...(in a bitterly sad voice):*I was living quite a lot of time all by*
myself in the grandma's and grandpa's stove room. At that time I had
two hobbies: all day long I was playing the old harmonium and on the
other hand I was reading an awful lot of books, which I was allowed to
borrow from the library. I was the old people's fat boy, who was
dressed in an old-fashioned way...At that time I always tried to be
well-behaved and obedient, on the other hand I also detested myself,
because in that period of jeans the fellows at school made fun of my
club coat and my terylene trousers, which were so worn out that you
could see your own picture at the back of them..."

The development of latency age in the granny's tender but strongly restrictive education aroused strong hidden aggressions. That period also involved strong distress and helplessness in respect of the future. The decisive change took place in Frank's school party, where his best friend managed to persuade him to come quite reluctantly:

Frank:
"It was there that I really heard rock music for the first time in my life. At home there was that old harmonium and the piperadio, in which however you always had to listen to the national programme, because the granny always got nervous of light music and especially of rock music. She kept on saying that she has got such an old head that she can't listen to any light music".

The therapist: (doubtful)
"Can that be true? You heard rock music for the first time at that age. Well,what was it like and how did it influence you"?

Frank:
"They were playing Rolling Stones, Mountain, Cream and Hendrix. Afterwards I have got the feeling that I fell into a kind of trance there. In that music all my emotions were sounding completely genuine and authentic. I got a damned good feeling.

After this I started immediately to put aside some of my weekly money and ordered a record-player from "Hobby Hall". Granny was first against it, but when grandpa said that let the boy have his interests, I was allowed to have it. I remember when I went to a record store for the first time that I got the same kind of feeling as I had had with granny in the church. I even remember the scent of the vinyl. At the beginning I bought a couple of old jazz records,which were the only sufficiently cheap ones that I could afford. I was then revolving them happily through the old radio. In that stage national programmes vanished well somewhere very far...

A little later grandpa brought me his workmate's old Czechoslovakian guitar, for which I even spared such holemike of "Ideal"make. There was nothing more left to do than to fix wires and then we let it swing at full speed through the old radio..."

Frank's puberty was difficult. His good-natured and adaptable child habitus changed strongly into its opposite. The shy and well-behaved "granny's own darling", who was dressed in the club jacket and terylene trousers, changed quickly into a long-haired hippie, who was wearing round colourful sunglasses. Frank's attitude towards external institutions changed; the earlier markedly good-natured and retiring school kid became an apparently

141

indifferent and critical school kid. Frank drifted in a quick tempo further and further off from his granny's sphere of influence starting to "hang around" in the gang formed by the school kids having an interest in rock music and whose central place was the orchestra's practicing cave, a "bunkhouse", in the basement of one apartment building:

Frank:

"That was the crazy period at the end of the1960's, when the swingers and the rockers were using a lot of stuff. I remember thoseTimothy Learys and Allen Ginsbergs, Jim Morrisons and all the others. Our gang drank mostly medium strength beer.Then the hash and Valium pills along with the beer came into picture. I was hanging around in those gangs, but I never really got involved with that kind of stuff. Somehow I still had left that old phrase "not granny's Frank" - mentality.

On the other hand my certain outsider's tendency and diversity I was well aware of influenced the fact that I didn't want to go into those pictures, where, to tell the truth, many people burnt their fingers".

Frank solved the problem by withdrawing further off from the gang and by starting the studies of classical guitar and musical theory, which continued actively for several years. According to Frank's description the "classical music studies" were in a notable way forming "a grip of something meaningful" at the moment when the external reality and the fellow gang were in a certain kind of chaos. Abundant daily practice lasting several hours formed in the case of Frank an important bursting channel of energy and emotions. At the same time systematic studying and musical activity gave him strong experiences of success. Simultaneously also other artistic activities were activated. Frank started writing poems and composing:

Frank:

"The time in conservatory was a pretty hard experience. It felt good to me to be bustling among all those brats, who came mostly from so-called better families. Well, there were girls and boys, who were wearing fashionable clothes and whose father or mother was driving them to their music lessons. I was sitting there with too short velvet trousers on wearing purple-coloured sunglasses with my tangled hair stretching to the shoulders covering my eyes. Yet I managed all right with them and I always got into public demonstrations.

When we are talking about that period of time I can only state that it was the most alienating time in my life. I was a tourist in the world where I didn't belong at all. I guess it was a some sort of "Sunshine and Earth Sprite"-story. On the other hand I'm still grateful to my guitar teacher, who probably besides the granny was the first person who ever understood me. A granny can't really be a model for the boy. But my guitar teacher was well one. Damn it, he knew how to encourage in the right way and be critical. We also became good buddies. He was like a big brother or father to me, who always managed to stimulate and motivate me.It was through this way that I finally got rid of those gangs using pills. I realized that there are surely some other things in this world than deceiving one's own self with some crazy fools.

What was essential to Frank's development was the use of "identification relationships borrowed from elsewhere". The first male identification objects were rock- and pop idols, whom Frank's gang admired collectively. In the case of Frank the "borrowed identification objects" were shown in an interesting way. When he was telling about his early identication objects, the first thing that came to his mind was the big, overweight and bearded guitarist, Leslie West, "from the band Mountain", to whose sounds Frank told he had taken a fancy when still a teenager. When examining Frank's outer appearance one could easily notice a clear external correspondence.

Frank was also big and rather fat, he had a thick full beard and he loved to dress himself in tent-like clothes, which rather emphasized his large size. Frank's main instrument was also a similar small light-coloured "Gibson Les Paul TV-guitar", which against Frank's massive being looked like a some kind of too small a toy.

In the case of Frank music came out very strongly especially in the foams of puberty, where it as a transitional object formed a significant outer "Screen", with the use of which Frank could handle his difficult emotions in the safe non-verbal form. On the other hand the meaning of music as the continuation of ego was emphasized in its meaning. In very difficult and distressing situations Frank used to withdraw to practice very intensively. According to what Frank told he was literally speaking playing till his fingers were bleeding.

Frank:

"When now afterwards I'm thinking about that case, I guess it was the question about the fact that I was doing that music business in a kind of distressed state. It was the way with which you could invest all your energy into a certain meaningful direction. When I was practicing that way, it kind of cleaned my brains from depression and distress.When I finished that kind of extremely crisis-like playing period, some kind of relaxation took place. I got a good and satisfied feeling when I also fell easily asleep. I kind of felt that I was playing myself integrated".

In the case of Frank music had got nearly a magic meaning as he sadly stated himself: "Music is my father and playing my mother". Frank had managed fairly far by handling the different contradictions in his life with the help of music. His abundant collection of records, which contained several thousand records, had also been in the key position. According to Frank's own words it was soothing to know that for each and every emotional state you could at home find some records, by the listening of which you could approach difficult emotions. On the other hand the excessive use of music had started to disturb Frank. He had started to feel that even if music for him represented the safe and distress- free channel to difficult emotional states, he on the other hand experienced it as a some kind of non-verbal fortress, to whose prisoner he was about to remain. Musical communication no longer functioned in his important human relationships. Frank's wife experienced the blues records connected with Frank's depression as strongly disturbing, when they also caused discordance and difficulties at home. Frank described his relation to music as a some kind of "private world", where it was difficult to find place for the others:

Frank:

> *"Earlier I somehow experienced the guys of our band as another family of mine. Nowadays I rather feel disgusted with the thought. We are similar vagabonds without any home or land. It is a mere illusion to think that way and at the same time gulp down beer to distress. In fact I have never had a home. All my life I have been like a leaf in the wind* (also Frank's sparklingly sad instrumental composition), *whom the wind of life has been blowing here and there. There are no roots anywhere. Actually I am a real "selfmade man", I have been my father and my mother myself. I have made myself into what I am right now".*

In this stage of therapy Frank started to be afflicted by the nightmare, where a big black dog repeatedly appears to him. According to Frank's nearly magic idea the appearance of the dog in his dream "knew evil". For him it represented the continuous and disturbing presence of death in his experience world. In the handling process of dreams it became clear in an interesting way that Frank was working up his speech and dreams in the same way "thematically" as music. Frank joins his separate dreams to chains, which in a certain way illuminate some common theme at the same time bringing new dimensions into it or increasing the tension of the theme.

Frank:

> *"At night I once again saw a very real-like dream, where that dog came quite close to me with its head turned down. It kind of asked me to follow it. I was frightened but I started to follow it. All of a sudden we were on the back yard of my childhood, where the granny, who had died some time ago, was sitting old and pale, looking the same as when I saw her in that coffin. She said to me, Frank I have been waiting for*

you to get here. I realized in the dream that granny had been waiting for my death so that I would come back to her again. I woke up into my own shouting" (starts crying)

The mythic "black dog" acted as a kind of messenger, through which different contents inside psyche unite into new entireties. Frank's dream, where the black dog led him to his granny, gave him at the same time the opportunity to see his own destructivity in new light. After the conversation Frank cryingly confessed that the idea of dying and committing suicide had repeatedly come to his mind. His contact to life was however constructed very strongly through his family; the relationship to his son and wife seemed to be the decisive factor "for Eros, in other words in behalf of life", which had to fight continuously against "Thanatos" representing psychic pain and distress as well as against final peacefulness representing death.

The terror of the mythic "black dog" was clearly linked with a certain kind of frightening and integrated "truthfulness" represented by it. The appearance of the dog into Frank's "internal world" expressly in dreams, represented a certain kind of integration opportunity. The dog came from the area, which in Fran's psychic "topography" represented unexplored and unconscious content, into which was also very clearly anchored the wordless and targetless distress often afflicting Frank. He himself started to describe the black dog using as a comparison point Boris and Argadi Strugatski's book "Stalker", which he strongly experienced as an attempt to conquer hidden (subconscious) psychic meaningful contents:

Frank:
"Last night again I saw that dog. It came again towards me from the dark. It seemed somehow different and it came directly towards me. Even though I was afraid of it, I pushed my hand toward it. Guess what? It started to lick my hands. At the same time I noticed that it was a big grey wolf. Okay, it was a steppenwolf. I remember how in the puberty I was devouring Hesse's "Steppenwolf" and at the same time listening to the band "Steppenwolf". Good Lord I have been that kind of wolf myself, which has been creeping in the dark aside from all the "mainstreams". On the other hand that dog lives in the area, where I have all my difficult images. Now I am pretty sure. On that white point in the map there are my father and mother, whom I have been trying not to think about ever since I was a small child".

From this stage onwards we started an intensive stage of therapy, where there began to appear strong unconscious and extremely traumatic experiences with great intensity. The action was often connected with associations to art and music. Frank was an interesting case in the very sense that he had constructed a very real and vital world out of music and art, with the help of which he had

145

quite far managed to replace and correct the defects and distortions in his own social istory. This was to be seen for instance in the fact that whatever we were talking about, he always had associations, which connected the matter with music, composers, books, films or other works of art. Art and the fiction represented by it had given Frank a comforting transitional refuge in his difficulties of childhood and youth.

Simultaneously when his problems started to discharge themselves, also some other changes took place in his life. He gave up the consuming life of a gig musician starting to teach music (an identification to his own guitar teacher). At the same time the life at home, which was in quite a bad crisis, started to have new dimensions and meaningfulness.

Frank's relationship to his wife became gradually better. Along with music therapy Frank started to shape more and more clearly his willingness of starting his own psychoanalysis, to which he moved after about a year. In the case of Frank "the healing grief" contained and mobilized by music had been the keyword in his getting through many growth difficulties and distressing life situations. Frank's personal way of handling his own emotions was fictive in a similar way resembling art. He handled his different emotions as different colours and symbolic human figures (the black dog, the wounded angel) forming out of them kind of illustrated imaginary texture.

Reference:

Stewen, R.(1989) *Hugo Simberg - Unien maalari.* Helsinki: Otava.

Hugo Simberg *"The Wounded Angel"*

Music as a Means of Contact and Communication with the Physically and Mentally Handicapped

- an attempt to describe the different levels of contact achieved when working with people with severe communication disabilities.

Anne Steen Møller (DK)

Introduction

I have been employed at a residential home, Sølund, in Skanderborg since 1987. Sølund has 220 residents - children, young people and adults, all with severe mental, and often also physical disabilities. I am employed full time, which is 37 hours a week, but I use half of my time working with children from 0-7 years old who live at home. These children have varying degrees of physical and mental disabilities.

The types of people I work with vary. As well as the differences involved in working with adults or children, and with people living in a residential home or at home, there are also great discrepancies with regard to their development and diagnoses.

There are for example diagnoses such as DAMP, Down's syndrome, Autism, Cerebral Palsy, people who are both blind and deaf, and many others.

In some cases there is the added difficulty of violent and/or self-abusive reactions, massive stereotype movements and sounds, sucking of fingers, or anything else for that matter. - These are all individual expressions, expressions which we must act on and perhaps work specifically with in order to get closer to the person concerned.

Moreover, epilepsy and psychiatric disorders mean that many patients are given medicine which can cause side effects.

Considerations concerning the use of music therapy with the physically and mentally handicapped

What the people I work with have in common are perception difficulties owing to developmental disorders - proven or unproven, - that is to say problems concerned with sensory integration in the central nervous system. This inhibits their ability to express themselves and thus their contact to other people.

There are two aspects of the disabled person's problem to consider:
their limited ability to understand and interpret experiences and impressions, and their limited ability to express themselves and communicate with the world around them. And this is where I find music extremely relevant,

because to a high degree music gives them the opportunity to work impressively and expressively.

Over the years in the area of music therapy I have seen much evidence that music and sound create spontaneous, meaningful experience, even for the severely mentally handicapped. And I have often found that the motivation to create sound is very strong, in spite of the great amount of effort required to use the voice, beat a drum or produce sound in one way or another.

I can conclude from this that:

"Sound in itself has meaning", both for the listener and the creator.

To *"listen to"* and to *"create"* sound, - are part of communication.

And communication is a basic concept in music therapy, also when working with the most severely handicapped. Working with this marginal group is exciting. Discovering what experiences music can give these people, and not least finding out how I can use music to build up contact and communication with them. For this reason I have called my paper:

MUSIC AS A MEANS OF CONTACT AND COMMUNICATION WITH THE PHYSICALLY AND MENTALLY HANDICAPPED

Presentation of my subject

Treatment using music therapy naturally varies from case to case. In this paper I have chosen to concentrate on the group which can broadly be described as "poor communicators". And I have chosen to concentrate on the area of therapy specifically concerned with contact and communication. - For this I use what I call *contact music.*

(Another area of therapy which I will not go into in detail here involves *music for experience,* where the focus is primarily to give the participants many varied experiences through themedium of music.)

In my work with music therapy it was quite clear from the very beginning that it was necessary to use a wide variety of musical approaches in order to gain contact to this group of poor communicators.

My experiences have by degrees formed a pattern, and I now use 5 levels of contact in music therapy, 4 of which are relevant to this group. The division into these levels has emerged from the response I get when I contact each individual through the medium of music.

THE 5 LEVELS OF CONTACT

1. I feel contact between us.

2. I see/hear the contact.

3. You control the contact.

4. Our contact takes the form of dialogue.

(5. We contact each other through free, improvised music.)

(I have put brackets round number 5, partly because I seldom experience interaction with a client in this way, partly because it is debateable whether this level of contact is attainable for the group of "poor communicators").

LEVEL OF CONTACT 1 - *"I feel contact between us".*

At this level there is a very low level of contact, barely noticeable or audible between myself and the client.
I can *feel* the connection, and describe the contact at this level as follows:
"When I feel that you can sense me, I assume you also feel that I can sense you".
At this level of contact wherever possible I use the client's own way of expression - when there is one - in my music.These can be sounds, movements or breathing, which I put into a musical framework and return to her.- I use my own voice for this, and often a pentatonic harp.

The aim of the music therapy at this level is partly to communicate myself to the client. In addition, I must give her the possibility of wanting and daring to direct her attention outwardly, so that we can meet on common ground.
The prerequisite for this is that the client feels secure, that she feels my acceptance of her, and senses that I am not making any kind of demand or expectation in our interaction.

Observations:
I sense the person I am working with both physically and mentally. Does she feel comfortable? Is she relaxed or tense? Do I feel that her attention is introspective or extroverted? And myself? Have I got the necessary calm to earn her acceptance, and give her assurance and tenderness.Am I receptive to any signals, or outward-going awareness on her part? Are there any reactions to my music? - For example, are there changes in her sounds, movements or breathing? Is she more relaxed? Is there a change in her level of attention?

149

I experience the role of the music at this level as a symbiotic form of contact. It is the client's form of expression - sounds, movements, possibly also rate of breathing, which I glide into and which creates an area of "affinity".

And I have to be physically close to the client for my sounds to reach her. Her attention span is very short and sporadic.

My experience is that our mode of expression must be familiar and shared by both of us in order to create the platform of acceptance and reassurance - and perhaps even curiosity - for the client, which is necessary if she is to direct her attention towards the outside world. And this is where we can meet.

I feel that music used in this way is "enveloping". It surrounds us and it is our interaction and it *creates a frame* for our interaction.

It can be difficult to discern whether or not there is any development in the contact at this level.

The reactions are very slight and often sporadic. The effort required to turn her attention outwards can swing from time to time, from minute to minute.

It is important to recognize the value of the "here-and-now experience".

LEVEL OF CONTACT 2 - *"I hear and see the contact"*.

At this level there are obvious reactions to my approach in sound and music. It can be a body movement. Or a turning of the head towards the sound, following the instrument with the eyes. It can be a vocal sound, facial expression, smiles and laughter. And sometimes tears. - Here it is the case of the beginning of a self-awareness - and perhaps, in particular, an awareness of the outside world.

The reactions are often expressed in the pauses I make in the music.

In this interaction I am consciously aware of a rule where I ascribe an intention to the client's reaction, for example: "I will play when you look at me", or "I will play when you make a movement, sound etc."

The aim of using the music in this way is to make the client conscious of her *own* expressions by hearing my musical reactions. I also work on extending the client's *attention span* in my use of music,

Observations:
Reactions to my music vary from person to person.

It is important to imitate vocal sounds, and movements - also stereotypes - must be supported and possibly extended, for instance, by placing instruments so that she can produce sounds on them. There may be a beat in her mode of expression which I stress musically. I note whether the client seems to be able to differentiate between the various sounds. For example, whether there are different reactions to different instruments. And whether, in the course of the music therapy there is any sign of recognition at all, (my voice when I come in and say hello, the guitar, any other instrument sounds etc.).

The role of the music
Here I use the music as a direct approach. In this way I am able to create the beginnings of communicative interplay. The source of the sound is usually simple and easy to perceive.The drum and the calimba have very strong vibrations and I use them to work with "in-depth sensing " which intensifies the level of attention.

A **development** can often be observed in the following 3 areas:

Time: reactions are faster, and pauses become shorter.
Quality: more marked - though not necessarily new, - reactions, greater attention.
Recognition: showing that the client remembers and learns from experience.

LEVEL OF CONTACT 3 - *"You now control the contact"*

Here the client is aware of herself through her ability to make sounds - either vocally or by clapping, stamping etc. This is a personal expression (as averse to a stereotype) which she uses partly to make contact and partly as a reaction to her surroundings.

The contact music now becomes my response to the client's expressions. She is now aware that by making sounds she can provoke a reaction from me. But she is still unaware of the basic rule of communication, "your turn, my turn". That is to say, she does not understand that I expect her to return my expression again when I have "answered" her sound. My experience is that the client's attention is focused on me and on provoking my reaction.

The rules of our interaction are the client's . They are:
"When I make my sound/movement, the therapist plays."

The aim of using the contact music is to increase the client's awareness of communicating and motivating this awareness.

Observations:
I note whether there is a possibility of increasing the client's patterns of movement using different instruments. We can also make the movements together - here I note if the client imitates me, and if she can synchronize her movements with mine.

The role of the music
is now increasingly a reaction to the client's active participation.
For the client, an expansion of her repertoire regarding sound and movement is a help to directing her attention away from her body and towards her surroundings.

Development at this level can be seen in increasing activity in our interaction. The method of using the various instruments becomes more relevant, that is to say new patterns of movement are incorporated. - There is also development with regard to time and quality.

LEVEL OF CONTACT 4 - *"Our contact takes the form of dialogue"*

The client is now conscious of our interaction. We can take turns at producing sound and listening, The client can direct her attention on me and on herself in our interaction.. That is to say that the interaction now takes the form of a dialogue. The rules are the same for both of us and are: "We take turns at producing sound and listening"

The aim of the contact music is thus to create two-way communication in which the client experiences that her mode of expressing herself becomes the starting point of our dialogue. I am working towards the stage where her experience in communicating can be transferred to her relations with other people.

Observations:
I observe whether or not there is equilibrium in our interaction with regard to length of play and breaks. I test if the interaction can take place using other instruments. And if in the course of the interaction it is possible for me to change my mode of expression, for example change to a different instrument, instead of imitating the client's mode ofexpression.
I might move farther away to see whether or not increased physical distance reduces herconcentration on our interaction.

The role of the music
Here the music is used as reciprocal communication. It originates in the client's mode of expression, which I imitate and perhaps even expand. The music gives the client the possibility to enter into a dialogue. Thus the client's awareness of what communication is all about materializes through the music.

The object of using the 5 levels of contact
As a music therapist the job of describing non-verbal communication is difficult but essential. Working with the group of clients I am describing here requires a thorough knowledge of the client, the way she expresses herself,

her patterns of reaction, her stereotype and pause reactions, etc., in order to know and recognize how and when the music becomes a link between us.

Moreover, it is necessary to make systematic observations in music therapy. Partly to start at the level where the client finds herself. Partly in order to retain an overall view and to see where the possibilities and developments in our relationship are.

We must see the level of contact as a tool which puts a developmental perspective into the music therapeutic work with the group of poor communicators. It is my experience that when keeping the levels of contact in mind music therapy sessions become more intensive. At the same time I think that the relevance of music therapy as a viable possiblity within this area becomes more obvious both to myself and to other professional groups.

Conclusion

So what is left for me to say?

I have learnt a lot about myself in my meeting with the people I describe here. - Thoughts about my own life, what values I attach most importance to, and how I cherish them - what I really live for.

These are important questions which invariably come to mind and which stay with me in my work at Sølund, - because my way of life and my view of life have been put into perspective in my meeting with people who have not had the same possibilities of spreading their wings and experiencing life, as I have. There are, however, some primary, basic needs which we all have in common. The need for close contact with another person, which is the most fundamental psychological need. After which the need for experience, which is the prerequisite for any kind of development. In my work I am reminded that not everyone has these dimensions in their lives as a matter of course. And that I have a responsibility to contribute to giving my clients a life that is worth living and which I can vouch for. But it is not just a question of giving. To an equal extent it is a matter of taking from the other person.

They have a right to be seen and respected for who they are. And in spite of their handicap or bizarre behaviour, I must find the essence in myself and in the other person - the essence which is openness and a desire to be together.

When this is successful we can meet, and this can be a wonderful experience both for me and for the physically and mentally handicapped person.

What kind of Mother am I?
The Role of Music Therapy within the Context of a
Multi-Disciplinary Team Based in a Child Development Centre

Alison Levinge (GB)

Introduction

Through discussion of one mother and child together in music therapy I hope to show something of the way in which the powerful feelings engendered between them, became transferred into the dynamics of a multi-professional team based in a Child Development Centre.

My understanding of the case material, reflects the thinking and writings of Donald Winnicott. His work with mothers and children, led him to focus on the importance of the role of mother in a child's development. He emphasized that the baby's ability for working towards a "personal way of being", is at first totally reliant on the mother's capacity to present the world in manageable doses. Winnicott identified and described what he saw as essential aspects of a mother's care if she were to be a "good enough mother". This term has almost become a catch phrase, but I feel it encapsulates both Winnicott's recognition, and value of what he termed ordinary mothering. It embodies his belief, which he continuously expressed that in the main, "mothering grows naturally out of being a mother". Winnicott felt that in the early stages of a child's life, if a mother can be supported and protected, then she can spontaneously come to discover her mothering skills. Both in his theoretical writings and his talks given to other professionals, as well as the general public, Winnicott was diligent in affirming mothers. In the introduction to his book "The Child, Family And The Outside World" he states, "I hope to give them (that is mothers) support in their reliance on their natural tendencies..." Perhaps Winnicott's dedication to observing and understanding the process of mothering, coupled with the conspicuousness of fathers by their absence, reflects an aspect of his own childhood. Winnicott himself came from a family dominated by women. He grew up as he wrote, "in a sense, an only child with multiple mothers and with father extremely preoccupied in my younger years with town as well as business matters". The youngest of three and the only boy, Winnicott's family consisted of a mother, father, two older sisters, as well as a nanny and a governess. It is difficult to imagine that Winnicott could be anything but affected by this family group of multiple mothers and this must surely have influenced his work. It is also this term multiple mothers, which I feel illuminates aspects of the Child Development Team's functioning, which I see as analogous to a family, as well as featuring as one of the main issues in my family case study. The term multiple mothers, seems to me to very well describe both a feature and process, which I saw as central to the Child Development Team as well as reflecting an aspect of the family process described in my case study.

The Team

Firstly I will describe the team. One finds, that it is often females who choose to work professionally with children and in particular, children under the age of eleven. The Child Development Centre in which I worked was no exception. It was begun and directed by a charismatic and internationally known male consultant paediatrician. His idea, was to create a centre of excellence and in order to support this, he expected that all those employed were to engage in some form of research. He led every case conference, insisting that the parents were sat by his side. Together they faced an array of professionals, who were instructed by the consultant to make their remarks directly to him. He would then discuss the comments with the parents in such a way, that it both affirmed his powerful position, whilst keeping the female professionals in their place. After his retirement, he was replaced by another male consultant, who announced from the beginning that he did not wish to be seen as a leader. However, despite this different approach, the ethos of the previous consultation lingered on and the main component of the team remained the same, totally female. There was a wide range of professional skills which included, a consultant paediatrician, a clinical psychologist, a social worker, a physiotherapist, an occupational therapist, a speech therapist, a teacher and a music therapist. As I have already said, all but the consultant were women. Music Therapy had been introduced to the Centre ten years prior to my arrival. It was a part-time post, and funded by the education department. I feel that these two components contributed to my feeling, that somehow, Music Therapy did not quite fit as a profession. I often felt that it was not taken totally seriously. This perhaps provided an opportunity for projections in the team to find a safe place. That is, within a less established rather unusual form of therapy. I also feel, that my particular approach, that is psychodynamic, continually brought into focus the unconscious and often painful feelings of the families, which the more physically or behaviourally orientated therapies found difficulty in addressing. There was only one time within the week, when all the team members met together. This was the once weekly allocation meeting, where new referrals were discussed and a decision made as to which profession should be involved.

The Children

Children were referred from a range of external agencies and attended the Centre on an out-patient bases. The difficulties presenting were wide-ranging and included physical, developmental and emotional problems. Once the appointments had been arranged and the child had been seen for assessment, the parents would be invited to attend a case conference. Naturally, it is distressing and bewildering for parents who are making their initial visit to a centre such as this and it may be the first time that they have had to face the possibility that their child has a problem. They may appear angry, distressed, confused or in denial. However, as well as the obvious external reactions, I also feel that there are more unconscious processes which come into play. These are hidden and more subtle, and can effect how the team functions. It is these unspoken responses upon which I wish to focus.

The Unconscious Feelings

A mother who has for nine months nurtured and nourished her baby safely in her womb, has perhaps also nurtured desires and dreams for her baby, which she hopes will be fulfilled as they develop. If then once the pain of birth is over, whether due to a genetic defect or birth trauma her child is damaged, mother may feel that in some way she is also damaged or damaging. If the mother is then forced to find her way to a Child Development Centre, she is faced with what in her unconscious mind, may be perceived as healthy mothers. The female experts. At this point, I feel there is an unconscious challenge to this mother's capacity for being a "good-enough mother". The professional - who appears as the one who knows - may then unconsciously tune into mother's vulnerability and unknowingly support her fantasies that somehow she has failed. It is the professional who then appears as the potentially healthy mother. The particular mother and child about whom I wish to talk, connected with these unconscious feelings in a very powerful way. What then arose, manifest itself firstly, amongst the team members and secondly within my music therapy sessions with them both.

Mother and James

At eighteen months, James had been seen by a GP for sleep and feeding problems. At his twenty month review, mother raised the issue of his speech. At first, he saw a community speech therapist, but at the age of two and a half he was referred to the Centre. From the beginning, a conflict arose between team members, and what seemed like a fight ensued over who would be the most appropriate profession to assess and offer treatment. Because some team members appeared to be saying that they had the answers, or could offer just what was needed, this led others into feeling that they had nothing to offer. Feelings of omnipotence and impotence were rife. The team therefore became divided into two opposing factions and this became replicated in how the assessment and treatment of the mother and child was carried out. It was decided, that James should join a speech therapy group, whilst mother should see the psychologist. I had felt that they should been seen together, yet as I seemed to be given no choice in the matter by the team as a whole, I felt pushed out and impotent. A music mother with little to offer. However, after a few months of speech therapy, James did not seem to be improving. As a result, the speech therapist decided to end treatment and suggested that I take over. There was no real team discussion. Rather something of, "I've failed, now it's your turn". My decision had been to work with mother and child together. This seemed to suggest, that the two previous professional mothers, ie. speech therapist and psychologist, were now being replaced by one. Even from our first session however, I experienced both the omnipotent and impotent feelings which had until then been split and fed into the team's pathology. By bringing James and mother together, these powerful feelings now met. Was I going to provide the answers that nobody seemed to have? Or, would I fail and therefore confirm the fantasy that no mother is good-enough?

It is perhaps important at this stage to draw attention to the fact, that James's mother was strongly attached to her own mother. She had to pass her house in order to bring James for therapy, and on occasions would invite mother to come along. Grandma stayed in the waiting area, although later on mother confessed that she had wanted her to come into the therapy. In some way, however, Grandma was present as James continually referred to her. It seemed that he was questioning his own mother's capacity for being good enough. James's mother told me early on in therapy, that James would relate only to Grandma and not his grandfather, that is mother's father. James's inability to connect to his grandfather, seemed to link with the real absence of James's own father who lived in America. In discussion with mother, she had given the impression that this man was of little consequence. Within the team, the only male the consultant, also now appeared to have become redundant to the process of treatment.

After our first session of music therapy, mother expressed surprise and disappointment that therapy was not what she had expected. When I asked her what she had imagined, she replied that she had thought that it would be like LA Law. This is a slick, fast moving American series showing clever, smartly-dressed lawyers solving cases. Is this what mother wanted for James? A fast-acting, smooth, painless form of treatment. I feared I was bound to fail.

Music Therapy Sessions

Introduction
I shall now refer to two sessions, which I feel highlighted in particular, the difficulties of the relationship between this mother and child and perhaps something of what became evoked in the team.

Session A
Mother usually arrived carrying James and the session would often begin with him sat on her lap. One immediately had the impression of a vulnerable couple, clinging to each other for security. The quality of my initial music I

158

feel reflects this vulnerability, yet it also clearly begins to challenge something which seemed at a deep and primitive level of both mother and James's psyche.

Almost immediately, the music and me as music mother became an "I don't want" mother. For James continually repeated that he did not want it. Yet I feel it was mother's passive, apparently unmoved state, which then provoked in me the feeling that I had to be able to do something. Perhaps, this is why I persisted in my play and in an attempt to connect made use of that I had as the musical qualities behind James's verbal demonstrations.

*Description**
Following this, interestingly James swung between telling me that he did not like it, to actually hitting his own mother and telling her "I don't like you". He then tried to encourage me to end the session and repeated the words which I usually used when a session was coming to its conclusion. These were "Goodbye James, see you next week". As neither mother nor me complied, James's distress began to increase. The agony and developing terror in his voice seemed only to drive mother further into a helpless state. In turn, it became increasingly difficult for me to find a space in which I could play. Finally, James began to call for his blanket and then his dummy. It was as if his own mother was not present. Or at least what she had to offer could not be experienced as useful. In interview, mother had told me that James was eating predominantly pureed food as if still in a baby-attached state. This seemed to connect with his inability to separate and his incapacity to feel safe, as if he had not been able to build up and hold onto an internal sense of a mother.

It was towards the end of this session, after James had left the room and returned several times that mother told me how she had explained to her own mother what had been happening in therapy. Grandma herself had then suggested that she might also join us. I began to realise that mother was not only feeling totally overwhelmed by James's state, but she was also feeling that I too was helpless and perhaps hopeless. These feelings were enormously powerful, and I could imagine that by "passing-on" mother and child to me for therapy, the speech therapist with whom James had stopped working, had passed-on the enormously primitive feelings that this couple stirred up. As I attempted to contain them in music therapy I saw that the team were able to split themselves from the pain and helplessness and therefore maintain and protect their feelings of competence. The omnipotent feelings remained located in the team, as I increasingly began to experience the impotence of being in the presence of both mother's and my feelings of not being good enough.

Session B
Three months into therapy, the issue of multiple mothers both inadequate or all good, arose. In this next session, we see, that from the beginning, James repeatedly refers to Grandma. Despite being in the presence of his own

mother, as well as music-mother, neither of us seemed to be present enough for him. Only, the absent mother would suffice.

*Description**
James's repeated cry for Grandma was then exchanged for pleas for his mother, as if the two were interchangeable. At that moment, it was difficult for either mother or myself to feel we had anything to offer.
Later on, James was actually able to come into the music, albeit briefly. He began to explore other instruments. However, this seemed to provoke in him aggressive and rejecting feelings which were enacted when he took part of an instrument and threw it outside the door.

Once again, James returned to his thoughts about Grandma. However, he was able to suspend them briefly when he turned to attacking me. In the session he moved between holding onto our aggressive connection and looking again for Grandma. James's constant references to different mothers coupled with his attacking of me, seemed to suggest that he wanted a mother, yet one which he could choose. As bad mother in that moment, I was hit. By constantly referring to Grandma, James was torturing his own mother. However, he had been able to offer something of the music-mother's environment to his own mother in the form of a guitar. But this was not followed through, and mother was left to play on her own. Instead, James began once again to destroy the music.

The session ended, after James had become trapped (in his mind) on a chair. He became desperate, crying for help and seemed terrified, paralysed and abandoned. But this brought no movement from mother who stayed fixed in her chair. In this session, James had let us both experience his anger in different ways and this seemed to arise out of a need for him to have everything his way.

The Ending
It all came to a head in our final session which occurred after the long summer break. Unbeknown to me, mother had seen both the doctor and psychologist in the team. Without discussion, she had then left me a note saying that she did not wish to attend music therapy any more and would come to that day's session to explain. In taking this action, mother appeared to be expressing the idea that one mother-figure - that is music-mother - could be easily exchanged for another - the psychologist. It seemed that if she could not have her satisfaction immediately, then the answer was to find someone else. As they both arrived, mother told me that James had been saying "no music" all the way down the stairs, as well as during the holiday break. After we sat down however, for the first time, James spontaneously went over to the piano and played. For most of the session, whilst mother and I were in discussion, he continued to explore the instruments. Mother had interpreted James's words "no-music" as him not wanting it. But maybe, as he had now vividly

demonstrated that he wished to play, perhaps in fact, he had been expressing his awareness that the music had been missing, or not there, in the holiday break.

Later on in the session James attacked me, biting my legs, grabbing my breasts and looking up my skirt. It felt, that he was just beginning to find out if I could withstand his aggressive attacks. Perhaps after all, it was mother who had wished to end therapy. In response to mother's request the psychologist had offered mother individual sessions, which she had decided to take. As this request occurred after a long break, then it seemed to me, that it might be connected with the issue of separation. The psychologist had interpreted mother's anxiety as a need to change her therapist. I felt, that she had not been able to tolerate the break and had needed to have someone else. Separation is one of the most significant issues in dynamic psychotherapy. It is important for the therapist and patient to find a way of bearing the breaks and working through what they bring up. It is not necessarily such an important focus in other kinds of therapy and the team's collusion with mother's need to finish with me, supported and reinforced both the feelings I was not a good mother and my role in the team as impotent. By not discussing the difficulties with me, mother had once again fed into the team's predisposition to split. I was now the useless, perhaps even actively bad mother, who caused more pain. Whereas, the psychologist could protect her role as a potentially good mother professional. I found that it was difficult to discuss what had happened with the psychologist and as a result, I experienced persecutory feelings as well as a sense of helplessness.

Perhaps James's inability to engage with me was being supported by mother's passive resistance. As she had initially presented as being in control, it was difficult at first to see what was going on. As therapy progressed, it became clear that this resistance was also manifesting itself within the team, both in relation to the treatment process and the unconscious, rivalrous feelings which were being subtly acted out. Whatever else, in the middle of all of this was James, who remained caught in an unseparated and at times terrorized state. Perhaps I too was caught between both mother and James as well as between members of the team. In the sessions, it had felt that there was rivalry between mother and James, mother and grandmother, mother and music-mother and perhaps also James and me. This feeling became transferred into the team and expressed in the rivalrous, envious feelings now apparent. In the end, mother and James had been able to manipulate the whole team. The question that came to my mind was, What would have happened if I had succeeded, both in regard to mother and as well as the team? Equally, I wondered how James would have been in music therapy without mother present.

Conclusion
I think that when working with children and therefore usually mothers, enormously powerful and primitive feelings become evoked. If this occurs within a team of predominantly female professionals and there is no space in which to address these issues, then the team may find that they are unconsciously re-enacting the families pathology.

* All descriptions are related to video documentation, as presented at the conference.

Music Therapy: The Art of Relationship

Giulia Cremaschi Trovesi (I)

Introduction

My experience in Music Therapy began twenty years ago in an Institute for children up to the age of fifteen years, with insufficient mental capacity, psychosis or autism.

I entered my first experience with infantile deafness with a two years old deaf child who worked in a very small group of children of his same age, in a course of Musical Education for very small children. This child is now attending University and is studying for a degree in Economy. During the following year I began to collaborate with the Audiology Institute of The University of Milan.

Actually three Music Therapists associated to Associazione Pedagogia Musicale e Musicoterapia (APMM) are working at the Audiology Institute in Milan. In the meantime I have always worked with Musical Pedagogy also teaching in classes of Maternal and Elementary school. I have been teaching for ten years at the state ISTITUTO MAGISTRALE in Bergamo and now I give courses for music teachers.I'm teaching in "Corso Quadriennale di Musicoterapia" in Assisi (Italy).

My presentation today is accompanied with a video registration. From the analysis of results, aspects emerge regarding formation of Music Therapists. I now present in synthesis some theoretical aspects that characterizes our way of operating.

Sound and Life

In the absolute sense of the term, silence does not exist in nature. The term sound implies Man-Sound relationship. Sound is both production and reception. The new life that grows within the maternal womb is inside the interpersonal relationship through heart beat, breathing and sound vocal timbres. The sound timbres within the mother's body, in the liquid-sound-emotional transmission, are the FIRST ORCHESTRA that each of us experiences for nine months, without a single moment of interruption of ternary beat. The original way of playing music reproduces all these different rhythms, melodies, accents experienced within the maternal womb.

History of music documents the evolution of the primitive way of making music. The coming of the Alphabetical, Numerical and Musical writing is the synthesis through which the human being finds the symbols to represent his way of living his relationship with the world, with others, with himself.

Every human being lives and feels the same perceptive and emotional experiences. Every sound vibration inside the maternal womb comes to the new life through liquid transmission. Every liquid-sound vibration implies an emotional vibration. Every emotional vibration becomes a new experience and, thus, a new learning.

The human being has then begun a way of learning by PROGRESSIVE ASSIMILATION. This way of learning goes on for the rest of his whole life. Sound waves are waves of pressure and energy; they induce movement.The human being that grows within the maternal womb lives his experiences and learns through his whole being. The presence-absence of sound-liquid-emotional waves will never be experienced in the same way as in pre-natal lifer because birth brings AIR TRANSMISSION of sounds.

Every sound timbre exeperienced within the maternal womb (THE FIRST ORCHESTRA) is now found again in a different way through air transmission. The same sound timbres are EQUAL but DIFFERENT; the same timbres are now received with different harmonics.

Every acoustical-sound perception occours through RESONANCE.
Our hearing apparatus that begins to work after birth through air transmission of sounds, receives sound waves from the external world and transmits them to the internal one always through Resonance.These are the most important fundamentals on which the Music Therapist operates in a direct and active way without having to use words but giving rise to the spontaneous making of the word.

Learning to listen: The deaf child

Deaf children, when correctly diagnosed and prothesised at an early age (i. e. around first year), are for hearing people, a source of learning with relation to the wonderful listening process. They teach us how nothing can or must be taken for granted. In contrast to what is commonly believed, the world of sounds is accessible also for deaf children. One must be able to create those relational situations which can favour the evolution of listening attention in them. Music therapy is a process where the hearing aspect can be emphasised while separating it from the motory and visual aspects. Listening attention is the main issue on which the relationship with the deaf child must be based. Hearing may not be replaced by nor subordinated to other sense-organs.

RESONANCE, which is realised with the use of the huge soundbox of the grand piano, allows to start a relationship with a deaf child. The music therapist, noticing how the child perceives sound-waves in all their corporeality, leads the child towards the appreciation of the harmonical frequencies which he/she receives through the amplification of hearing aids. The intonation quality of the child's voice confirms that he/she is learning to appreciate frequencies which he/she would not receive without hearing aids.

The music therapist uses idiophonic musical instruments (specific idiom sound) to arouse the child's curiosity. Each timbre is highlighted in the game of musical arousing the child's curiosity. The child participate in improvisation, or SOUND DIALOGUE. The child manipulates instruments, compares and throws them away according to the typical exploration tecniques of childhood. The musi-therapist gives a meaning to every movement and manipulative action of the child by means of MUSICAL IMPROVISATION ON THE PIANO.

The child reacts with growing curiosity and attention. Emotions are disclosed naturally through vocal outbursts. The deaf child vocalizes, produces glissandos, articulates phonemes spontaneously because he/she is caught by fascination of the musical games. Words are born in accordance with the natural laws concerning all human beings. Words are born as need of interpersonal communication which can not be given up. The introduction of nursery rhytmes and popular songs completes the game. The PARENTS' PRESENCE is indispensable, because through the child's action they change their way of judging deafness and they open to a rediscovered faith in life. The child opens itself to verbal language naturally and spontaneously. Acting within a team of professionals facilitates growth and prepares the child to successful school and social life.

The natural development: Brain damage
It is important to understand the quality of lessons taught by deaf children to welcome the principle of the VIBRATING BODY. In the presence of sound waves, a body which does not vibrate even when reached by sounds and voice, either because it is too tense (hypertonicity) or because it is not tense enough (hypotonicity), is in a situation of poor participation possibilities. Words, in their natural making, are born in the game of discovering timbres.

Onomatopoetic sounds are the basis of human relationships in the world. The world is meant in the consistency between maternal womb and life on earth. When a trauma breaks this consistency, the music therapist acts musically with a SOUND DIALOGUE executed with RESONANCE, with MUSICAL IMPROVISATION.

A trauma entails pain and, in many cases, prolonged suffering. There are no words which can abliterate pain. Using resonance, the child can be influenced to restore the faith in the world which the pain had jeopardized. A child who undergoes intensive therapy will inevitably experience loneliness. The game of musical improvisation customised on each child, is a new experience which leads to overcome fear. Even encephalopathic children are restored to harmony with life through the rythmical, timbrical and vocal order they knew in their mothers' wombs. Resounding signifies being alive and vibrating in listening.

Each successive step is shown by the children themselves, who, in one lesson after another, open up to reveal the way the music therapist must follow.

The music therapist does not operate alone; he is flanked by another

165

professional with different and congruent assignments, so that the child can be sustained, supported in his/her evolution process to achieve an always better balanced bodily tone. EURHYTHMY, EUTONICITY and EUPHONY progress at the same pace.

To change the map of the world (Weltanschauung):
Psychotic and autistic children

Musical improvisation carried out in Sound Dialogue is a direct and immediate way of communication from which neither the psycotic or autistic child can escape. Resonance, through the sound board of a grand piano, makes the body vibrate, renewing the creation of positive emotion and feeling. Through the BODY SCRIPT the music therapist can match the child's positive energetic level without using verbal language. The method is based on these aspects: MATCHING, PACING, LEADING, a powerful way to deepen acknowledgement and acceptance of a person.

The music therapist observe the child as if he would be a "living score". In this way musical improvisation changes continuously, renewing the child's curiosity, interest and attention. As it happens in the musical game of imitations: with music you can repeat the same thing by playing it in different ways. So the child can't find a scheme to which he can refer. The interpersonal relationship is unpredictable.

In Music Therapy you don't have rules or schemes already written. Creativity is the substance of the interpersonal relationship. It is a double relationship:

- the music therapist plays observing the child
- the child observes because every action of the music therapist is unexpected
- the music therapist observes while he plays
- the music therapist plays while he observes
- SOUNDS FORM THE WORDS
- THE WORDS DO NOT EXPLAIN THE SOUNDS

Music Therapy with Severely Multiply Handicapped Children

Eyulfur Melsted (AU)

I feel I owe you an explanation why I choose to talk of handicapped children in this paper of mine, rather than using the definition, "developmentally disabled". The fact is, that the children referred to are so severely impaired from the causes of their disabilities, that through those they are additionally handicapped in so to say all other fields of their devolepement. Therefore I still choose to speak of handicaps. I also feel that I owe those of you who have never been professionally confronted whith these children a definition of this group. Perhaps some of you may even find a certain idendity with the participants in the Swiss psychologist's, Jörg Grond's, survey of how different groups of people looked upon this matter.The general trends of his study showed that:

- special teachers, therapists, nurses and caretakers immediately thought of *their own* weakest clients or pupils. In most cases they could hardly inlagille that there were others weaker and more disabled than "their own most difficult cases".
- on the other hand parents most often found "some other" children more severely impaired as *their own* multiply handicapped children.
  non affected people pointed generally non productive people or non consumers out.
- managers and directors - frequently: "people who are unable to do a "decent job"".

I wonder if such considerations are solely to be found among the Swiss population?

Who are they?
Therefore I'd like to quote the haedlines of two definitions of this group. The first one of the already mentioned, Jörg Grond, and the other, that of the german special education professors: Andreas Fröhlich and Ursula Haupt.

Grond: - they are disabled in a multiple sense and almost all of them are corporally disabled to the degree that their corporal control is severely impaired; - almost all suffer tram medically surveyed deseases (most frequently of epilepsy) and must therefore take drugs .

Fröhlich/Haupt: - they are children, who are in all main fields of development, i.e. psychomotoric, emotional, communicative, social and cognitive, severely impaired!. They seem not able to move themselves around on the floor on their own. They are still not able to aim the movements of their hands in order to eat alone , or for constructive playing.

Grond: - they seem to be lifelong dependent on steady medical care.

Fröhlich/Haupt: They are still not able to cornnunicate verbally - their perceptual field is limited to the nearest vicinity and they can neither give any feedback, by imitation, of what they see, nor hear; their reactions and assimilations are bound to present experience, but they are still unable to draw even the simplest abstract conclusion of what they have just experienced.

Grond: - as teenagers or adults they cannot be occupationally integrated; they don't fulfil the minimal demands of sheltered workshops or normal occupational day-care-centers, but have to be attended to in all daily activities. You try to keep them occupied all day longs but theirs contribution is meagre, to say the least. Still they participate passively in daily activities of others. They enjoy it obviously and seem to gain therefrom strength for their humour and will of life. Anyway, we can observe that by such attention and approach they are less ill.

Fröhlich/Haupt: - they are so impaired in their mobility, that they need to be helped by adults by any activity of daily living, such as: dressing and undressing, eating, toilette, moving around, communicating, fulfilling their emotional and social needs and stimulation to occupation.

Grond: - only few of them can speak or understand more than a couple of words, and communication with them is only possible in form of gesticulations, mimicry or alternation of pitch and breath and with signals.

Fröhlich/Haupt: - at best they react to offers of contact from related adults, but they are unable to establish relationship with other children. Therefore they must always be attended to individually.

Grond: - emotional approaches find a far better echo by them than a cognitive one. They are helplessly exposed to all affects of their surroundings. Some of them are bound to their instincts and can as such hardly allow any form of approach.

You may clearly see that this is certainly not the easiest group of clients to deal with - but who of us have easy clients - to deal with?

Why music?
It may be a good question to ask why music should do especially good in the developmental stimulation of these children. The answer is, sometimes music provides a unique means of establishing contact and communication with these children, as well as stimulating them to activity, where other disciplines do not so easy. Music may help these - in most cases severely spastic children to relax, and that even in a short time, so that they can have a longer period of active experience by the session. - Active experience being the absolute base for their further learning.

But why is it so? - The main reason is, that these children have had the same fetal, or intrauterine, musical experience as other, non handicapped, children. This, even if in some cases the causes of their impairment have presumably taken place already in the fetal stadium. Clauser described the fetus' experience of his mother as: "mainly acoustic, rhythmical, vibrational and as movement". To me it sounds more like a musical definition than a medical one. According to Lux Flanagan the development of the inner ear (the first of all our organs) is completed st the 37th day of pregnancy.

This, of course, does not mean that we ve already learned to hear. But one or two weeks later the navel string is there - still primitive, but "pulsating".

From the 10th up to 12th week of pregnancy we generally take for granted, that the fetus has developed so far, that he can "hear" the heartbeat and the murmur of his mother's digestive organs. In this case hearing may mean acoustic and vibrational perception in any form. We may therefore take for granted that all children can "hear", at least in this acoustical and vibrational manner, for at least 2/3s of pregnancy.

The influence of this intrauerine stimulation, as described by Clauser, is withheld as a corporal memory, sub- or nonconcious, after birth. The most obvious and the most affecting type of those memories is the pulse. Thereby one's own arterial beating is not necessarily referred to, but far more the emotional, psychological and musical phenomenon of pulsating beat and how we feel it.

One of the forms of this corporal memory can be seen from a study I made some 25 years ago. 100 persons were asked which beat they felt was slow and which was fast. To exclude answers such as "rather fast" or "relatively slow" the possibilty of answering "can't decide" was given. The beat-examples were played by a hidden metronome in the sequence shown. As we can see, people generally feel that tempo up to 60 beats/minute is slow. Frown then on we can see that the answers are mixed and overlapping, slow - fast - can't decide, up to the limit above 90 beats/minute. From that point on the participants are generally shure that the tempo is fast. There was no relation to be found between the normal pulse of the participants, measured at rest, and their answers. Trained musicians among them, however, gave the most accurate answers. With most of them you could notice a sharp turning point, most frequently at 72 and hardly any "can't decide" answers. In the group there were three marathon runners whith pulses: 42, 45 and 48 at rest. Their answers did not show any abnormalities. Therefore I conclude, that the relative sense of rhythmical speed is memory bound, or imprinted and rotates by ones decision around the axis of normal pulse and heartbeat, i.e. in the area between 60 and 90 beats/minute. We can also see that the most frequent turning points lie between 70 and 80.

I choose to call this phenomemon "memory pulse". This kind of memory the multiply handicapped children share with all other people. But the Posit important form of imprinted memory pulse for the music therapeutic work with these children is the "mother pulse". The important role of "mother pulse" in soothing of newborn babies was shown by Lee Salk. Infants who were allowed to listen to his synthetic heartbeat music in the clinic were more calm. They lost less weight in the first days and gained their birthweight faster. Mother's heartbeat therefore seems to be the most decisive musical imprinting factor in our prenatal and infant existence. It plays a significant role for our taste of music, at least in the first montns of life.

I quote only those two examples of pulse imprinting. There are many more - so many that they could deliver us stuff for a whole conference. As the experience of "motherpulse music" seems to be common with all developmentally disabled children as well as by the non disabled ones, it is a natural basis for the music therapeutic approach. Through years of work in this field I have realised that we have to divide the functions of pulse into five categories at least. They are:

1. *Ones own corporal pulse*
2. *The Mother pulse (memory)*
3. *Memory pulse*
4. *Efficiency (ergo)-pulse*
5. *Expression pulse*

The first form needs no explanation. The phenomena: mother and memory-pulse are already explained. Efficiency pulse is the speed or tempo in which the child is able to move its hands and is of great importance for the active part of the music therapy. Expression pulse can be heard and observed e.g. by the pulsating rhythm of ones speech or by ones habitual playing of music, singing etc.. It plays an important role by speech training with music e.g. in early intervention.

Recognizing the role of the different forms of pulse-imprinting is essential for music therapy with severely multiply handicapped children. The fact is, that in this sense they have learned the same things in their prenatal stage as all other children.

How?
Up to the emotional-developmental age of six months, the mother pulse is a ruling factor by soothing and relaxing of these, as well as all other children. At the threshold of six months of developmental age, the child begins to develop its own ISO and from then on we must look for other varieties of musical approaches. Still the most important commandment to the therapist is - "a careful approach". As many baroque composers who chose to compose their introductory toccatas in a very gentle manner, we too should make our toccatas - "the musical touch" - "molto tenero". It is also essential to form the music therapy session to a kind of a ritual because of the magical effect of the repetition. One should always start the session with the same theme. I play an individual opening theme for every child, which is a pure matter of privacy between my client and me - our song, which belongs only to the two of us and our musical sessions.

Toccata
The purpose of this choice is to mark the importance of the situation. In some cases I forbid other teachers and therapists to play these "private" tunes in order to prevent confusion. Therefore you should not wonder that I incline to choose foreign themes - in Austria non Austrian melodies - to preserve our musical privacy. They are songs who are less likely to be heard outside our music therapy sessions.

The choice of music follows, if possible, according to the background information given by the parents on the child's musical experience. Anyway, this kind of information is normally very scarce, so in most cases you have to start the touching with something that comes into your mind and if it hits - it is good music.

In the receptive phase tuning forks are outstanding instruments.
You can use them acupressurally to speed up the relieving of spasms and general relaxation of the client in order to have a longer phase of active experience. Through years of work with these children, I have learned that you can use high quality tuning forks where fingers are far too coarse instruments. This, for instance, in the oro-facial stimulation according to Castillo Morales. Only when relaxed can these children take part in an active experience play, which is the absolute basis for their learning.

Campanara
The first activities are normally those with gross motoric movements. Holding a stick and swinging the arms - striking a sounding bowl might be considered

171

a typical discipline for this part. The bowl gives a strong, but a very pleasant feedback in form of sound as well as vibrations, which are accurately converted and amplified over the Lili Nielsen plate. In our case the plate provides the optimal "musical platform" and I always work with these children on such a plate. The bowl may also be placed directly on the body in order to allow its vibrations to work directly on legs and knees. We must never forget the multilateral effect of music. When playing music we also enjoy it and these children do it just as anybody else. While playing you also sense their pride over the success if they are able to strike the bell without any help.

Alla marcia

The corporal condition of these children is generally not the very best. Therefore its important to switch over to receptive phases between the strong efforts of activity. These receptive phases can be both: informing and stimulating at the same time. We, who work with these children often ask ourselves whether they really know that they have feet. Therefore massage and other corporally informative skills are typical for the basic stimulation. For years I've also been observing colleagues having troubles by putting the feet of their clients into stays, another orthopaedic device. This, due to the lack of preparatory stimulation. A few preparatory "tuning in's" with the forks and marching with the foot soles on the "quica drum" may help to correct the position of the feet so that they glide smoothly into the orthopaedic device without frustration and pain. He who is allowed to march to the music of Mancini or good old Duke Ellington on the vibrating head of the quica may certainly know that he has feet. In the same way we can use the cabasa as a stimulating instrument. With this you can practically stimulate the whole body, just as well as with the tuning forks. One should not forget that a rhythmical touch of the body with suitable instruments provides a far richer experience of contact, communication and information than an ordinary massage.

Arpeggione et pizzicato

From the gross motoric skills we in most cases go over to the finer ones. It's very important that these children do not experience frustration, or even pain which may occur by their efforts of plucking the strings with their fingers. A non developmentally disabled child does not like to pluck guitar strings untill it has reached the developmental age of 7 1/2 to 8 months. Because of this fact, touching and plucking the fine strings of the guitar - even the softest types - is an unsuitable task untill the pupil has reached this developmental age. Most of my young clients have not yet reached this stage of developernent. They therefore apt to hook their fingers around the strings and may even hurt themselves thereby. Therefore one should be very careful by presenting fine strings untill the children have had the experience of thicker and coarser ones, like those on the Ulwila bass fretboard (or zither). The Ulwila instruments give a highly accurate feedback of sound and vibrations and they sound long after plucking. If correctly plucked, the bass fretboard may sound and vibrate up to four minutes. But the playing of pleasantly sounding and vibrating strings must not always be of the active type. Receptive music may lead to correction of positioning. The girl on this video* clip stretches her head constantly to the left. By covering her left ear and playing the tune on her right side, she changes the position of her head quite naturally. In this situation she gains the control of the normal head position without any difficulty.

Volare

I don't know if the picture of the world of a person who is mainly moved around by others in a wheelchair or carried about on the arms of grownups, is familiar to you from your own experience. In moss cases the vestibulary experience of the multiply handicapped children is of that sort. Therefore these children fear being swung around or being moved abruptly from one position to another. In this situation their spasms become extremely hard and often they react with obvious panic. This is due to their underdeveloped vestibulary sense. I'd like to suggest to anyone who is interested in working with these children that they have the experience of a couple of days sitting in a wheelchair - in order to understand the client's situation a little better. With music played to the beat of the mother-pulse and the change of chords marking the change of swinging direction they can be swung around without showing any signs of fear or panic. In this case, as in so many others correctly aimed music can provide a preparatory phase for the basic stimulation in other fields.

Stretching and swinging of the arms can also be enlightened by playing and watching the ocean drum. Hatching ones own playing leads to better hand-eye coordination - so in this case, one skill of musical playing leads to the stimulation of another skill.

Miau Miau

Due to their extremely retarded development, only few of my clients can be confronted with the task of playing the guitar. If they are ready for it, I of course misuse this gained ability and will of playing as I present other skills like that of assymmetric movements of the hands in combination with the already achieved one. This way we play some sort of cat music. It s still no "Cat Duet" of Rossini's or "The Blues of the Alley Cat", but the way to perfection starts with one little step.

Finale

Grasping - holding firm and releasing - is one of the most essential skills children have to learn. Normally non-professionals don't regard this as learning because these skills develop so quite naturally that you take them for granted. In our case this is a task of hard training - the fight against pathological movement patterns. Here we train these skills by the "Shower of balls and chestnuts". Patrick and I are rehearsing for a wedding. Next Saturday Patrick's pre-school teacher is going to be married. It is going to be a traditional Austrian farmers' wedding, with "pomp and circumstances". We plot a surprise in the church. We are going to play and sing the tune I hum (on this video* clip). Patrick will be one of four developmentally disabled children accompanying the singing of some colleagues together with six non disabled children. His ball and chestnut shower scale fits into the tune at any place. Thus music can provide one of the first chances of an up to standard participation in integrative playing.

Finally I'd like to try to summarize this paper in one sentence:
Provided you offer these children that accurately balanced mixture of aimed music and humane approach, which we in common language call music therapy, at their optimal level of perception, they seem to do better.

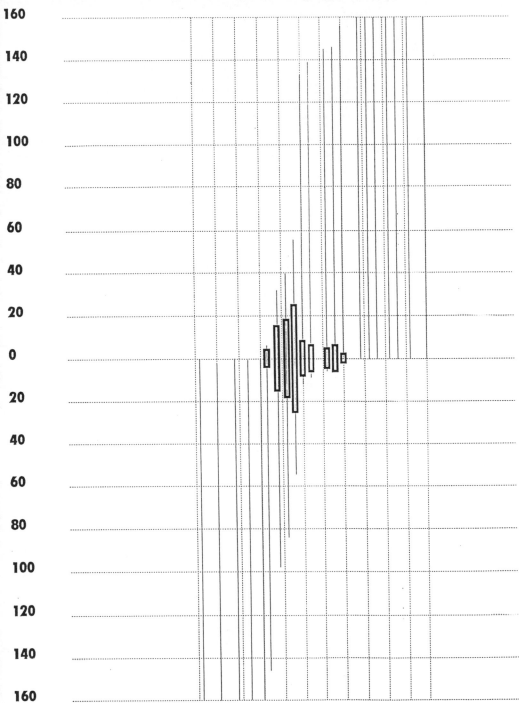

Individual Music Therapy in the "Integrative Primary School" in Hamburg - Ten Sessions with a Slow Learning Girl

Wolfgang Mahns (D)

1. The Context

Within the scope of a large city-wide project in Hamburg, called "Integrative Grundschule" (Integrative Primary School) I am working as Special Pedagogue and Music Therapist. Currently my work focuses mainly on the collaboration with one class as well as with a pre-school class. Furthermore I am doing music therapy with some children from other schools who could not be sufficiently stabilized with what is on offer. These lessons are financed by a so-called "resource pool".

There are 25 children in class 2 (ages 7 to 8) and I work very closely together with the class teacher. As a result and to enable efficient co-operation between ourselves we meet regularly once a week for a long session, other [female] teachers and the head master may be called to participate, when needed. We will discuss every pupil's knowledge and state of development and try to establish together the need for special attention with regards to certain "difficulties".

Alongside my participation within the system (class rituals, music, excursions etc.) my main opportunities lie in the following areas:

- Individual Music Therapy (10 to 50 sessions)
- Music Therapy in group work (6 - 10 sessions)
- Integrative stimulation of speech (including breathing exercises, voice and body awareness)
- Talking sessions and consulting.

Initially it is essential to be convinced of the specific qualities of improvisation in music therapy, with regards to

- Reintegration of any split off feelings
- Developing the ability of dialogue
- Developing curiosity
- Encourage new experiences.

2. Extraordinary Behaviour in the Normal School Class

What kind of children may be offered and could benefit from music therapy ? Instead of a catalogue of indications or diagnoses, I would just like to give three examples:

Example 1

Ralf's father is in prison for attempted murder. Since then, Ralf is mainly preoccupied with death, ghosts, zombies and similar subjects. He finds it very difficult to direct his feelings towards the outside. He might just trip somebody up when he feels like it, kick him or her in the stomach or strangle the person.

Example 2

Metin came to Hamburg a few years ago from Izmir in Turkey. He is now due to start class 1 in primary school. Straight from the beginning he would not talk to anybody, he fell silent. At home he is a lively little boy, at school it seems to be his way of punishing everybody. Metin has chosen his own method of expression after the shock he suffered: two different worlds, separation from home, different laws and rules than at home are in force.

Example 3

Nadine is a single child. Her mother accompanies her to school daily and picks her up afterwards - occasionally even straight from the class room. Mother and daughter regularly perform partly touching partly displeasing welcoming and farewell rituals . Nadine participates nicely in class. However, she never talks about herself i.e. during our talking sessions. She actually only comments when someone else has done "something bad", or when she doesn't know what she "must" do. She would burst into tears for example at the slightest spelling mistake or if her exercise book has a little stain.

Existing difficulties of children at school can be enhanced or make the person suffer for many different reasons: In some cases because of traumatic and neurotisizing childhood experiences, other children are not prepared for the size of the group, and even learning conditions as well as the class and school atmosphere can play a part. These difficulties can show up in form of elective mutism, uncontrolled actions on impulse, slow learning, exaggerated adaptability, speech problems as well as behavioural disturbances or learning problems.

As a result of his study about the situation of conspicuous children in primary school, HURRELMANN (Bielefeld) suggests that 15% of children are hyperactive, aggressive and are having learning difficulties. There has been however, a dramatic increase in children with allergies and psychosomatic symptoms. In 1992 this problem was investigated in Hamburg in 116 primary school classes. The results of this investigation are even more alarming.

Depending on the different catchment areas there will be approx. 5 mostly socially conspicuous children per class. With class numbers between 20 and 25 children this means 20 to 25%.

The investigation also brought to light the extremely high difference in figures between boys and girls i.e. 82.5% versus 17.5%.

3. School, Language and Relationship Problems
Boys and girls spend a very big part of their childhood and youth in and around school. The "School-Life" is therefore of major importance.

Learning procedures within the school are mainly composed of linguistic interactions. Difficulties in experiencing life as well as behavioural problems often show up at speech level. Outrageous and unpronounceable things, often expressed by means of "bad words", sexual fantasies, day dreaming and even violence, are more or less suppressed and therefore look for other outlets. This is often the "normal" price to pay for the process of integration into society. But for some children this course of events may have fatal consequences if the outlets are of uneconomical or pathological nature.

If the school puts too much emphasis on rational language and therefore becomes partly initiator of some troubles, it is important for integration purposes to create a certain balance. Where the child is only partly assessed it is necessary to reestablish integrity. Within the school set-up it must be possible for a child like Ralf to open up to a trustworthy person a little group or inside the classroom to express himself through play, painting or music.

In some cases, just a few conversations along with special support and training are not sufficient, in particular if the developmental impairment started at an early age. Nicole was such a case.

4. Case Study - "Nicole discovers autonomy"

4.1 Cause (Instruction for treatment)
Nicole is seven years old and in class 2 at primary school. She is a single child. Nicole is good looking, slim, and has long black hair and dark brown eyes. During several observation sessions, I noticed that Nicole often gets carried away dreaming, that she has a little smile on her face for everything even if there is nothing to smile or laugh about.

From time to time she is subjected to Bernd's impetuous and aggressive attacks who always goes for the "nice girls". Bernd pulls her hair or just suddenly punches her in the stomach . Nicole accepts all this quietly and without defending herself.

Nicole is well accepted by most children especially by the girls. Right from the beginning she established a certain closeness between her and myself. Even at the beginning of class 2 when I newly arrived as teacher for special needs and we therefore hardly knew each other, she often cuddled up to me, looked for my hand or touched me in an almost erotic way. To me this seemed to be a little more than just the normal trustworthy behaviour of a seven year old.

After a while it became more and more apparent that Nicole had difficulties assimilating the teaching material. During group teaching, such as general knowledge and class discussions, where talking predominates the lesson, she frequently drifts away into her dream worlds. Her speed in maths is extremely slow and gets worse when we work out the course of writing. Sometimes the class teacher wonders if Nicole might be 'a little thick' or stretched too far intellectually. Should she be sent to a special school for children with learning difficulties.?

In the first instance I was trying to help Nicole during lesson time, and often had to go over the various tasks again with her, explaining, demonstrating generally giving her a helping hand. However, the more I devoted myself to her the more she seemed to turn inside herself, and as a result she slowed down even further. I could sense in her a certain feeling of paralysis and a big scream for help. In fact, I felt just as 'stupid' as her because my efforts didn't get me anywhere. At the same time I witnessed her aggressions on account of the power she has over me. She would probably have liked to see me deal with all her tasks instead of having to do it herself.

I am starting to fantasize: Nicole is a little princess from a foreign country. She wants to break out and go for a little walk around the castle. Unfortunately she has got the wrong shoes on for such a sandy road, full of stones and tree roots. I have been ordered to be at her side as a servant, to help her overcome all obstacles so that she doesn't hurt herself.

4.2 Exploration Contracting

In the beginning I talked with the class teacher and the parents. Then, during a first interview with Nicole, I tried to find out where her strengths and weaknesses were. First musical contacts and a projective test ("family as animals") round the first impression off.

Furthermore, I met Nicole various times during music lessons in a class situation, where she was able to demonstrate her hidden vitality through dancing and singing. She also 'dared' to ask me, if she could have individual lessons, which to me proved her motivation to move into this direction.

During the first discussion we talked about the necessary agreements such as reasons for Individual Music Therapy, length of sessions, obligation to secrecy, recordings on cassettes).

4.3 The Process of Treatment
Nicole is undecided {First Session}
Nicole and I met on the way to the therapy room. I was carrying a bag and some musical instruments. Nicole offered to help carry my things. The session

starts with a short talk about things which happened during the week. Nicole reports openly about an argument at home between mother and father. Then she talks about the difficulty of always having to decide between mother and father: "I don't know who I like best ..." I am confused about this formation of opinion by Nicole. I simply let her know that I can imagine how difficult it must be for her having to make such decisions.

The instruments are ready to be used and I invite Nicole to try them out. To begin with, Nicole chooses the little instruments which are spread out on the floor, she quickly lifts up one after the other, almost as if they were made from fragile porcelain, but she only wants to know what 'the thing' is called. With some instruments she also enquires about how they are being used. First of all I oblige and answer all her questions. Finally, as Nicole 'knows' all the answers our dialogue grinds to a halt. I indicated to Nicole that she was very welcome to try out everything but it could not prompt her to make sounds with the instruments. The situation did not change when I requested her decision for one instrument. This proposition does not even seem to reach her. As far as I am concerned I am almost under Nicole's spell through all these questions, a spell which prevents me from being active myself and playing a tune.

My impressions after this session: A great many things are happening alongside each other and there is no real (musical) dialogue. I feel Nicole is in conflict with herself, partly fragile - partly weak, paralysed in her inability to grab things, to make decisions or to play, but sometimes she can also be powerful in determining certain situations.

Guess-Work (Second to Fourth Session)
The next session is being taken up at this point. Nicole does not want to play "just like that". She suggests the following: "You shut your eyes, I shall hide an instrument and you have to guess which one is missing". There is no mistaking the rules of her game and we therefore play hiding, guessing and seeking in many different versions. To follow on, we have another guessing game. I must think about a word or a sentence, then present the thought musically and she wants to guess what it is called. I think of "autumn leaves" and play the glockenspiel. Nicole guesses: "Will you stay here a little longer?"

I now realise that there seem to hide some serious questions behind this suggestion of "guessing game", for example: "How long do we have these individual sessions for ? What can I rely upon ?"

I confirm to Nicole once more that we are to meet 10 times and this answer seems to satisfy her. We end this session with an improvisation in which Nicole plays triangle, key-ring and whistle. I play tone bars and guitar. We create rather a trendy farewell song, which I identify as the beginning of dialogue and uniform rhythm, whereby the key-ring would be heavily symbolic for the beginning and the whistle for the end. Nicole seems to have understood that this is a situation limited in time during which however, lots of things may happen.

A Fantasy Store (Fifth Session)
In the fifth session I made a suggestion to Nicole: "Let's play a fantasy story which we make up as we go along. At some stage whilst the music is playing a magician comes along (when we hear the Glockenspiel) and everything changes". We start straight away.

In the beginning Nicole plays very loudly on the handdrum and the cymbals. Finally, after a softly played improvisation with short melodical parts, almost like a seduction, she determines herself that the magician should start at this point. The next improvisation is short and not very fast.

In our little discussion that follows, Nicole describes to me what she saw inside herself during the improvisation: "There was a horse riding through the forest. I think, it probably ran away and could not find its way back. Then it met the magician. He enchanted the horse so it could find its way back into the stable.

If we look at fantasies symbolically as fulfilments of desires, Nicole shows us three aspects of her personality in this game:

* the desire to break free, to follow her inner instincts and the desire
  for freedom (the horse which runs away)
* the power to exorcize and calm down previously released aggressions,
  just as if nothing had happened (role of the magician)
* the desire for domesticity, home, harmony (horses in the stable).

Secret desires become apparent, but immediately dismissed in the fantasy.

Being a shadow (Sixth to Eighth Session)
Nicole follows me musically like a shadow. Through music I make contact with her as a "shadow" and try to get rid of it by playing faster and faster. In this way the music increases speed all the time and becomes incredibly lively, almost ecstatic. For the first time Nicole has tried the drumsticks on the snare-drum. This little episode was followed by tension releasing laughter.

We continue with the "shadow" theme. Things will be getting even more exciting.

Incidentally, Nicole's class teacher requests to let Nicole leave a little earlier from the therapy session so that she won't miss the instructions for the homework in German.

We enter the therapy room together. The instrument are scattered all over the room ready to be played as in previous sessions. Today Nicole does not feel like sitting down one could almost say 'she keeps her coat on for protection'.

I ask her: *"With what would you like to begin"?*
Nicole answers this question with another question: *"What would you like to play ?"*
Me: *"You tell me what I should play."* Another echo:
Nicole: *"You tell me."* Long silence.
Me: *"Allright then, after all it is your lesson."*
Nicole seems surprised: *"Why ?"*
Me: *"This is your time and you can decide what to do with it."*
Nicole stops to think for a moment. Then she smiles enigmatically.
Nicole: *"Does this mean that I am allowed to do anything ?"*
Me: *"What were you thinking of ?"*
Nicole: *"Well, would it be allright to throw that chair out of the window, through that glass window there ...?"*
She thinks up other ways of letting go of her aggressive impulses.
Finally I add:*"You see, if I don't like something you do or if I find it too dangerous, I shall let you know. But you are correct you have lots of possibilities."*

Nicole is now ready for a musical game. She chooses glockenspiel and the big cymbal. I am playing melodika and rattles. The noise is deafening, and later in the teachers' room two colleagues complain about it.
After this session I get some really nice feed-back from Nicole's class teacher.

To her great surprise, during the German lesson Nicole managed to finish off everything within a few minutes at the end of the lesson, for which her classmates almost took the whole time of the lesson. It sounds like a parallel to the music-therapy session: Breakthrough.

The next meeting starts with Nicole's information that she got her swimming certificate. This is a further indication of development from an existence in the shadow, from a 'copy-cat' behaviour towards slow and gradual independence.

Farewell - Knowing what is needed (ninth to tenth session)
I soon started to talk about the farewell. Nicole always knew throughout the whole process of therapy which session we were at, despite the holiday breaks. In fact she told me once that she would always count how many times she had been to a session. She did not want to extend the individual sessions.
In the lesson before last (9th) we therefore invited her best friend Mareike. Nicole passes on a lot of the acquired information, her knowledge of musical instruments, ideas for games, even ways on how best to play.

The last session begins with a little dialogue.

Nicole: (is choosing certain instruments only)
"Therefore, I still need....." She hesitates and thinks.

Nicole: (to me) *"Do you know what I still need ?"*
Me: *"You alone know what you need"*.
Nicole: *"Oh yes"*. - In fact, Nicole knows very well what she wants.
We play an improvisation on the topic of "travelling" with the aim to retrace once more our route together.

I quote from my notes:
At the beginning certain sounds, then excitement, vivacious movements. Quieter sounds in another part of the music sneaking through the grass birds in the forest secret things. During the further course of the therapy something breaks through: wildness and temperament, still stumbling along clumsily but without giving up. To finish off we play the electric organ together. An almost solemn fugue, the melodies melt into each other. Right at the end Nicole plays the electric organ on her own and I play drums. A little unaided walk by Nicole.

With the help of the music we talk about the reasons and the end off the Individual Music Therapy. Nicole is well aware about her progress and manages to talk easily about her experience during the various stages.

4.4. *Effects*
The class teacher keeps me informed about certain observations concerning changes in Nicole's' behaviour. During physical education classes par example she now defends herself against dominating boys and even shows the strength to protect other girls. At one occasion in particular I happened to be present: Fatima sprained her ankle.

Her crutches are in their usual place. Bernd turns up picks up Fatima's crutches without asking and starts clowning around. Fatima wants them back but cannot run after him. She senses her helplessness and starts crying. Nicole now takes Bernd to task, which is followed by a scuffle. Bernd chokes Nicole, who frees herself with a punch into Bernd's face. Since then Bernd seems to be a bit more careful with his little "jokes".

Even in her learning behaviour Nicole give the impression to be more alert: when talking in class or following instructions during German lessons. She dares to read aloud and is already able to write little fantasy stories.

However, Nicole has mood swings, dreams sometimes, is irritable or conforms too much. She is more aware of her feelings concerning her home situation or if she doesn't find anybody to play with during break time. But she is now able to express all these things verbally in a way that the teacher and her class mates are able to take part and look for a solution.

5. Concept of Treatment
At the beginning of the individual therapy the teacher showed her awareness of the problem by making the following general comment:: "Something is the matter with her, she needs something, she raises questions ..." I first thought

of using a prophylactic approach: offer a little chat, encourage, guessing games, bring a little 'inside' to the 'outside'. At a second glance, however, it became apparent that in Nicole's case a neurotic conflict was the cause, a worry to let aggressions go, an inhibition to think of the own self as important, which resulted in a learning difficulty. My way off proceeding is possibly both prophylactic and psychotherapeutic work as far as the time of the intervention is concerned. (Because of the special quality of the 'integration model', there is a good chance to reach a child before things go completely wrong.) In Nicole's case it was almost music psychotherapy, in as much as I could get to her neurotic conflict.

6. Final Thoughts

As for so many school children the question for Nicole must be: Is it true that her possibilities are generally limited, or are emotional conflicts culpable for her inability to develop her potentials.?

You might think: "Well, Nicole does not really seem to be a very conspicuous child or a child which needs to be offered special treatment.
But this is just the job of the 'integrative task', to understand at a very early stage even slight obstructions in character and to eradicate these in prevention with the help of careful interventions within class lessons or through special, timely offers (additional or alternative) so that these slight obstructions do not become manifest.

I see my own intervention with Nicole more as personality strengthening. In other words: Nicole should be encouraged to clear the obstacles out of her own way.

Finally I would like to take up some points by Herman Schwarz. Herman Schwarz is a former school inspector responsible for structuring educational matters in primary schools and has played an important part in implementing integration in Hamburg.
Schwarz indicates:
"Integrative education can only be complete when it also includes opportunities for additional therapy and support for specific handicaps."

Therefore the main concern is not about education or therapy, individual or group lessons, process or programme orientation. These items must of course be looked at. But in order to increase individuality and therefore difference, it is necessary to apply flexible offers or settings to the individual child and to link them together.

In the end this can also serve humanization of schools as a whole. For this position, however, we have to enlist support again, especially in times of cuts in resources.

185

Music Therapy: A Supervision Project

Gianluigi Di Franco (I)

Introduction

When I stay on a stage always my problem is connected to a question:
"Am I musical performer or am I a music therapist giving to the audience some feelings and feedbacks about my clinical experience ? "

Plus, really often all the people when they are listening to a presentation of mine they guess to practice sounds, knowing me as vocals trainer in M.T., but in this occasion unfortunately I'm going to express me through words referring to experiences derived from my clinical activity in M.T. .

I'd like to start this presentation making a connection between:

Different professionals

MULTIDISCIPLINARY TEAM

MULTI-DISCIPLINARY APPROACH

Music Psychology Medicine Psychotherapy

Figure 1

When I heard that the announced central argument was "multi-disciplinary teams" I began to think and feel things which could be around this concept-word.

While I was wandering at this level came to my mind the words "multi-disciplinary approach" which became like a sledge hammer giving me the chance to make a comparison between the two levels.

I started to work with Music Therapy in the 1978 with the psychotic patients inside of one of the largest Psychiatric Hospital in the South of Italy and there I had the chance to bound my clinical background with my musical one. It was possible because my head-physician was largely open to creative experiences that could make a larger "container"for the patients' needs of expression and the professional anxieties.

During this experience I made between 1978 and 1983 I was very involved with the two earlier mentioned terms. I derived a sort of general consciousness where the work inside this équipe was very useful to me. There I had the possibility to live different cultural backgrounds close to my experimental idea to use the musical language inside of a clinical project with the adult psychotic clients.

So I had from one side the music (like a "quantitative" object helping me to treat the problem); and on the other side: a) psychoanalytical background and b) a clinical background (like a "qualitative" aspect helping me to read the events treated with the music).

The relationships between all these different elements I found again when I understood that it would be a useful starting point in my geographical area within a Training Course for the professionals interested in getting competency in Music Therapy as a methodology applied at specific clinical needs. That's why it for me was quite natural to think that the basic concept of the training in Music Therapy should be within a "multidisciplinary approach", derived from a balancing work between: Music, Medicine and Psychology:

Music   as a concrete tool in order to get in touch with oneself and then with the others especially where the communication through the words is deeply difficult : so it's a way to overcome the verbal language.

Medicine   as an instrument which helps us to know different pathologies we're treating and plus the features with which they showe themselves. More, it is a way to distinguish different symptoms of different clinical problems.

Psychology as a key of reading can help us to understand why some events happen inside of the M.T.relationship between the client and the therapist. Plus, psychology gives us a chance more to reveal the significance of music as language and then to better make M.T. as a specific and evolutive project.

*   *   *

We could use *"Psychology"* and *"Psychotherapy"* as keys to help us to read the events we established using the music as a tool of relationship with the client.
After this introduction now the topic I wish to discuss as human being is how we can check and how we can give support to young music therapists in order to get in touch with their own problems of relationship with the internal world, especially if we are going to apply Music Therapy in mental health with deep pathologies.

Referring to this I can say that my experience at the clinical level is with real severe pathologies, where the involvment in the emotional relationship is obliged. So we can't think that the only level on which we're going to work is the musical one as a tool of relationship, but we need also to take into account the possibility to read this events and put the therapist in the place to observe, understand and treat that .

Now I would like to introduce the principal topic of my writing that is the **Supervision:** Supervision as a box of Sound, Words, Emotions, as a uterus membrane which protects the therapist and feeds him as he makes with his client.

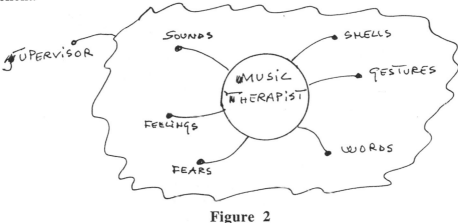

Figure 2

It could be a precise space where you can have precise details from the senior music therapist also trained at a psychotherapeutic level .

In the Supervision we'll have the therapist becomes a client of the supervisor ; so he is in the centre of setting :

Supervision Setting   M.T. Setting

THERAPIST   CLIENT

I think it is really useful to have this kind of picture in our mind because this is the level we can use, referring to a psychodynamic cultural background, in the perspective to read all the problems this therapist started to have in his internal side .

It is really important to check for examples of how the musictherapist gives an answer to these following questions:

a) how is my reaction to the problem the client brought to me ?
b) how can I manage my feelings and transform them in musical answers ?

The external line of figure 2 is a sort of "membrane" of Supervision where you have a precise space like the room where you work, but also from symbolic point of view a sort of warm environment in which the supervisor could contain all things the therapist brings. In the centre of the circle (see figure 2) you can watch the relationship between significant (French: *signifiant*) and significance (*signifié*) referring to the concept of F. de Saussure. In M.T. we could consider "significant" as the sound and "significance" is the emotion is behind the sound itself. The most principal work of the M.T. is to deeply go inside the relationship between these two terms.

Especially if we consider the psychosis, we have an enormous disruption (gap) between significant and significance, where the patient brings us a lot of things in a confusive way; so at this level our countertransference could be totally confused if I'm not able to manage it and understand how I can use it in the perspective of a M.T. treatment.

If I don't have this control the risk could be to get crazy !
I used to work with nurses and some-times some of them had psychotic problems themselves; they stayed close to psychotic patients but afterwards they became psychotics. So, if you are not able to give a "containment" at this level could be really dangeurous. This problem is bigger for the musictherapists who work often with really regressive levels. We have two chances : either we become blind and we just try to establish relationships through the sounds and we can't get in touch with the emotional reactions as therapists we have or we are able to watch these problems and front them in the best way.

What the therapist brings into the Supervision ?
Sounds, questions, words, his fears, his feelings and plus the smells and non verbal sensations he got from the clients , that sometimes could create a lot of problems inside of him, especially with psychotic patients don't have a control of their body functions.

Then, *what are the must important things that therapist could bring in Supervision ?*

1) Assessment details about clinical case he is treating
2) Modalities he uses to conduct his treatment
3) Methodology he's using to manage the specific needs of that specific pathology.

On the other hand *what are the most important things that supervisor could make in Supervision?*

a) To give a sort of "holding" of all the dates brought, not just from musical but also from an emotional point of view; that's why it is very important with the emotional relationship between the therapist and the supervisor:

b) To make a "digestion" of all the elements brought, using the emotional aspects grown up inside of the history of relationship between the therapist and supervisor;

c) To give a work perpective for the next future about what kind of direction the therapeutic project can have.

Going a little bit more inside of the specific point of Supervision topic, I want to underline some details about what I call Supervision Process :

SUPERVISION PROCESS

Cultural background

* "Setting" concept (things to make/things to observe)
* different "hic et nunc" (here and now)
  in an evolutive and systematic project, considering each
  session and each session after the other one

but also

* how is the Music Therapy setting evaluated?
  Here we must consider:
  a) level of emotional investment the client makes toward the therapist
  and viceversa;
  b) a prevalent non directive and fluid attitude of the therapist.

Figure   3

Regarding Figure 3 I'm really well surprised sometimes today, when the people in our M.T. world talk more easily about "defenses", "emotions", "setting", "transference and countertransference"; in other terms they are words depending on a psychodynamic background. I'm so well surprised, because I remember when I participated in the 1983 Paris M.T. World Conference, organized by Prof. J. Jost at Salpretière, where most of the audience started to laugh as I started to talk about "transitional object" and "transitional area" referring to the Winnicott's concepts.

Nowadays I guess anyway that the idea of M.T. is grown up a lot at this level too.

Now I'd like to describe briefly something more about the methodology I use in M.T. and my students use when they make M.T.; it's clear that all the datas they bring in Supervision refer to this operative and methodologic scheme:

Methodology

1) SONOROUS ANAMNESIS
    1.a   *a colloquium* with the client and his family in order to :
    1.a bis collect details and informations from client's musical world
    1.a tris understand which is the communicational problem inside the family-group

    1.b   a *receptive test*
            in order to check the reactions of the client to different sonorous stimuli
            - rhythmic one
            - melodic one
            - harmonic one
            - electronic one
            - sounds of nature

    1.c   *Active sessions of investigation*
            in order to start understanding how the musical production and listening could be related to M.T. setting and to the therapist "holding" disposability.

2) TREATMENT

    2.a Sonorous "holding" phase where the therapist tries to contain all the expressive and not expressive elements brought by the client in the session, mostly listening to him.
    2.b Imitation phase where the therapist makes a sort of mirroring of the sounds brought by the client in order to build a "sonorous feeding" like the one the mother makes with her child givin' him the milk through the breast.
         Then it 's a sort of sonorous " maternage ".
    2.c Improvisation and dialogue phase where the therapist takes musical datas the client gives him and elaborate them and afterwards the client re-elaborates them again.

Third part of methodology regards to Evaluation Criterias of M.T. setting; in other terms they are things I ask to the student to observe and write down in a protocol :

3)   EVALUATION CRITERAS

 1) *The position of the bodies in relation to the instruments*
 2) *The chioce of the instruments and the meaning of such a choice*
 3) *Gestures and mimical aspects*
 4) *Musical production (intensity/timber/musical octades and so on)*
 5) *The way of approaching the instruments (traditional or not)*
 6) *The emotional attitude behind the musical performance*
 7) *The interaction between rhytmin and melody*
 8) *The capacity to listen to themselves and to the others*
 9) *The capacity to live the silence*
 10) *The capacity to be integrated with the others or deny the others*
 11) *The capacity to extend and contract musical phrases*
 12) *Parallel creative aspects (paintings, dancing and so on)*
 13) *Sound dialogue potentialities (rhytmic and melodic cells,
      harmonic sequences)*
 14) *Intermediary/transitional object (individual session)*
 15) *Groupal Intermediary object (groupal session)*

Regarding to the Supervision modalities :

How does the musictherapist work in Supervision?

 *   1 supervision pr. 4 M.T. sessions
 *   2 hours (work in Supervision)

Protocol from musictherapist to supervisor :
 a) *colloque with the client family*
 b) *receptive test*
 c) *report about 3 or 4 investigation sessions*

                ****

 1) *which kind of musical creativity is proposed*
 2) *which kind of contract is established with the client*
        * Time (30 min./40 min.)
        * Modalities of information around the treatment evolution
        * Results

- Reading and comment the 16 parameters protocol (see below)
- Listening to sonorous important moments in order to support and
  validate the things said
-Watching video fragments to understand better what happened in
  that specific moment.
- Bringing sentences about his countertransference
- Problems of relationship with the Institution where M.T. is done

Plus, **How does the supervisor work in Supervision ?**

1) MUSICAL PRODUCTION
   Analysis of sonorous aspects emerged during the sessions where
   the attention is focused on the way the therapist uses the music
   to approach and catch the patient.

2) COUNTERTRANSFERENCE LEVEL
   The Supervisor "contains" the problems and gives a feedback about
   the emotional attitude of the therapist regarding specifically to :
   - level of comprehension the therapist has of his reaction in that
   specific moment;
   - level of understanding of his capability to observe what's happening
                    relating to the other one
                              and
               relating to the M.T. project

3) WORK PERSPECTIVE
   Suggestions and feedbacks related to the things to be made in the future .

Moreover, **How does the supervisor evaluate the musictherapist in Supervision ?**

EVALUATION PARAMETERS OF THE MUSIC THERAPIST IN SUPERVISION

QUANTITATIVE PARAMETERS

1) Respect of the rules of Supervision setting (time, methodology, and so on).
2) Ability to compile the protocols.
3) Ability to organize sonorous and video materials of case study.
4) Capability to plan and follow all the structural problems.

QUALITATIVE PARAMETERS

a) Capability to underline the musical aspects emerged in the M.T. relationship.
b) Capability to be compromised with the client at musical level.
c) Capability to have memory of sounds: to remind all the musical features brough by the client.
d) Capability of expressing himself through objects used like instruments.
e) Capability of expressing and creating through the voice.
f) Capability to use his own body as instrument to better be in touch with himself and with the client
g) Capability to express his experience using word: make concepts.
h) Capability to transfer feeling in "playing" activities with sounds.
i) Capability to feel what's hidden behind the sonorous "significant".
l) Capability to observe and report his own countertransferential level.
m) Capability to use in the relationship with the client his countertransferential level of consciouness.
n) Capability to be in the role and function of "maternage" or "container" through the sounds.
o) Capability to create a "warm" environment more easily workable as "transitional area".
p) Creative capabilities to establish with the client different musical shapes and structures during
the evolutive process of therapy.
q) Capability to be in touch with the other one through a clear musical dialogue.
r) Capability to carry on with the difficult moments of therapy.
s) Capability to follow and apply the supervisor suggestions.

I'd like to close with this sentence :

We were children inside our mother's womb, and the music therapist in
Supervision is a little bit like a child, because Supervision is like an "uterus";
that means a warm and containing environment of all the problems he could
have in his M.T. experiences :
the supervisor as significant;
the supervision as significance.

To recreate a primary symbolic relationship inside a professional evolution of a therapist in his last part: that is the supervision. It could be perhaps a way to definitively teach something to him through an experience made by scientifical details and human exchangements.

References

D. Anzieu (1979) *"Il gruppo e l'inconscio"*, Borla, Roma

R.O. Benenzon (1983) *"Manuale di Musicoterapia"*, Borla, Roma

W. R. Bion (1971) *"Esperienze nei gruppi"*, Armando, Roma

K. Bruscia (1993) *"Definire la Musicoterapia"*, Ismez, Roma

F. De Saussure (1991) *"Corso di linguistica generale"* , Laterza, Roma

G. Di Franco (1993) "Music Therapy: a Methodological approach in mental health field", in: *Music Therapy Health and Education* (edited by M. Heal, T. Wigram, J. Kingsley, Londra)

G. Di Franco/D. Facchini/F. Laccetti (1991) " Musicoterapia per la psicosi: un modello per la salutementale" in Atti del Convegno: *"Una tecnica di supporto per le strutture sanitarie territoriali"* Editnews, Napoli,

E. Lecourt (1993) *"Analyse de groupe et musicothérapie"*, ESF , Parigi

D. W. Winnicott (1990) *"Gioco e realtà"*, Armando, Roma

"Becoming Clients"
Role Playing a Clinical Situation as an Experiental Technique in the Training of Advanced Level Music Therapy Students

Tony Wigram (DK)

Introduction

This paper explores the process of training music therapy students, and some of the possibilities of undertaking experiential role play work as a method of training.Thinking back to my own training in music therapy, I was aware that there was a big difference between what we undertook on the course in music therapy, and what happened when we went into clinical practice. I have always been aware of the problem that music therapists are trained to improvise, but their clients are not. Not only that, but music therapists go through a process of training where they loosen inhibitions, discard rigid or inflexible musical training and structure in order to open themselves to be free and responsive at an intuitive and sensitive level to the needs of clients who may produce very simple music, or even just sounds.

On the other hand, the clients have not gone through this process, and many of them may come to a music therapy session with considerable defence and resistance both to being involved in music making, and also to the process of opening up their feelings through a musical dialogue or relationship.

From this point of view, I remember that in the training I undertook, we at times focused on the repertoire that you could use in music therapy, techniques or ideas that you could use in sessions, and explored our own feelings as well as trying to understand the feelings of the clients. Going into improvisational experiences with ones fellow music therapy students is often a very exciting process, where fellow musicians gather together to use the power and language of music to make contact with each other at quite a skilled level. The realisation that comes when you embark on the first clinical experience with real clients is that they are not able to respond or to participate at the same level, and quite often have considerable problems in participating in music therapy experiences, let alone the problems that they themselves have as clients. So there should be a stage that students can move through where they address and go into the problems of clients with pathological problems before they actually begin working with them.

Preparation for clinical practice

For some years I believed that maybe the most effective way of helping music therapy students get in touch with the clients problems and needs was first of all to address the area of clinical knowledge. In this way, by teaching music therapy students as much as possible about the pathology of all the different clients they might come into contact with, the etiology, the epidemiology and the pathological and symptomatic condition of the clients, as well as considering their prognosis, they would become well prepared for undertaking music therapy. In addition, extensive teaching in the areas of therapy theory and music therapy theory would prepare them for the approaches and styles of work that they needed to use.

This is really only half the work necessary to prepare music therapy students for the daunting and difficult challenge of working with real clients. They may be prepared with their knowledge of the clients condition, they may well have learnt and even put into practice themselves some of the techniques and ways of approaching clients that they could draw from existing literature and experiential workshops in various therapeutic or music therapy approaches. However, there is a danger that students can become "flooded" or "over powered" with so much information, and they will go into a situation constricted by a great deal of knowledge and theoretical information engendering in them a feeling where they may have to know everything and be able to do everything. When I began teaching full time in music therapy, it therefore occurred to me that somehow I was going to have to give the students the experience of working with clinical problems before they actually went into practicum and faced those problems in the real environment. I was doubtful of the valididty of this approach. My own experiences from training on the few occasions what we undertook "role playing" sessions, where we tried to become an "autistic client" for a few minutes to explore the possibilities of music therapy work, were clouded by memories of embarrassment, humour, and frustration. I didn't find it a satisfying experience, and I had no reason to believe that the students that I tried it on would feel any different.

However in the music therapy programme at Aalborg University self experience had been developed as an important part of the training, and there was already a tradition of the students going into the role of student-clients. In group leading, individual music therapy, intertherap and group music therapy during the first three years of training, students experience both group and individual therapy. Developing music therapy skills to use with the *clinical population* had mainly been taught with an orientation on finding appropriate musical material, and the role playing undertaken in these sessions focussed on evaluating the value and use of musical arrangments, songs, and musical material coming out of the parts of the programme that taught musical skills. I felt it was necessary to develop this into a therapeutically oriented process, where the students could go deeply into the clients' and the therapists' experience of music therapy.

I therefore decided that if it was going to be successful, it would have to be undertaken of a very experiential way, yet with very clear structure and guidelines in a safe environment. In fact, it would have to have the same boundaries as a therapy session has, and all aspects of both the students playing the role of clients as well as the students playing the role of therapist would need to be carefully considered. Their feelings, thoughts and process would need to be respected and protected. So I set out to establish a structured programme, undertaken over a whole year, of clinically oriented therapeutic work, mainly with groups, but dealing also within the groups with individual problems (kliniske gruppemusikterapifædighider).

It was going to be necessary to set up situations that came as close as possible to the real situation. I decided to create cameo portraits of real clients, using many clients from my own experiences as well as clients documented in the literature.

I wanted the students to have an experience during these sessions of working with a variety of different client populations, and to be prepared for the needs of those clients as well as possible. I decided that the students would benefit not only from undertaking the role as therapists but also from going into the role of being clients and assuming a new personality for a period of time in order to understand the process of music therapy.

Clinically related therapy work - Role playing
In the masters programme at Aalborg university, I developed a course for fifth and sixth semester students which consisted of twenty, 4 hour sessions where the students went into the experience of setting up, running and then analysing therapy sessions. The students role-play clients and therapists and are observed doing this by other students as well as being recorded on video for subsequent analysis. A wide range of clinical pathologies are explored during the course of this year, from psychiatry. learning disability, social areas and general medicine. This course mainly aims to equip students to undertake group work with clients, and to teach them how to make use of musical material and musical frameworks for the purpose of group therapy work.

The groups covered so far include :

* Blind Clients
* Deaf Clients
* Deaf & Blind Clients
* Autistic Individuals
* Autistic Groups
* Profound Mental Handicap / Learning Disability
* Moderate Mental Handicap / Learning Disability
* Cerebral Palsied clients
* Muscular Dystrophy / Multiple Sclerosis

*   Psychiatric Open Group
*   Psychiatric Closed Group
*   Schizophrenic Clients (paranoid)
*   Schizophrenic Clients (thoughts disorder)
*   Anxiety Neurosis
*   Depressed Clients
*   By polar manic depressives
*   Elderly clients, Senile Dementure / Alzheimer
*   Psychiatric / Substance Abuse
*   Eating Disorders
*   Family Therapy
*   Terminal Illness

The students are expected to do some background reading on the clinical pathologies that they will experience each week in order to have a clear understanding of the aetiology, pathology and difficulties of these client groups. Literature from the theory of music therapy course is relevant for this course, and the students receive some teaching on these client groups, wherever possible with video examples. Recommended literature also includes Case Studies in Music Therapy (Bruscia), Improvisational Models of Music Therapy (Bruscia), Music Therapy in Health and Education (Heal & Wigram), Analytical Music Therapy (Priestley) and The Art and Science of Music Therapy (Wigram et al).

Preparation for the session

Each week, the students are given a client group of between three and five clients. The students undertaking the role of clients are expected to learn and memorise the information about the client that they have been assigned. They are always given a different name, and during the session, this name is written on a white label which wear. Taking a different name is quite important to the process in order to have a real feeling of change of identity.

The students acting as therapists (either individually, in pairs or in pairs with a helper) plan and prepare the therapy session. Supervision to prepare the session for at least an hour is also given to the students two or three days before each session. During this supervision, I first of all expect the students to have studied the clients they are going to be working with, consider their needs, and how they might structure the music therapy session. I expect them to have worked out some ideas of how they may approach the clients in this session and what they may do. We then discuss other possibilities, and look at the need for some frameworks and freedom within those frameworks. Special attention is paid to finding the most appropriate therapeutic approach and musical material to meet the needs of each client individually in a group, and the group as a whole.

The session

The students then prepare the room prior to the session, and prepare musical material where appropriate. The student therapists describe their group to all the students present. We revise the descriptions of the clients that have been given, in order to have that very present in our minds from the beginning of the session. Any instructions that are necessary are given for the beginning of the session, such as the parameters of the room, the instruments that are included within the musical space, and any issues about whether or not the clients may leave the session. Sometimes during this period of time, additional information may be necessary on exactly how the students will role play the clients. As they have frequently not encountered some of these clients, this is a necessary part of the process.

The therapy session always begins with the students undertaking the role of clients leaving the room and waiting outside some minutes and getting into their roles in a quiet space. When the therapists are ready to begin their session, they go outside the room, collect their client group and bring them into the room. From that moment on the session is a protected, safe environment in which the therapy takes place, and everybody is very much in the role. The session may last 45 to 90 minutes, and at the end of the session, the student therapists will take their clients out of the room. Only when they are out of the room and the door is closed is the therapy session considered finished.

Feedback

The feedback time is a very important part of this process. The order may vary, but typically, the feedback occurs in the following way :

1. The students playing clients give feedback.
2. The students playing therapists give feedback
3. The observers give feedback.
4. Sections of the video are analysed.

I give feedback during the whole process, and also at the end. After the feedback period we sometimes go over some situations to find out what else could have been done. Role-playing exercises are again used to model some different styles of work. In this way, exercises can be done on techniques that were used during the session, or on techniques that could be used in future sessions.

Student therapists' process

The students acting as music therapists are developing their musical skills, their therapeutic skills, their creative skills, their group leading skills and also their observational skills. They are also having to develop memory, as in the feedback session, they need to remember what happened in the session, particularly what musical material was used, and what musical material the clients themselves produced during the session. They are in the position of having to interact with a group of their own students who are playing the role of clients and this rather "false" situation can create specific problems for them. Countertransferential issues centre around their feelings towards the students / clients and to a large extent the stage they are in their own process. Difficulties in building relationships are therefore obvious, and it is clearly more difficult to act in the role of therapist in this situation than that of a client.

Students acting as clients
The students who take the role of clients are going through two processes. They are beginning to try to get inside the role of clients with different disorders, illness or disabilities. They are also trying to explore how such clients would act and interact in music therapy sessions. This is a very difficult role and requires a total commitment and trust both in the therapists, each other and the teacher. Over the period of three years that I have been undertaking these sessions at Aalborg University, it is clear that getting the role of clients is easier for the students than being the therapist. I give the students a certain amount of information, but not too much, as they can't be expected to remember a whole history of a persons life. At the same time, they can be creative in the session, and bring their own ideas into the role they are undertaking, perhaps adding some aspects to the patient that they are being.

One example of a client group I have created for the students is ANXIETY NEUROSIS:

1. **KAREN** - A 42 year old women who is phobic. She is frightened of crowd.. She has a problem with social situations, and she doesn't like talking to people. She can become very agitated when under pressure. She has been in a hospital for 2 years since a major breakdown.

2. **MARTA** - A 51 year old women who is an obsessional neurotic. She thinks about dirt and filth all the time, and she talks about it a lot. Anything or anybody she comes into contact with is a threat to her health. She checks her clothes, objects around her and furniture for dirt of any sort. Frequently she needs to wash her hands.

3. **ERIKA** - A 35 year old women with general neurotic anxiety. She is restless, often walking around and has difficulty sitting for too long. She sleeps bad. She constantly worries about everyday problems.She asks a lot of questions all the time - for example "have you turned the water off in the bathroom?", and many other trivial matters. She has been in the hospital for 7 months.

This is a group with varied problems centerred around the pathology of neurotic anxiety. They are hospitalised patients, but the objective may be to help them find ways of controlling and containing their neurotic anxieties so that they may have a possibility to live more normal lives in the community, as well as helping them gain insight into their condition.

Another group is : PROFOUNDLY HANDICAPPED CLIENTS

1. **NIELS** - 31 Year old man. He has no language, and it is difficult to tell if he understands anything. He has lived in the hospital for 18 years, and is very institutionalise.. He has Down's syndrome and his IQ is approximately 35. He likes music, rocks and plays with a steady monotonous beat. He is slow, has poor perception, and is not very creative. His is friendly.

2. **KAREN** - 27 year old woman. She is profoundly handicapped, sits in a foetal position and doesn't move much. She shakes her head slowly, plays with her clothes and has no language. She responds to physical contact, is quite tactile and is aware of people around her.

3. **HELLE** - 34 year old woman. She has been in the hospital for 19 years. She is blind, profoundly handicapped, and is very closed. She often sits on the floor, in a foetal position, with her arms around her. She hums to herself, she enjoy contact, but squeezes or grabs things near her. She listens to what is happening, but doesn't respond to her name.

4. **BENTE** - 32 year old woman. She has lived in the hospital for 12 years. She has phenylketonuria, and can be nervous and active. She doesn't understand language. She will use musical instruments, and is responsive to musical interaction. She can also be active, wandering around the room, but happy to come and sit with the group if you encourage her.

BI-POLAR DISORDER

1. **CARL** - A 30 year old man. He lives at home with his parents, and works on a farm. He is mildly depressed and he feels he has lost direction in his life. In the past he has been suicidal and he feels guilty about this. He has poor self-esteem and is very shy with women.

2. **KIRSTI** - A 34 year old married lady. She works in a library, and married when she was 31. She is anxious, mildly manic and is worried about becoming depressed again. Her husband expects a lot of her, so she often tried too hard. She is frightened of failing and comes to music therapy because she feels successful at relating to other people in this situation.

3. **ULLA** - A 38 year old single woman. She runs a clothes shop with a partner. She is mildly depressed, and anxious about her business being a success/ Two years ago she was very depressed and was in hospital for two months. She is frightened of this happening again and is always asking for reassurance that she is alright. She has a bad relationship with her family and blames herself for this. She is a good pianist and finds music therapy a very effective way of lifting her mood and spirits.

4. **HANNE** - A 35 year old woman. She has recently come out of hospital after a severe period of depression for three months. She is married to be successful businessman and feels very bad that she has had to go to hospital. She pretends she is OK but inside she has much anxiety. She is not optimistic about the future and has attempted suicide twice. Her husband loves her and is very supportive but she has difficulty in responding.

The clients in this group are all suffering mildly from manic/depressive affective disorder. They are not in hospital but attend a day hospital for a therapy session twice a week. The group has been meeting regularly and they know each other. All of them have a history of Bi-Polar disorder, whereby they have experienced both manic and depressive episodes. They also continue to have persistent mild symptoms of depressive / manic illness.

Students acting as observers

The observers have a definite role in every session. They need to make careful notes of the musical interactions going on in the session, the way the therapists are approaching and working with the group at a musical level, and also at an interactive, personal level, and the way the clients are responding. All aspects of the group process need to be observed, and in the feedback session the observers play an important role in giving an objective view of what has happened. Also, their own countertraferential issues can be addressed in the way they experience the session, and the feelings it creates in them.

Creating the music therapy session
Providing the students with a model for making a role play, and the descriptions of the clients givs them the setting for the therapy. What they try to do in the session is addressed in the supervision session. There is no "recipe" for a music therapy session. Each session will develop in the way that most appropriately meets the needs of the clients. But students need a framework, and many possibilities suggested to them of approaches and musical material they can use in the session. What follows is an attempt to provide a framework for considering the many elements that go to make up a music therapy session or couse of sessions, and the many aspects that will have to be considered.

This can provide a format for setting up a session and taking various things into consideration:

1. NEEDS OF THE CLIENTS
2. OBJECTIVES OF THE SESSION
3. STRUCTURE OF THE SESSION :
        ACTIVITIES
        IMPROVISATIONS
        PASSIVE / ACTIVE
        DIRECTED / NON - DIRECTED
        THERAPIST / CO THERAPIST / HELPER ROLES
4. EQUIPMENT NEEDED AND LOCATED
5. OPENING
6. SUSTAINING, DEVELOPING , JUDGING, CONTAINING, CHANGING
7. CLOSING
8 THERAPIST

The area needing most discussion is usually the structure of the session. The students are often sensitive and informed about the needs of the clients, and also the objectives of the session. But what to incorporate in the session presents problems. Below in figure 1 is an attempt to provide a range of ideas, albeit incomplete, for developing a session.

Figure 1: Techniques and dynamics of improvisational music therapy

IMPROVISATION		
FREE & UNSTRUCTURED	THEMATIC	ACTIVITY STRUCTURED
	GUIDED FANTASY	WARM UP TECHNQIUES
	STORY	INSTRUMENTALLY ORGANISED
	OBJECT	MUSICALLY ORGANISED
	PAINTING	
	WEATHER	
	CONCEPT	
	EMOTION	
MEDIUM	MUSIC	CONTROL
INSTRUMENTS	ATONAL	FREE
PERCUSSION	TONAL	WITH INITIAL PLAYING FILES OR GIVENTS
+ PIANO	MODAL	
+ PITCHED PERCUSSION	PENTATONIC	PARTIAL STRUCTURE
VOCAL DIALOGUE	STYLISTIC	FULL STRUCTURE
VOCAL + INSTRUMENTS	THEMATIC EXTEMPORISATION	PARTIAL / FULL DIRECTION
VOCAL ALONE	EXTEMPORISATION	GESTURE
RECORDED MUSIC / RECEPTIVE		MUSIC
MOVEMENT		VERBAL
MOVEMENT + INSTRUMENT		CONDUCTED

The material one might choose, or the client may introduce into the session will very much depend on the nature of the theraputic process that is going on.

Improvisation
1. Free and unstructured -
In a session without any prerequired or given rules, musical structures or concrete material. The expression of feeling, emotion and state through musical improvisation without any specific framework.

2. Thematic material -
Examples can include a guided fantasy, where the therapist, with or without the client's involvement creates a fantasy in the music making, possibly using the idea of "tone-poem", or story. The client may tell a story verbally to start with, and then take this into an improvised experience; an object or painting, the weather on particular day as you would like it to be; an idea or an emotion such as improvising on the theme of anger or fear. Themes can vary from concrete to very abstract ideas.

3. Activity
a. I have begun sessions in a variety of ways: by listening to a piece of recorded music, offering the client an instrument or group of clients an instrument and asking everyone individually to experiment with their instrument; passing messages to someone in the group, or from a client to a therapist in individual work using the instrument; improvising to a client on the piano or on another instrument in an empathic way to reflect their mood.

b. Instrumentally organised activity
Examples of this include focusing improvisation purely on drums, on pitched percussion instruments such as xylophones or metallophones, or creatively exploring instruments together with the client.

c. Musically organised activity
This may involve giving some musical structure to an improvisation such as starting piano, crescending to forte, then returning back to a piano; structured turn taking, where the therapist and the client alternatively play; matching rhythmic structures; matching melodic styles.

d. Medium
This will depend on the client's own choice, but also on some decision making by the therapist to what might by the most effective way of building a musical dialogue with the client. Working exclusively in a vocal dialogue or with voices can be quite threatening for clients, and may for example may be facilitated by an instrumental accompaniment. If the client chooses to play simple percussion instruments, then the therapist may choose to support them

on the same instruments, or may work from the piano in establishing a dialogue. The piano can be a very dominating instrument, and also highlight the different musical skill level between the therapist and the client. Receptive techniques with recorded or live music include listening to some music that either the client or the therapist has brought, or the active technique of moving or dancing to recorded music.

4. Music
The music used may be atonal, tonal, or modal, but could also have additional stylistic frameworks such as melodic improvisation, pentatonic improvisation, or Spanish and Middle Eastern styles of improvisation.

5. Control
The control of what is happening musically in the session may be determined by the client or the therapist. The range shown in Fig 1. varies from free improvisation without any form of control to conducted improvisation which involves almost complete control. Initial structure may be determined by "playing rules" or "givens" (Brusica 1987) which can be defined by the client or the therapist together, where they may decide there are some elements that they are going to include in the improvisation. For example, they might decide that they want to respond to each other by splitting their roles or possibly by splitting the two parts of the client's personality e.g. the therapist may represent the contained or controlled part of the client , and the client might musically represent the excited, manic or aggressive part of themselves.

Partial structure leading to full structure is a technqiue where the therapist and the client decide how they are going to begin playing, what might happen in the middle of their improvisation, and how they are going to end, and could also include defined musical elements, such as beginning with a steady pulse, accelerating to an uneven tempo and chaotic rhythmic structures.

Partial to full direction gives the control element either to the client or the therapist who can, during improvisation, direct their partner in a specific way. For example, I might give the client the opportunity to decide when he would like me to play at any time during the improvisation, and indicate this by touching me or looking at me, or by stopping playing himself.

A conducted form of control involves the client or the therapist actively conducting an individual with some basic symbols or signs indicating how they want them to play - for example, raising their arms above their head when they want the volume to increase, crouching down and making small movements with their hands if they want a soft, gentle sound. This must be differentiated from what is understood as convential conducting, and does not involve beating in time or controlling in the same way as an orchestral conducter.

So combinations of elements could result in the following frameworks:

- *Free and unstructured improvisation through a vocal dialogue using an internal medium.*

- *An improvisation of a picture using pitched percussion instruments in a pentatonic mode, with some partial structure.*

- *Using an emotional theme, listening to recorded, tonal precomposed music with a feedback period afterwards.*

The style of improvisation with containing thematic material, structure, medium, musical style and level of control can vary considerably.

The material I have included in Fig.2 and the explanations of some of this material form only a part of the wide variety of techniques and ideas one can introduce into music therapy sessions. These techniques can be at a conceptual level, or they can be specifically musical or interactively structured. The choice depends entirely on the clients needs, the point which therapy has reached, the therapists intuition or the process or musical relationship that is being developed.

Closing a music therapy sessions can present particular problems, and a number of alternative ways can be used:

CLOSING

- RESOLVING ISSUES

- ALLOWING ENOUGH TIME

- PREPERATION FOR NEXT SESSION

- MUSICAL CLOSURE: GOODBYE SONG

        GOODBYE IMPROVISATION

        RECORDED MUSIC

        PHYSICAL

- VERBAL CLOSURE

- POST-SESSION ISSUES

Conclusion

Music therapy is difficult to teach because there are great limitations in giving students recipes for the work. There are models, theories, and techniques, but great variability in the practical application. The method of teaching through experiential work role-playing clients described in this paper has proven effective in bringing students closer to an understanding of the problems clients present and appropriate ways of developing their approaches and musical skills, as well as increasing their awareness of the needs of clients.

Contributors

Keynote Speakers of the Conference

PROF. DR. EVEN RUUD has a MA within musicology.He has taken music therapy training in USA based on learning theories. He is the former head of the Music Therapy Programme at Østlandets Musikkonservatorium, Oslo, Norway. Now he is a professor at Oslo University, institute of Musicology, and he is functioning as a teacher and researcher within musicology (music sociology and anthropology) and music therapy. he has been a significant figure in developing theory of music therapy in Scandinavia and he has been the main author and publisher of the present Scandinavian litterature on music therapy. His publications are broadly based and he has developed the theory of music therapy from a sociological and anthropological point of view. His doctoral dissertation was a study of "Music as Communication and Interactions". He has lectured widely in Scandinavia, Europe and USA and is a wellknown Keynote Speaker.

PROF. DR. DAVID ALDRIDGE is trained as a teacher of art and has worked as a community arts organiser. from this work he realized young peoples' need for specific counselling for personal and social problems. After gaining his doctoral qualification in psychology for a study of suicidal behaiviour as an ecosystematic approach in 1984, he has worked as a research consultant. he was Senior Research Fellow at St. Mary's Hospital medical school in London where he was responsible for implementing a research project in general medical practice. This project developed research methods suitable for complementary medicine, one of which was music therapy. From there, he moved to Germany, where he is now professor for Clinical research methods in the Faculty of medicine at the university of Witten, Herdecke.
He has published a wide range of articles in Europe and USA.

PROF. HELEN ODELL-MILLER is Course Director of the MA-Programme in Music Therapy at Anglia Polytechnic University, Cambridge, England. She is also manager of the Art Therapy Service in the Mental Health Service in Cambridge and a specialist music therapist working with adults such as clients with depression, schizophrenia and dementia. She has a M.Phil. in music therapy research on:"The effect of Music Therapy with elderly mentally ill."
She has published and lectured widely in the UK, Europe, USA and Australia. She is advisor to Department of Health on Music Therapy.

CANDIDATE IN MUSIC THERAPY ANNE STEEN MØLLER was educated in the first group of students at the MA-Programme at Aalborg University. She has worked with music therapy with clients with profoundly developmental diseases for nine years and is a specialist music therapist within this client population. Her work is based on a psychodynamic foundation. She has developed new ways on working with musical contact with this group of clients on one of the biggest institutions for clients with developmental disabilities in denmark, and she is used as a consultant for music therapists at other similar institutions.

Other contributors:

Claus Bang
Working area:

Music Therapist. Special Teacher.
Music Therapy & Musical Voice Treatment,
Speech Therapy with Hard of Hearing, Deaf and
Deaf-blind children & Youngsters

Working place:

Aalborgskolen, Aalborg. Denmark.

Ruth Eckhoff
Working area:

Music Therapist
Adult psychiatrtic patients in a school setting.
Training M.T. - students

Working place:

Kongsskogen Vid. Skole,Oslo, Norway.

Guianluigi di Franco
Working area:

Prof., Music Therapist. Psychiatrist.
Music Therapy in Psychiatry.
Treatment and Research

Working place:

C.R.M. Music Therapy Center. Naples, Italy.

Edith Lecourt
Working area:
Working place:

Prof., Music Therapist. Psychoanalyst.
Research within Music Therapy
University Paris V (Sorbonne), Laboratory of
Clinical and pathological psychology.
Paris, France.

Kimmo Lehtonen
Working area:

Ass. Prof. Music Therapist.
Music Therapy with children and adolescents
with severe psychic and social problems

Working place:

University of Turku/Dept. of Education.
University of Jüväskylä. Suomi Finland.

Alison Levinge
Working area:

Working place:

Music Therapist.
Children presenting with emotionally based
communication difficulties. Mental Illness.
Blackberry Hill Hospital. Bristol. Great Britain.

Helle Nystrup Lund
Working area:
Working place:

MA-Music Therapist.
Training M.T.students' piano-skills
Aalborg University. Aalborg. Denmark.

Wolfgang Mahns
Working area:
Working place:

Music therapist. Special teacher
Music Therapy with children in public school.
Integrative Grundschule Fahrenkrön.
Hamburg. Germany

Eyjolfur Melsted
Working area:

Working place:

Music Therapist. Teacher
Basal-stimulative music therapy with severely
multiply handicapped children.
Freelance consultant. Kindergarten & Preeschools.
Austria

Anne Olofsson
Working area:
Working place:

Music Therapist. Pedagogue
Music Therapy within cancer care
Karolinska Sjukhuset, Psychosocial Unit
Stockholm, Sweden.

Gabriella G. Perilli
Working area:

Working place:

Prof.Music Therapist. Psychologist.
Psychiatry. (youth and adult) with rehabilitative
and therapeutic purposes.
Supervising MT-students. Researcher.
S.I.M. Societá Italiana di Musicoterapia.
Rome. Italy.

Almut Pioch &
Albert Berman
Working area:
Working place:

Music Therapists.
Music Therapy in psychiatry
Psychiatric Center "Zon en Schild".
Amersfoort. The Netherlands

Katie Santos
Working area:

Working place:

Music Therapist.
Forensic Psychiatry. Mentally Disordered
Offenders
Richard Dadds Centre, Broadmoor Hospital.
Berkshire. Great Britain.

Henk Smejsters

Working area:
Working place:

Ass. Professor. Head of Studies.
Director of Research
Training and Research.
Hogeschool Enschede Conservatory.
Music Therapy Laboratory, Hogeschool Nijmegen.
The Netherlands

Guilia C. Trovesi

Working area:

Working place:

Music Therapist.
Research - Training, Mental health,
Developmental Disabilities.
A.P.M.M. Ponteranica. Italy